广东省新材料产业标准体系规划与路线图

王璐玲　主　编
刘圆圆　副主编
林浩　孙帅　编　委

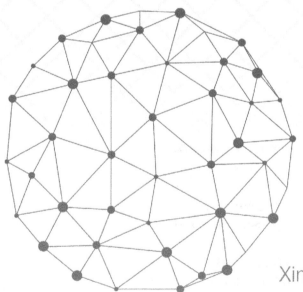

Guangdongsheng
Xincailiao Chanye Biaozhun
Tixi Guihua Yu Luxiantu

·广州·

版权所有　翻印必究

图书在版编目（CIP）数据

广东省新材料产业标准体系规划与路线图/王璐玲主编；刘圆圆副主编．—广州：中山大学出版社，2015.5
ISBN 978-7-306-05262-9

Ⅰ.①广…　Ⅱ.①王…②刘…　Ⅲ.①材料工业—标准体系—研究—广东省　Ⅳ.①F426—65

中国版本图书馆 CIP 数据核字（2015）第 087990 号

出版人：	徐　劲
策划编辑：	廖丽玲
责任编辑：	廖丽玲
封面设计：	林绵华
责任校对：	黄浩佳
责任技编：	何雅涛
出版发行：	中山大学出版社
电　　话：	编辑部 020-84111996，84113349，84111997，84110779
	发行部 020-84111998，84111981，84111160
地　　址：	广州市新港西路 135 号
邮　　编：	510275　　传　真：020-84036565
网　　址：	http://www.zsup.com.cn　　E-mail:zdcbs@mail.sysu.edu.cn
印 刷 者：	虎彩印艺股份有限公司
规　　格：	787mm×1092mm　1/16　13.25 印张　323 千字
版次印次：	2015 年 5 月第 1 版　2015 年 5 月第 1 次印刷
定　　价：	35.00 元

如发现本书因印装质量影响阅读，请与出版社发行部联系调换

目　录

第一章　概　述 ··· 1
　一、产业概况 ··· 1
　　（一）新材料的概念 ··· 1
　　（二）新材料的种类 ··· 1
　　（三）发展新材料产业的重大意义 ··· 2
　　（四）常见新材料的主要应用 ··· 4
　二、全球新材料产业现状和发展趋势 ··· 6
　　（一）全球新材料产业发展现状 ·· 6
　　（二）全球新材料产业发展趋势 ·· 10
　三、国内新材料产业现状和发展趋势 ······································· 13
　　（一）国内新材料产业发展现状 ·· 14
　　（二）存在的主要问题 ·· 16
　　（三）国内新材料产业发展趋势 ·· 17
　四、广东省新材料产业现状和发展趋势 ··································· 19
　　（一）广东省新材料产业发展现状 ······································· 19
　　（二）存在的主要问题 ·· 21
　　（三）广东省新材料产业发展趋势 ······································· 22

第二章　新材料产业标准化发展现状 ··· 24
　一、标准化与技术应用、产业发展的关系 ······························· 24
　　（一）促进企业技术创新 ··· 24
　　（二）提高产品质量水平 ··· 24
　　（三）保证产品的通用互换 ··· 25
　　（四）应对技术性贸易壁垒 ··· 25
　二、国内外新材料产业标准建设现状 ······································· 25
　　（一）先进金属材料 ··· 26
　　（二）新型无机非金属材料 ··· 28
　　（三）高性能有机高分子材料及复合材料 ···························· 30
　　（四）特种精细化工材料 ··· 31
　　（五）前沿新型材料 ··· 35

第三章　新材料产业标准体系 ··· 37
　一、新材料产业标准体系概述 ··· 37

二、新材料产业标准体系框架 ··· 38
　　三、新材料产业标准体系编制说明 ··· 40
　　　　（一）标准类型 ·· 40
　　　　（二）材料类型 ·· 40
　　　　（三）材料分类交叉的处理 ··· 40
　　四、新材料产业标准体系明细表 ··· 41
　　五、新材料标准体系统计与分析 ··· 61

第四章　广东省新材料产业标准体系规划 ······································ 64
　　一、广东省新材料产业标准体系概述 ······································ 64
　　二、广东省新材料产业标准体系框架 ······································ 64
　　三、广东省新材料产业标准体系编写说明 ································ 66
　　　　（一）预立项标准项目来源 ·· 66
　　　　（二）标准项目优先级 ·· 67
　　　　（三）标准项目选择过程 ··· 67
　　四、广东省新材料产业标准体系的任务 ··································· 68
　　五、广东省新材料产业标准体系标准制修订建议 ······················ 70

第五章　广东省新材料产业标准体系实施环境分析与产业标准化路线图 ··· 90
　　一、标准体系规划实施环境分析 ··· 90
　　二、SWOT 分析 ··· 94
　　　　（一）优势 ·· 95
　　　　（二）劣势 ·· 95
　　　　（三）发展机遇 ·· 98
　　　　（四）威胁因素 ·· 98
　　三、广东省新材料产业联盟与政策推动 ··································· 100
　　四、广东省新材料产业标准化路线图 ······································ 107

附录1　ISO 标准列表 ·· 113
　　1. 先进金属标准 ·· 113
　　2. 新型无机非金属材料 ··· 137
　　3. 高性能有机高分子材料 ·· 144
　　4. 特种精细化工材料 ·· 151
　　5. 前沿新型材料 ··· 155

附录2　IEC 标准列表 ·· 170
　　1. 先进金属材料 ··· 170
　　2. 新型无机非金属材料 ··· 174
　　3. 高性能有机高分子材料及复合材料 ···································· 182
　　4. 特种精细化工材料 ·· 188
　　5. 前沿新型材料 ··· 191

第一章 概 述

一、产业概况

(一) 新材料的概念

材料是人们用来制成各种机器、器件、构件、物品或其他产品的具有某种特性的物质实体，是人类社会生活的物质基础。随着科学技术的快速发展，材料的种类也发生了很大的变化，相对于传统材料，开发出了很多新材料。目前，国内外对新材料的定义主要是新出现的或正在发展中的具有优异性能和特殊功能的材料，或是传统材料改进后性能明显提高和产生新功能的材料。新材料不仅应用在高端行业，在基础性产业中也应用得很广泛。从我们穿的衣服、用的餐具、乘坐的交通工具、栖居的住宅到工作的场所，可能都正使用着新型材料；从大飞机、高速铁路、新能源汽车等重点工程，到三网融合、物联网、节能环保等重要产业，都需要一系列新材料技术的突破和应用。历史证明，材料是人类社会发展的物质基础和先导，那新材料便是人类社会进步的里程碑。

新材料产业是国家确定的七个重点发展的战略性新兴产业之一，也是我省重点培育的八大战略性新兴产业之一。2012年1月4日，工业和信息化部（以下简称"工信部"）印发了《新材料产业"十二五"发展规划》，明确指出"新材料是材料工业发展的先导，是重要的战略性新兴产业"。进入21世纪以来，我国新材料产业发展迅速，2010年我国新材料产业规模超过6500亿元，与2005年相比年均增长约20%。

(二) 新材料的种类

新材料根据不同的分类方法，可分成不同的种类。按照材料的性能来进行分类，新材料主要包括结构材料和功能材料。结构材料主要是利用材料的力学和理化性能，以满足高强度、高刚度、高硬度、耐高温、耐磨、耐蚀、抗辐照等性能要求；功能材料主要是利用材料具有的电、磁、声、光热等效应，以实现某种功能，如半导体材料、磁性材料、光敏材料、热敏材料、隐身材料和制造原子弹、氢弹的核材料等。按照材料的属性来分类，我们可以把新材料划分为新型金属材料、新型无机非金属材料和新型高分子材料等。新型金属材料当中主要有新型合金材料，比如铝合金、镁合金、钛合金、稀贵金属合金等；新型无机非金属材料中典型的有玻璃纤维、碳纤维、光导纤维、记忆玻璃、防弹玻璃、防辐射玻璃等；新型高分子材料当中主要包括医用高分子材料和聚合物基复合材料。此外，随着纳米技术的提出和发展，纳米技术在材料领域的研究，促使纳米材料成为新材料的一个热点。

根据工信部《新材料产业"十二五"发展规划》，列入规划的新材料主要包括以下六大类：① 特种金属功能材料。具有独特的声、光、电、热、磁等性能的金属材料。② 高端金属结构材料。较传统金属结构材料具有更高的强度、韧性和耐高温、抗腐蚀等性能的金属材料。③ 先进高分子材料。具有相对独特物理化学性能、适宜在特殊领域或特定环境下应用的人工合成高分子新材料。④ 新型无机非金属材料。在传统无机非金属材料基础上新出现的具有耐磨、耐腐蚀、光电等特殊性能的材料。⑤ 高性能复合材料。由两种或两种以上异质、异型、异性材料（一种作为基体，其他作为增强体）复合而成的具有特殊功能和结构的新型材料。⑥ 前沿新材料。当前以基础研究为主，未来市场前景广阔，代表新材料科技发展方向，具有重要引领作用的材料。

根据《广东省新材料产业发展"十二五"专项规划》（粤经信材料〔2011〕666号），广东省现阶段重点发展先进金属材料、新型无机非金属材料、高性能有机高分子材料及复合材料、特种精细化工材料、新型稀土功能材料五大领域。根据2012年3月由广东省政府办公厅印发的《广东省战略性新兴产业发展"十二五"规划》，在新材料领域的分类中，增加了"前沿新型材料"一类。如将稀土功能材料列入先进金属材料分类中，可将新材料种类分为五类，即先进金属材料、新型无机非金属材料、高性能有机高分子材料及复合材料、特种精细化工材料、前沿新型材料。

（三）发展新材料产业的重大意义

随着科学技术的发展，新材料技术也在不断发展，当前，新材料产业已渗透到国民经济、国防建设和社会生活的各个领域，新材料作为高新技术的基础和先导，应用范围极其广泛，它同信息技术、生物技术一起成为21世纪最重要和最具发展潜力的领域。我们对新材料的研究以及对新材料的应用开发，是人类对物质性质认识和应用向更深层次的进军。

1. 新材料是促进传统产业转型升级的重要基础

新材料产业的发展对中国成为世界制造强国至关重要。一方面，新材料是材料工业发展的先导。我国是材料工业大国，但远不是材料工业强国，高端产品发展滞后、精深加工能力不强等问题十分突出。2013年我国粗钢产量已达6.8亿吨，但每年仍需进口上千万吨高性能钢铁材料；我国电解铝产能占世界总产能的40%，但大飞机所需关键铝合金及碳纤维材料仍未完全突破。因此，加快发展技术密集、附加值高的新材料产业，对于提升我国材料工业发展水平具有重要的现实意义。

另一方面，新材料也是传统工业实现转型发展的助推剂。工业转型升级要求传统工业向更加注重资源节约、环境友好、节能降耗、质量效益的可持续发展路径转变。材料是工业的食粮，消耗量巨大，资源环境影响明显。新材料具有绿色、低碳、智能、延寿、可循环等新的特征，对于传统工业转型升级具有重要作用。

2. 新材料是战略性新兴产业发展的支撑和保障

战略性新兴产业是以重大技术突破和重大发展需求为基础，对经济社会全局和长远发展具有重大引领带动作用，知识技术密集、物质资源消耗少、成长潜力大、综合效益好的产业。当今世界，新技术、新产业迅猛发展，新兴产业正在成为引领未来经济社会发展的重要力量，推动全球经济与竞争格局发生深刻变化。加快培育和发展战略性新兴产业对推进我国构建国际竞争新优势、掌握未来发展主动权具有战略意义。

新材料产业既是重要的战略性新兴产业，也是发展新一代信息技术、节能环保、新能源、生物、高端装备制造、新能源汽车等其他战略性新兴产业的支撑和保障。以新能源汽车为例，要真正实现产业化和规模化，关键是要在动力电池的能量密度、充放电次数、安全性等方面取得重大突破，归根结底还是要提升电池正/负极材料、电解液和隔膜的性能，发现一种新的高性能储能材料。因此，新材料产业对于支撑战略性新兴产业发展具有重要基础性作用。

3. 新材料是新技术革命的催化剂

材料科学的变革和进步的外溢性极强，往往带动其他行业和领域随之发生翻天覆地的变化，可以看作是技术革命的催化剂，被誉为"发明之母"和"产业粮食"。新材料是当前世界新技术革命的三大支柱（材料、信息、能源）之一，新材料与信息、能源、医疗卫生、交通、建筑等产业结合越来越紧密，与其他学科的交叉领域和规模都在不断扩大。正是因为半导体材料的工业化生产，才催生了规模庞大的电子信息产业；正是因为有了液晶材料、发光材料，才产生了蓬勃发展的新型显示工业；正是因为有了光导纤维，才会有今天的光纤通信和高速互联网。

新材料是具有传统材料所不具备的优异性能的材料，它可以带动和促进基础材料和传统材料的改进与更新，对其他行业、高新技术行业的发展形成支撑和先导。以国防军工为例，新材料的运用和突破是驱动国防军工装备升级的基础，也是改变战场形态的直接诱因（见表1-1）。正所谓"一代材料、一代装备"。航空工业是制造业的"皇冠"，航空发动机是"皇冠"上的"明珠"，但如果没有新材料作为支撑，"皇冠"和"明珠"都会黯然失色。航空工业的飞速发展，很大程度上归功于先进钛合金、高温合金、高性能复合材料的革新应用。有数据表明，现代航空发动机"推重比"的不断提升，有70%的贡献来源于关键材料的创新和使用。

表1-1 新材料的突破驱动军事装备更新

新材料的突破	新产品	武器装备的性能提升
超纯硅、砷化镓	大规模和超大规模集成电路	计算机运算速度从每秒几十万次提高到每秒百亿次以上，使得C4ISR等出现
耐高温材料	高性能航空发动机	航空发动机材料的工作温度每提高100℃，推力可增大24%
超高强度钢	大潜深潜艇	潜艇潜深加大减少自身暴露的可能，大大提高隐蔽性
隐身材料	隐身装备	吸收电磁波或降低武器装备的红外辐射，使敌方探测系统难以发现我方目标

资料来源：民生证券研究院根据公开资料整理。

（四）常见新材料的主要应用

材料科学技术的迅速发展，促进了新材料设计与制造加工工艺时代的到来，包括先进制造技术、加工与成形技术在国内的发展，反过来也促进了国民经济和国防建设等各个领域高新技术的发展，促进了人类社会的繁荣和人们生活水平、质量的提高。在当今世界科技发展的大背景下，为了使材料加工技术和应用更加节能、高效和优质，对新材料的研究是我们不得不重视和关心的重大问题。

1. 半导体材料

当前半导体材料的应用主要体现在三个方面：第一，半导体材料在照明技术领域的迅猛发展。由于半导体发光二极管（LED）的半导体光源的优点较突出，例如它的体积和消耗的电量很小，同时又能兼顾环保的价值，目前在照明技术领域具有重大的市场价值。第二，半导体材料在汽车光电子市场的应用。这主要体现在汽车雷达技术，现在越来越多的汽车安装的防撞雷达就是半导体材料技术的应用。第三，半导体材料和移动通信技术发展的结合。随着移动通信技术的发展，目前第四代（4G）移动通信技术已推广使用中，这个也为半导体材料的发展带来了新的发展。

2. 磁性材料

随着信息技术日新月异的发展，磁性材料在市场中的应用也得到了快速的发展，当前磁性材料在以下几个领域发挥着重要的作用。第一，磁性材料在通信领域的应用和发展。随着移动通信技术的发展，手机功能的增加必然要求移动技术的发展和提高，而磁性材料技术的发展给移动通信技术提供了有力的支持。第二，磁性材料在计算机领域的应用。计算机是磁性材料的主要应用领域之一，计算机的普及和应用给磁性材料的发展带来了新的机遇和挑战。

3. 隐身材料

隐身材料（stealth material）是隐身技术的重要组成部分，在装备外形不能改变的前提下，隐身材料是实现隐身技术的物质基础。武器系统采用隐身材料可以降低被探测率，提高自身的生存率，增加攻击性，获得最直接的军事效益。因此，隐身材料的发展及其在飞机、主战坦克、舰船、箭弹上的应用，将成为国防高技术的重要组成部分。对于地面武器装备，主要防止空中雷达或红外设备探测、雷达制导武器和激光制导炸弹的攻击；对于作战飞机，主要防止空中预警机雷达、机载火控雷达和红外设备的探测，主动和半主动雷达、空对空导弹和红外格斗导弹的攻击。为此，常需要雷达、红外和激光隐身技术。

4. 碳纤维

碳纤维是一种含碳量在95%以上的高强度、高模量纤维的新型纤维材料，质量比金属铝轻，但强度却高于钢铁，并且具有耐腐蚀、高模量的特性，在国防军工和民用（汽车、体育休闲等）方面都是重要材料。

2015 年前，全球碳纤维市场需求都保持了13%的增长，我国对碳纤维的需求增速则快于全球（新闻来源：轻工纺织服装网），碳纤维行业正处高速发展期。但我国工艺技术水平相对较低，尚难以满足国内需求，数据显示，2013 年我国碳纤维及其制品进口量12386.2吨，同比增长了34.5%。

西方国家将碳纤维视为战略物资，曾对中国禁售、禁运，足见碳纤维材料的重要性、急迫性。碳纤维在军工领域的应用很广，被广泛应用于火箭的助推器、防护罩、发动机罩和导弹壳体、发射筒等结构，还被用在战斗机和直升机的机体、主翼、尾翼、刹车片及蒙皮等部位，可见碳纤维的通用性。

在民用方面，民航客机所用复合材料，主要为碳纤维复合材料。碳纤维复合材料主要用在机翼部件、垂直尾翼、机头罩等部位上，且其在风机叶片和汽车上的使用也越来越普遍。

国家对碳纤维的发展高度重视和扶持。2013年11月，工信部印发《加快推进碳纤维行业发展行动计划》，要求经过3年努力，初步建立碳纤维及其复合材料产业体系，应用市场初具规模；到2020年，我国碳纤维品种规格齐全，基本满足国民经济和国防科技工业的需求。

5. 石墨烯

石墨烯被认为是改变世界未来的12项变革性技术之一，也是联合国2013年初认定的人类未来两大领军产业之一。

石墨烯是一种由碳原子构成的单层片状结构的新材料，为已知的世上最薄、最坚硬的纳米材料。石墨烯的应用范围广泛，包括"太空电梯"缆线、微电子、超级计算机、光子传感器、液晶显示材料、触摸屏、超薄超轻飞机材料、新能源（超级电容、锂电池、新一代太阳能电池）、基因测序等方面，可见其重要性和通用性。

石墨烯目前在全世界均处于研发试验阶段，但在各国政府和企业的积极推动下，相当数量的研发项目正在进入商业化准备期。研究机构IDTechEx发布最新报告预测，全球石墨烯材料市场在2024年将超过3.9亿美元，比2014年的2000万美元增长近20倍。

目前我国有关石墨烯的专利数量居于世界第一的位置，我国石墨矿储量占世界总储量的75%，产量占世界总产量的72%，石墨烯产业发展的基础条件优势明显。据称，工信部等相关部门正在考虑统筹研究石墨烯材料，其有望进入我国新材料"十三五"规划。

6. 特种钢

与普通钢相比，特种钢具有更高的强韧性、物理性能、化学性能和工艺性能。特种钢的应用领域广泛，包括汽车行业、能源行业、工程机械、船舶海工、高层建筑、铁路行业、国防工业等，属于重大、通用、牵涉面极广的新材料领域。

特种钢在国内还有广阔的开拓空间，我国虽然是钢铁生产大国，但在高品质特种钢生产上并非强国，很多高附加值、高品质产品依然依赖进口。按照《新材料产业"十二五"发展规划》目标，以及《高品质特殊钢科技发展"十二五"专项规划》，到2015年我国特种钢占比提高到10%，产品质量达到国际先进水平的比例由现有的15%以下提高到30%以上。

未来与核电、海洋工程、航空航天、国防军工等重大装备制造业相关的高品质特种钢生产企业有望成为政府政策扶持的重点。

7. 建筑节能材料

新型建筑材料主要包括新型墙体材料、保温绝热材料、建筑防水材料、建筑装饰装修材料四大类基础材料及部品。在节能环保方面，新型墙体材料、保湿绝热材料的使用能够大大减少建筑的能耗。

我国现有的住宅建筑95%都是高耗能建筑，建筑能耗占全国总能耗的27%以上，节能环保提升为新型建筑材料发展提供了广阔空间。据统计，在同等气候条件下或同纬度条件下，我国住宅的单位使用能耗是发达国家的2～3倍。近年来，国家对绿色建筑的规划目标不断提升，建筑材料的政策扶持力度不断加大。

二、全球新材料产业现状和发展趋势

（一）全球新材料产业发展现状

随着新材料产业规模的迅速扩大，产业发展逐渐呈现明显的交叉联合化、民用市场化、区域集中化、绿色低碳化四大趋势并表现出以下四大特点：一是上下游进一步融合、多学科交叉和多部门联合进一步加强，产业重组和融合继续推进；二是产业规模持续扩大，新品种、新技术不断涌现，主要生产技术被杜邦、巴斯夫、拜耳、GE塑料、Ticona、陶氏化学、日本帝人、韩国LG化学等大型跨国公司垄断；三是亚太地区成为新的投资热点，随着国际新材料巨头在全球范围内产能的扩张，新材料产业链的中低端逐渐向亚太地区转移，亚太地区成为国际巨头的投资热门地区；四是材料的高性能、低成本趋势明显，新材料在制造业、民用领域的普及应用，对材料的性能和成本提出了更高的要求，提高产品性能、降低产品成本成为新材料发展方向之一。

若干前沿新材料科技的发展动向：

1. 纳米科技研发形成国际浪潮，纳米材料生物效应引起关注

纳米材料和纳米技术是20世纪末兴起的一个高新科技领域，基于纳米材料和纳米科技在电子、信息、新型陶瓷、生物、化工、医药、机械、交通、能源、国防等领域有着重要意义和广泛的应用前景，21世纪前20年，纳电子代替微电子、纳米加工代替传统加工、纳米材料代替微米材料、纳米生物技术代替微米生物技术是未来发展趋势，因此，纳米材料和纳米技术备受世界各发达国家的重视和支持（见表1-2）。美国总统克林顿亲自过问纳米材料和纳米技术的研究，决定加大投资，这说明纳米材料和纳米结构的研究热潮将在接下来相当长的一段时间内保持继续发展的势头。美国在《21世纪纳米技术研究开发法案》中批准联邦政府从2005年以后的4年中投入约37亿美元用于纳米材料与技术的研究开发。欧盟、日本、韩国等国家相继投入大量经费用于支持本国纳米科技研究领域。

表1-2 2012年全球新材料产业重大政策

序号	国别	重大政策
1	美国	2012年2月,白宫发布了"先进制造业国家战略计划",创建包括先进材料在内的4个领域的联邦政府投资组合,以调整优化联邦投资,促进先进材料发展
2	美国	2012年2月,白宫发布了"国家纳米计划",规划沿袭了老版的整体战略目标和重点领域,仅在具体战略部署方面进行了微调,规划确定了纳米材料、纳米制造等八大主要支持领域
3	欧盟	2012年7月,欧盟出台"第7框架计划"(FP7),其中的"纳米科学、纳米技术、材料与新产品技术"主题计划在2013年部署12项优先项目
4	欧盟	2012年9月,欧盟科研与创新理事会出台欧盟飞机制造业"2050战略研发新议程",旨在集成纳米新材料技术、光电技术和先进机械制造技术等来推进绿色航空航天技术的研究
5	德国	2012年6月,德国联邦环境部、德国联邦职业与健康安全研究所与巴斯夫研究所联合启动实施了"纳米材料安全性"长期研究项目。该项目的目标是要了解各类纳米材料可能对周边环境产生的影响,通过定量化方法对纳米材料进行安全性风险评估
6	德国	2012年11月,德国联邦教研部宣布启动"原材料经济战略"科研项目,目的在于开发高效利用并回收原材料的特殊工艺,加强稀土、铟、镓、铂族金属等的回收利用,促进资源循环使用
7	韩国	2012年6月,韩国知识经济部和教育科学技术部表示,韩国到2020年将投入5130亿韩元(约合人民币28.2亿元)推动"纳米融合2020项目"

资料来源:赛迪智库原材料工业研究所整理。

随着纳米科技的发展,如何有效避免潜在的风险成为世界各国日益关注的课题,相应的研究也随之开展,目的是寻求降低风险的渠道,最终保证纳米技术的安全应用。值得一提的是,我国从事纳米生物效应研究的单位,已成功地将纳米材料的生物效应应用到肿瘤的医学诊断和治疗技术的探索上,并取得了多项重要成果。

2. 新型结构材料应用广泛,发展前景乐观

低成本、高性能先进钢铁材料仍然是21世纪的主要结构材料。钢铁材料性能优异、价格低廉,易于循环利用,是最传统和最主要的结构材料。从世界各国钢铁材料的发展状况看,特别是随着发展中国家钢铁材料需求的增长,在可预见的将来,低成本、高性能、高附加值的先进钢铁材料是新一代钢铁材料的发展方向,并将成为在许多领域广泛应用的主要结构材料。

铝合金材料发展迅猛,孕育着巨大的市场潜力。铝合金由于密度小、导热性好、易于成形、价格低廉等优点,在轻金属及合金中应用最广、用量最多。21世纪初,交通运输业消耗的铝占全世界原铝产量的27.6%,日本在交通运输业等领域对铝的消费达

30%以上。随着交通运输业现代化进程的加快，低成本、高性能的铝及铝合金材料在航空、航天和汽车三大领域的应用日益增加。

镁合金材料的应用领域逐渐拓宽，市场前景广阔。镁合金被业内公认为"最有前途的轻量化材料"之一，未来几十年内镁将成为需求增长最快的有色金属。欧洲汽车制造商提出的"3公升汽油轿车"新概念，以及美国提出的"PNGV"（新一代交通工具）合作计划，推动了镁合金在汽车、摩托车等交通类产品上的应用，使镁合金零件成为世界各大汽车公司零件的重要发展方向。随着镁合金生产技术的多项突破，电子及家电用镁合金消费量剧增。

钛合金材料的发展将由军工领域逐步向民用转化。钛和钛合金因其密度小、强度高和耐蚀性好等优良特性，备受世人瞩目。从世界主要钛生产国的产量及所占比例来看，美国、独联体国家、日本的钛产量占全球总产量的83%。钛和钛合金在航空航天领域的使用量占产量的40%～50%，在非航空领域的应用比例为50%～60%。随着钛和钛合金在化学工业、油气田钻探装置以及体育用品等方面的推广应用，钛和钛合金产业前景广阔。

高温结构材料作为宇航领域的主导材料之一，用量逐渐增加。随着航空航天技术的发展，对材料性能的要求越来越高。美国的先进发动机计划AFT和IHPTET的总目标是将发动机的推重比提高到20。发动机零件应力水平越来越高，为适应航空发动机的涡轮叶片、涡轮盘和燃烧室等材料的需求，各国均建立了各自的高温结构材料体系。高温合金、难熔金属、金属间化合物、金属基复合材料等成为高温结构材料的重要组成部分。其中Inconel 718（GH4169）和Hastoloyx合金的应用量，已占先进发动机用高温合金的60%，研制的高温结构复合材料，满足了航空航天领域对高温材料的需要。国外新一代运载火箭、战略导弹及其推进系统的关键结构材料几乎全部复合材料化。C/C复合材料已成为对宇航发动机减重、节油、提高推重比、增大飞行半径与航程、提高战技术比能不可替代的材料。

高分子结构材料的发展及应用出现新契机。高分子材料、金属材料、无机非金属材料是三大基本原材料。高分子材料主要包括合成树脂、合成橡胶和合成纤维等，在经济发展和科技创新领域得到了广泛的应用，发挥着越来越重要的作用。最近，日本科学家用高分子材料代替无毒性的病毒作载体，进行基因治疗实验获得了成功，大大拓展了高分子材料在生物医用材料领域的应用范围。发达国家在药物控制释放体系、骨科固定、组织工程和医用手术缝合线等方面，部分已经产业化。

3. 新型功能材料及其应用技术面临新突破

超导材料的临界温度在逐步提高，超导材料正向低成本和实用化方向发展。目前国际上高温超导产业化应用正从以军事领域为主向民用领域扩展，例如，超导滤波系统在第三代移动通信中得到了应用，并将在能源、信息、交通、仪器等领域发挥重大作用。此外，在继续改善BSCCO带材（也称为第一代带材）的同时，各国正在努力研究开发在柔性金属基带上涂以YBCO（$YBa_2Cu_3O_x$，$x=6\sim7$，钇—钡—铜氧化物）厚膜的涂层导体（第二代高温超导带材）。铋系高温超导线材目前已实现商品化。

新能源材料发展前景广阔。新能源材料是指实现新能源的转化和利用以及发展新能源技术中所要用到的关键材料，主要包括以储氢材料、燃料电池材料、Si 半导体材料为代表的太阳能电池材料以及反应堆核能材料等。当前的研究热点和前沿技术包括高能储氢材料、聚合物电池材料、中温固体氧化物燃料电池电解质材料、多晶薄膜太阳能电池材料等。21 世纪，人类将面临世界范围的能源危机，各国对新能源材料发展的高度重视，极大地推动了新能源材料的发展。

生物医用材料的发展面临重大的技术突破。生物医用材料是用于诊断、治疗、修复或替换病损组织、器官或增进功能的天然或人造高技术新材料。生物医用材料应用广泛，全世界仅高分子材料在医学上的应用就有 90 多个品种、1800 余种制品。最近日本科学家用高分子材料代替无毒性的病毒作载体，进行基因治疗实验获得了成功。西方国家在医学上消耗的高分子材料每年以 10%～20% 的速度增长。随着现代科学技术的发展尤其是生物技术的重大突破，生物医用材料的应用将更加广泛。

先进复合材料进入规模化应用时代，例如，日本正在制造碳纤维—酚醛树脂复合材料车身，将其用在新一代高超列车上，可降低噪音，减少振动和低能耗地保持车厢温度。战斗机的隐身技术主要使用具有隐身功能（吸收雷达波和红外线）的吸波碳化硅纤维、碳纤维复合材料等。

智能材料代表了材料科学较为活跃的发展方向。智能材料是能随周围环境的变化而自动调节自身功能与特性的一种材料，它可以满足人类的特定要求，达到自诊断、自适应甚至自修复的目的。智能材料的构想来源于仿生（仿生就是模仿大自然中生物的一些独特功能），一般由两种或两种以上的材料复合构成一个智能材料系统。目前具有传感与传动特性的智能材料，如形状记忆合金、磁感应材料、智能高分子材料和芯片化的材料多功能技术等得到飞速发展，这就使得智能材料的设计、制造、加工和性能结构特征均涉及材料学的最前沿领域。

4. 电子信息材料发展呈现新趋势

随着电子学向光电子学、光子学迈进，业内普遍认为微电子材料在未来 10～15 年仍是最基本的信息材料，光电子材料、光子材料将成为发展最快和最有前途的电子信息材料。电子、光电子用功能单晶将以大尺寸、高均匀性、晶格高完整性为主要发展方向，而新型元器件将向低维化、多功能化、片式化、超高集成度和低能耗方向发展。

纳米电子学是当今电子学发展的一个重要方向。随着固体器件朝着小尺度、低维方向的发展，它已经发展成为一种纳米量子结构。由于纳米量子结构中受限电子呈现出许多与它们在三维结构中十分不同的、物理内涵十分丰富的新量子现象和效应，它不断地被人们用来研制具有新功能和新原理的电子器件，不断地从最基础层面上为开拓电子信息技术的潜力提供新机遇。因此，世界上的科技大国和大财团都对这个领域的研究投入大量资金，组织大型研究项目，力求在电子学的新时代占据制高点。其中准一维材料——纳米管、纳米线和分子、电子功能器件成为研究热点。纳米电子学近年来的主要进展有定向排列的纳米管和纳米线、可集成在塑料上的薄膜晶体管、纳米线交叉电路等。

集成电路和半导体器件用材料由单片集成向系统集成发展。微电子技术发展的主要途径是通过不断缩小器件的特征尺寸，增加芯片面积以提高集成度和信息处理速度。当前美国 AMD 公司已开始量产 90 nm（纳米）的高性能集成电路芯片，而国际上对 65 nm 技术的开发也趋于成熟。

光电子材料向纳米结构、非均质、非线性和非平衡态发展。光电集成将是 21 世纪光电子技术发展的一个重要方向，而光电子材料是发展光电信息技术的先导和基础。材料尺度发展是逐步低维化的，即由体材料向薄层、超薄层和纳米结构材料的方向发展，材料系统由均质到非均质、工作特性由线性向非线性、由平衡态向非平衡态发展是其最明显的特征。

新型电子元器件材料主要向小型化、片式化、集成化方向发展。目前，电子元器件正进入以新型电子元器件为主体的新一代元器件时代，它将基本上取代传统元器件。电子元器件由原来以适应整机小型化及新工艺要求为主的改进，变成以满足数字技术、微电子技术发展所提出的特性要求为主，而且是成套满足的产业化发展阶段。

（二）全球新材料产业发展趋势

新材料在发展高新技术、改造和提升传统产业、增强综合国力和国防实力方面起着重要的作用，世界各发达国家都非常重视新材料的发展。随着社会和经济的发展、全球化趋势的加快，新材料产业的发展呈现出以下主要特点和趋势：

1. 新材料多学科交叉，前沿性技术不断突破，产业进一步融合

随着新材料技术发展日新月异、转化速度不断加快，前沿技术的突破使得新兴材料产业不断涌现。同时新材料与信息、能源、医疗卫生、交通、建筑等产业结合越来越紧密，材料科学工程与其他学科交叉的领域和规模都在不断扩大。特别是纳米技术的发展，加速了新材料多学科的交叉，这在生物学、医学、电子学、光学等领域更为凸显。因此，对学科交叉的认知和有力推动将对一个国家新材料产业超前发展起到举足轻重的作用。

基础材料产业正向新材料产业拓展。伴随着元器件微型化、集成化的趋势，新材料技术与器件的制造一体化趋势日趋明显，新材料产业与上下游产业相互合作与融合更加紧密，产业结构出现垂直扩散趋势。

2. 各国政府高度重视新材料产业发展

美国、日本、欧盟是世界新材料生产的主要国家和地区，在加强对量大面广的传统材料改造的同时，高度重视新材料产业发展。各国政府、部门相继制订了推动新材料产业和科技发展的相关计划，如美国的"国家纳米计划"、"光电子计划"、"太阳能电池（光伏）发电计划"、"下一代照明光源计划"、"先进汽车材料计划"等，日本的"纳米材料计划"、"21 世纪之光计划"，德国的"21 世纪新材料计划"，欧盟的"纳米计划"等。目前，世界新材料产业的重点发展方向主要集中在信息材料、生物医用材料、新能源材料、航空航天材料、生态环境材料、纳米材料、超导材料等领域。

3. 新材料发展由以军事需求为主转向民用需求

从 20 世纪来看，国防和战争的需要、核能的利用和航空航天技术的发展是新材料发展的主要动力。而在 21 世纪，生命科学技术、信息科学技术的发展和经济持续增长将成为新材料发展的最根本动力，工业的全球化更加注重材料的经济性、知识产权价值与商业战略的关系,新材料在发展绿色工业方面也会起重要作用。未来新材料的发展将在满足军事需求的同时,在很大程度上围绕如何提高人类的生活质量展开。寓军于民、军民两用材料是国际新材料产业发展的一个重要趋势。

4. 新材料市场需求旺盛,产业规模迅猛发展

随着社会科技的进步和新兴产业的快速发展,人类对新材料种类和数量的需求日益增加,新材料产业的发展前景十分广阔。以新材料为支撑的新兴产业,如计算机、通信、绿色能源、生物医药、纳米产业等的快速发展,对新材料种类和数量的需求也将进一步扩大。

目前,全球生物医用材料的产值超过 4000 亿美元,世界纳米技术的年产值为 2000 亿美元。预计纳米材料产业将成为仅次于芯片制造的世界第二大产业,年产值将达 14400 亿美元。全世界功能陶瓷的市场总规模预计可达 800 亿美元。

5. 跨国公司对新材料产业发展的影响力加强

跨国公司对新材料产业发展的推动作用显著,这些企业规模大、研发能力强、产业链完善,主要通过战略联盟、大量的研发投入、产业技术、制定市场标准并控制知识产权,在竞争中处于优势甚至垄断地位。其中半导体硅材料市场和生产已经形成垄断。目前,信越、瓦克、住友、MEMC 公司、三菱材料公司 5 家企业硅片销售额占国际销售额的 80% 以上。有机硅材料则是 Dow Corning 公司、GE 公司、Wacker 公司和 Rhone-Poulenc 公司及日本一些公司基本控制了全球市场。另外,有机氟材料则是 Du Pont、Daikin、DN-Hoechst、3M、Ausimont、ATO 和 ICI 7 家公司占据全球 90% 的生产能力,在全球居于统治地位。

6. 高性能、低成本及绿色化发展趋势明显

21 世纪,新材料技术的突破将使新材料产品实现高性能化、多功能化、智能化,从而降低生产成本、延长使用寿命、提高新材料产品的附加值和市场竞争力。如新型结构材料主要通过提高强韧性、提高温度适应性、延长寿命以及材料的复合化设计等来降低成本;功能材料以向微型化、多功能化、模块集成化、智能化等方向发展来提升材料的性能。面对资源、环境和人口的巨大压力,生态环境材料及其相关产业的发展日益受到关注。短流程、低污染、低能耗、绿色化生产制造,节约资源以及材料回收循环再利用,是新材料产业满足经济社会可持续发展的必然选择。

7. 新材料产品标准呈现全球化趋势

在世界经济全球化日益增强的背景下,要求世界不同地方对同一材料采用相同的标准,克服各国材料及其产品数据标准不一的矛盾,避免引起混乱、低效并增加成本,以利于市场应用的国际化。为此,对材料供应商和用户来说,世界不同的国家、地区以相同方式测试材料特性尤为重要,对于新兴市场上的新材料,这种要求意义重大。

新材料作为 21 世纪最重要和最具发展潜力的三大领域之一,受到各国的广泛重视,多国制订了推动本国、本地区新材料技术和产业发展的计划,在资金上给予大力支持。在政策和资金的推动下,世界材料产业的产值以每年约 30% 的速度增长。其中,微电子、光电子、新能源等是研究最活跃、发展最快、应用前景最好的新材料领域。部分国家和地区促进新材料科技和产业发展的战略和举措如下(见表 1-3):

表1-3 新材料是各国竞相发展的21世纪希望领域

国家	重点发展方向	发展规划
美国	信息材料、生物医用材料、纳米材料、环境材料及材料技术学等	国家纳米计划、未来工业材料计划、21世纪纳米技术研究开发法案、光电子计划、太阳能电池（光伏）发电计划、下一代照明光源计划、先进汽车材料计划、美国氢染料电池研究计划、光电子计划、建筑材料计划等
日本	信息通信、环境、生命科学、纳米材料等	信息通信、环境、生命科学、纳米材料等
欧盟	光电、有机电子、超导复合、催化剂、光学、磁性、仿生、纳米、生物医药和智能材料等	框架协议、纳米计划、尤里卡计划等。欧盟在2009年3月宣布，在2013年之前投资1050亿欧元支持欧盟地区以新材料突破为代表的"绿色经济"
德国	激光、纳米、电子、生物、信息通信等技术领域	从1994年启动国家级新材料研究计划。在新材料制造装备、加工和应用3个方面确保德国在国际上的领先地位。进入21世纪，德国在9大重点发展领域均将新材料放在首位
韩国	下一代高密度存储、生态、生物、自组装的纳米、未来碳素、高性能高效结构材料、智能卫星传感器、仿生、控制生物功能等材料	2025年构想、新产业发展战略、纳米科技推广计划、NT（纳米技术）综合发展计划、G7计划（先导技术开发计划）、生物工程科学发展计划、重点国家研究开发计划、原子能开发计划等
俄罗斯	高分子材料、复合材料、金属材料、陶瓷材料、高纯度材料、生物材料、超导材料、纳米材料	新材料与化学产品是俄罗斯多年来的年度9项科技规划之一

资料来源：民生证券研究院根据公开资料整理。

1. 美国保持新材料科技领域的全球领先地位

美国把生物医用材料、信息材料、纳米材料、极端环境材料及材料计算科学列为主要前沿研究领域，支撑生命科学、信息技术、环境科学和纳米技术等发展，以满足国防、能源、电子信息等重要部门和领域的需求。为此，美国制订了一系列与新材料相关的计划，主要包括"21世纪国家纳米纲要"、"国家纳米技术计划（NNI）"、"未来工业材料计划"、"光电子计划"、"光伏计划"、"下一代照明光源计划"、"先进汽车材料计划"、"化石能材料计划"、"建筑材料计划"、"NSF先进材料与工艺过程计划"等。

2. 日本注重实用性、先进性及资源、环境的协调发展

目前，日本将纳米技术与纳米材料列为四大重点发展领域之一，对新材料的研发与传统材料的改进采取了并进的策略，注重于已有材料的性能提高、合理利用及回收再生，并在这些方面领先于世界。

日本在 21 世纪新材料发展规划中主要考虑环境、资源与能源问题，将研究开发资源与环境协调性的材料以及减轻环境污染且有利于再生利用的材料等作为主要考核指标。制定的发展规划主要包括"科学技术基本计划"、"纳米材料计划"、"21 世纪之光计划"、"超级钢铁材料开发计划"等。

3. 欧盟将保持在航空航天材料等某些领域的领先优势

欧盟在"第六个框架计划"中确定了 7 项优先发展主题，而与新材料有关的就有信息社会技术，纳米技术和多功能材料及其新的生产工艺和设施，航空和航天，可持续发展、全球变化和生态系统 4 项。2003 年 9 月，欧盟科研总司决定着力推动"催化剂、光学材料和光电材料、有机电子学和光电学、磁性材料、仿生学、纳米生物技术、超导体、复合材料、生物医用材料以及智能纺织原料"十大材料研究领域的发展。

欧盟还制订了多个与新材料相关的计划，主要包括"第六个框架计划（7 项优先发展主题中有 4 项与材料有关）"、"欧盟纳米计划"、"COST 计划（欧洲科学和技术研究领域合作计划）"、"尤里卡计划"、"欧洲新材料研究规划"等。欧盟各成员国也都有自己的新材料相关发展规划。如德国、法国、英国等的"纳米计划"、"光产业发展计划"等。

4. 韩国力争成为世界新材料科技产业强国

韩国新材料科技发展战略目标是继美国、日本、德国之后，成为世界新材料产业的强国，把材料科技作为确保 2025 年国家竞争力的 6 项核心技术之一。

韩国在 2025 年构想中列出了为未来建立产业竞争力开发必需的材料加工技术清单，包括"下一代高密度存储材料、生态材料、生物材料、自组装的纳米材料技术、未来碳材料技术、高性能结构材料、用于人工感觉系统的智能卫星传感器、利用分子工程的仿生化学加工方法、控制生物功能的材料"。同时，韩国还制定了与新材料相关的主要发展规划，如"韩国科技发展长远规划——2025 年构想"、"新产业发展战略"、"纳米科技推广计划"、"NT（纳米技术）综合发展计划"等。

5. 俄罗斯将新材料与化学工艺作为优先发展的科技方向之一

俄罗斯为了提高国家经济竞争力，在航空与国防方面与美国抗衡，将新材料与化学工艺作为其科技 9 个优先发展方向之一，并列出发展新材料的关键技术，即陶瓷和玻璃材料，膜技术，特种性能的金属和合金，重要战略原料的评估、综合开采和深加工技术，聚合材料和复合材料，超硬合成材料，超导技术，微型冶金生产技术模型等。

三、国内新材料产业现状和发展趋势

当前，我国新材料产业在国际产业布局中正处于由低级向高级发展的阶段，随着对外开放的扩大和与全球业界交流合作的深入，我国新材料产业逐步发展壮大，技术水平也已经得到大幅提升。截至 2012 年年底，全国 20 多个省市将新材料作为重点发展的高新技术产业之一，北京市、湖南省、山东省等地新材料产业发展势头强劲，新材料产业正逐步成为这些地区经济的重要增长极之一。

（一）国内新材料产业发展现状

我国新材料产业从无到有，不断壮大，据不完全统计，2012年我国新材料产业实现产值突破1万亿元，已经成为名副其实的材料大国。我国的钢产量十多年稳居世界第一，2011年已突破6亿吨；我国的十种有色金属产量以及高分子材料产量多年居世界前列，由中国材料支撑的"中国制造"遍布全球。目前，我国新材料产业每年都以10%的发展速度快速增长，在一些重点材料方面，如电子信息材料增长速度达20%～30%，生物医用材料增长速度达20%。其中稀土功能材料、先进储能材料、光伏材料、有机硅、超硬材料、特种不锈钢、玻璃纤维及复合材料等产能居世界前列。全国范围内从事新材料开发的企业超过12000家。

1. 特种金属功能材料

稀土功能材料的主流研究方向是改进工艺，以进一步提升稀土功能材料的性能。我国稀土永磁材料、储氢材料、发光材料等已经实现规模化生产，供应量占全球的80%以上，但与国外领先水平相比仍有差距，磁性材料、发光材料、催化材料等领域缺乏核心的知识产权。半导体材料方面，目前硅材料是最重要的半导体材料，应用最广，用量占半导体材料总用量的95%左右。我国的硅材料加工技术已经取得了很多重要进展，硅晶体生产方面如12英寸硅单晶生产技术已经成熟，硅片加工方面如12英寸硅单晶抛光片加工技术已经成熟，但总体来看，我国半导体硅材料产业仍处于成长期。

产业规模方面，2012年，受全球经济低迷影响，国内特种金属功能材料领域中的稀土产品价格大幅下跌，消费疲软，稀土冶炼企业实现利润95.13亿元，同比下降37.8%，稀有稀土金属加工企业实现利润29.18亿元，同比下降13.4%；多晶硅、钽铌产业同样受市场低迷影响，产量降低；硬质合金产量2.35万吨，同比下降17.6%，但硬质合金产品结构得到进一步优化，产品档次有所提高。

2. 高端金属结构材料

特殊钢方面，我国特殊钢材品种不断增加，支撑了国防、航空航天、汽车、家电、能源、轨道交通等装备制造业的发展。其重点品种发展情况如下：部分核电用钢已基本具备产业化的条件；超超临界火电用钢中的高压锅炉低温段使用钢种（15CrMo、12Cr1MoVG、12Cr2MoVTiG）基本实现了国产化，开发出了连铸T91、连铸T92、T92、P92、S30432、S31042等超超临界火电用钢新钢种，迫使国外进口锅炉管产品大幅度降价50%以上，为国家节省了外汇，降低了火电机组的建设成本；高品质不锈钢使我国不锈钢品种消费结构发生了显著变化；原油轮耐蚀钢完成了工业试验和生产，相关的应用研究也在同步进行；高强度汽车板已具备批量生产能力，改写了知名品牌汽车用钢板全部依赖进口的历史；轴承钢国内主要生产企业工艺装备已达到世界先进水平。新型轻合金材料方面，商用汽车轻量化带动了铝材料的大量应用，飞机专用第三代新型铝锂合金试制成功；具有完全知识产权的普通乘用车（家庭轿车）通用系列——16英寸/17英寸/18英寸规格的全镁合金轮毂正式实现批量化生产；成功研发了特种镁合金材料，连续保证了航空航天的需要；肇庆多罗山蓝宝石稀有金属有限公司湿法冶炼钛产品产量已达到国内总产量1/2以上，公司还是全球最大的钽丝供应商，其航空航天用钽铌材料在国际市场占有相当一部分比例。

产业规模方面，高品质特殊钢行业，我国已形成了以太钢、中信泰富特钢集团、东北特钢、西宁特钢、宝钢特材、宝钢不锈钢为代表的大型特殊钢企业，6家特钢企业2012年产能总计达到2800万吨。特种合金材料行业，2012年，我国重点统计企业特种合金材料产量15855吨，其中高温合金8259吨、精密合金6492吨、耐蚀合金1104吨。新型轻合金材料中，2012年，铝材料生产稳定增长，产量3039.5万吨，同比增长14.6%；原镁产能152.25万吨，同比减少3.82%，产量69.83万吨，同比增长5.71%；镁合金产量20.75万吨，同比减少13.25%；钛板、钛管等钛加工材产品出现大幅下滑，下降幅度分别达到13.4%和10.7%，而钛棒材和钛锻件分别以21.1%和88%的增长幅度成为推动钛加工材产量增长的主要品种。

3. 先进高分子材料

合成橡胶方面，SBR（丁苯橡胶）仍是国内最大的通用橡胶，2012年产能达到148.2万吨/年，产量为118.4万吨；BR（顺丁橡胶）产能达到109.5万吨/年，产量为70.3万吨；SBCs（苯乙烯类热塑性丁苯橡胶）产能达到78万吨/年，产量为52万吨。工程塑料方面，尼龙工程塑料、聚碳酸酯、聚甲醛、PBT（聚对苯二甲酸丁二醇酯）、聚苯醚树脂五大通用工程塑料均已建成装置，特种工程塑料中聚苯硫醚、聚酰亚胺、聚醚醚酮初步实现了产业化，新增产能集中在聚甲醛、PBT、聚碳酸酯。有机硅行业景气度下降，多个在建项目推迟投产，有机硅单体开工率为65%左右，产量约130万吨。截至2012年，国内多种氟化工产品产能均已达到世界第一，但存在低端产能过剩、高端供不应求的问题。

4. 新型无机非金属材料

国内已经具备玻璃新材料制造技术，但存在产学研用脱节、部分行业产业化规模不大、政策支持力度不够等问题。2012年，绝大多数摩擦、密封材料生产企业营业收入和净利润与2011年同期持平或下滑，但有近三成企业净利润增长超过10%。汽车摩擦材料产量在行业中居主导地位，占总产量的83.89%，其中盘式刹车片占35.49%，鼓式刹车片占32.66%，制动蹄总成占4.19%，离合器面片占5.59%。此外，刹车带、火车闸瓦、钻机闸瓦、摩托车用摩擦材料分别占总产量的0.62%、0.32%、0.05%和4.55%。

5. 高性能复合材料

航空航天领域的需求推动了复合材料向高端化发展，先进复合材料工艺装备水平和成型工艺技术有所提升，主要用于大飞机、宇航工程等领域。可再生能源风力发电用复合材料叶片、机舱罩产品竞争力加强并出现国际化发展趋势，脱硫、烟囱方面的玻璃钢/复合材料制品、复合材料电缆芯和杆塔的应用范围不断扩大。

我国三大高性能纤维（碳纤维、芳纶、UHMWPE纤维）产能合计约4.45万吨/年，但大部分高性能纤维装置的实际开工率较低，2012年，三大高性能纤维产量约1.35万吨，国内消费量约3.45万吨。2012年，玻璃钢/复合材料行业运行呈现下行迹象，同比增长5%，增幅首次低于全国GDP7.8%的增长水平。

6. 前沿新型材料

石墨烯、超导材料等部分关键技术研发取得新进展。石墨烯产业化发展取得进展，首条石墨烯生产线的开工建设解决了石墨烯量产问题，中国科学院宁波材料研究所研发出的石墨烯批量制备技术大大降低了石墨烯的生产成本，石墨烯产业链逐渐形成，应用市场有望扩大。

（二）存在的主要问题

我国虽然已成为材料大国，但还不是材料强国，我国新材料目前正处于由大到强转变的关键时期。我国新材料产业虽然得到了快速发展，但是从总体上看，与发达国家仍有很大差距，如何实现我国新材料由资源密集型向技术密集型、劳动密集型再向经济密集型的跨越，成为我国面临的迫切问题。我国新材料发展存在的主要问题表现为：

1. 自主研发、创新能力薄弱

我国新材料生产的高端技术装备和很多关键产品严重依赖进口，关键技术受制于人。大型材料企业创新动力不强，研发投入较少，新材料推广应用方面困难；企业对高端技术及先进装备制造的研发投入不足，对制备工艺、性质、性能的研究欠缺，技术储备相对匮乏，基础研究薄弱，导致整体产业竞争力不高。部分新材料企业"重市场轻科技、重硬件轻软件"，特别是在自主创新能力以及人才培养等软实力的建设和培育方面重视程度不够，严重制约了新材料产业的创新发展。

2. 产业集中度低，部分行业产能过剩现象严重

整个产业发展缺乏科学规划、统筹规划和政策引导。新材料企业数目多，规模小，布局分散。工业和信息化部统计数据显示，目前我国稀土冶炼产能为39.9万吨/年，但企业数量较多，有稀土冶炼分离企业99家，产业集中度较低。此外，部分新材料行业已经出现产能过剩迹象，产能利用率低。例如，我国钛加工材中低端产品严重过剩，而高技术含量的深加工产品却远远不能满足需求，厚板（50mm以上）和薄板（0.5mm以下）在我国还不能批量生产，焊管用钛带仍依赖进口。

3. 产品质量水平较低，产品结构有待调整

我国新材料产品以中低端产品为主，如我国硬质合金产量占世界总产量的40%以上，高性能超细合金、高精度高性能研磨涂层刀片、超硬工具材料、复杂大异制品、精密硬质合金数控刀具等高附加值产品产量较少、品种不全。

4. 产品回收利用率低，资源利用率有待提高

随着国家对可持续发展的重视，材料的可回收利用日益受到关注，环保、低碳成为新材料发展的方向。受技术所限，目前我国部分新材料的回收利用率不高，制约了行业的进一步发展，如热固性复合材料的回收利用率低成为制约复合材料行业持续发展的"瓶颈"。整个行业的发展仍然处于高投入、高消耗、低效益的粗放型发展阶段。

5. 新材料检测高端应用不足

材料检测是新材料技术的重要方面之一。按照技术手段通常可将材料检测分为物理检测、化学检测以及无损检测，具体包括光谱分析、色谱分析、X射线分析、核磁共振分析、热分析以及力学性能试验等，通过对材料的化学成分分析，热、光、电、磁、声

等物理性能的分析以及材料的力学性能试验，能准确地了解和掌握材料的化学成分以及性能和质量，对新材料的研发和应用都有着不可替代的作用。在中低端领域，我国的材料检测设备已基本能够满足国内需求，但在高端应用领域，国产检测设备与进口产品相比，从精度到性能仍有很大差距，在一些关键技术方面仍需突破，目前国产检测设备还不能完全满足国内高端应用领域的检测需求。

（三）国内新材料产业发展趋势

1. 特种金属功能材料

（1）稀土功能材料。以提高稀土新材料性能、扩大高端领域应用、增加产品附加值为重点，充分发挥我国稀土资源优势，壮大稀土新材料产业规模。大力发展超高性能稀土永磁材料、稀土发光材料，积极开发高比容量、低自放电、长寿命的新型储氢材料，提高研磨抛光材料产品档次，提升现有催化材料性能和制备技术水平。

（2）稀有金属材料。充分发挥我国稀有金属资源优势，提高产业竞争力。积极发展高纯稀有金属及靶材，大规格钼电极、高品质钼丝、高精度钨窄带、钨钼大型板材和制件、高纯铼及合金制品等高技术含量深加工材料。加快促进超细纳米晶、特粗晶粒等高性能硬质合金产业化，提高原子能级锆材和银铟镉控制棒、高比容钽粉、高效贵金属催化材料的发展水平。

（3）半导体材料。以高纯度、大尺寸、低缺陷、高性能和低成本为主攻方向，逐步提高关键材料自给率。开发电子级多晶硅、大尺寸单晶硅、抛光片、外延片等材料，积极开发氮化镓、砷化镓、碳化硅、磷化铟、锗、绝缘体上硅（SOI）等新型半导体材料，以及铜铟镓硒、铜铟硫、碲化镉等新型薄膜光伏材料，推进高效、低成本光伏材料产业化。

（4）其他功能合金。加快高磁感取向硅钢和铁基非晶合金带材推广应用。积极开发高导热铜合金引线框架、键合丝、稀贵金属钎焊材料、铟锡氧化物（ITO）靶材、电磁屏蔽材料，满足信息产业需要。促进高强高导、绿色无铅新型铜合金接触导线规模化发展，满足高速铁路需要。进一步推动高磁导率软磁材料、高导电率金属材料及相关型材的标准化和系列化，提高电磁兼容材料产业化水平。开发推广耐高温、耐腐蚀铁铬铝金属纤维多孔材料，满足高温烟气处理等需求。

2. 先进高分子材料

（1）特种橡胶。自主研发和技术引进并举，走精细化、系列化路线，大力开发新产品、新牌号，改善产品质量，努力扩大规模，力争到 2015 年国内市场满足率超过 70%。扩大丁基橡胶（IIR）、丁腈橡胶（NBR）、乙丙橡胶（EPR）、异戊橡胶（IR）、聚氨酯橡胶、氟橡胶及相关弹性体等生产规模，加快开发丙烯酸酯橡胶及弹性体、卤化丁基橡胶、氢化丁腈橡胶、耐寒氯丁橡胶和高端苯乙烯系弹性体、耐高低温硅橡胶、耐低温氟橡胶等品种，积极发展专用助剂，强化为汽车、高速铁路和高端装备制造配套的高性能密封、阻尼等专用材料开发。

（2）工程塑料。围绕提高宽耐温、高抗冲、抗老化、高耐磨和易加工等性能，加强改性及加工应用技术研发，扩大国内生产，尽快增强高端品种供应能力。加快发展聚碳酸酯（PC）、聚甲醛（POM）、聚酰胺（PA）、聚对苯二甲酸丁二醇酯（PBT）、聚苯醚（PPO）和聚苯硫醚（PPS）等产品，扩大应用范围，提高自给率。积极开发聚对苯二甲酸丙二醇酯（PTT）和聚萘二甲酸乙二醇酯（PEN）等新型聚酯、特种环氧树脂和长碳链聚酰胺、耐高温易加工聚酰亚胺等新产品或高端产品。力争到2015年国内市场满足率超过50%。

（3）其他功能性高分子材料。巩固有机硅单体生产优势，大力发展硅橡胶、硅树脂等有机硅聚合物产品。着力调整含氟聚合物产品结构，重点发展聚全氟乙丙烯（FEP）、聚偏氟乙烯（PVDF）及高性能聚四氟乙烯等高端含氟聚合物，积极开发含氟中间体及精细化学品。加快电解用离子交换膜、电池隔膜和光学聚酯膜的技术开发及产业化进程，鼓励液体、气体分离膜材料开发、生产及应用。大力发展环保型高性能涂料、长效防污涂料、防水材料、高性能润滑油脂和防火隔音泡沫材料等品种。

3. 新型无机非金属材料

（1）先进陶瓷。重点突破高纯超细陶瓷粉体及先驱体制备、配方开发、烧制成型和精密加工等关键环节，扩大耐高温、耐磨和高稳定性结构功能一体化陶瓷生产规模。重点发展精细熔融石英陶瓷坩埚、陶瓷过滤膜和新型无毒蜂窝陶瓷脱硝催化剂等产品。积极发展超大尺寸氮化硅陶瓷、烧结碳化硅陶瓷、高频多功能压电陶瓷及超声换能用压电陶瓷。大力发展无铅绿色陶瓷材料。建立高纯陶瓷原料保障体系。

（2）特种玻璃。开发超薄玻璃基板成型、低辐射镀膜玻璃膜系设计与制备、高纯石英粉（≥5N）合成和光纤管（金属杂质＜1ppm）制备技术、电子专用石英玻璃及制品制备技术、6代以上TFT-LCD玻璃基板及OLED玻璃基板制备技术。

（3）其他特种无机非金属材料。开发高纯石墨（≥4N）电加热连续式化学提纯、高温连续式绝氧气氛窑生产、柔性石墨碾压法和挤压法加工技术，半导体用石墨保温材料加工技术，人工晶体生长及加工等技术。

（4）新型无机非金属材料。开发6代以上TFT-LCD用玻璃基板窑炉，气氛加压陶瓷烧结炉，超硬材料用大型压机、大功率（30～100kW）微波等离子体和超大面积（150～300mm^2）热灯丝CVD金刚石膜成套装备，高纯石墨用高温（3000～3500℃）各项同性等静压机，（炉内氧含量≤1000ppm）连续式绝氧气氛窑，石墨负极材料包覆和炭化装备等。

4. 高性能复合材料

（1）树脂基复合材料。以低成本、高比强、高比模和高稳定性为目标，攻克树脂基复合材料的原料制备、工业化生产及配套装备等共性关键问题。加快发展碳纤维等高性能增强纤维，提高树脂性能，开发新型超大规格、特殊结构材料的一体化制备工艺，发展风电叶片、建筑工程、高压容器、复合导线及杆塔等专用材料，加强在航空航天、新能源、高速列车、海洋工程、节能与新能源汽车和防灾减灾等领域的应用。

（2）碳/碳复合材料。以耐高温、耐烧蚀、耐磨损及结构功能一体化为重点，加强材料预成型、浸渍渗碳及快速制备工艺研究。积极开发各类高温处理炉、气氛炉所需要的保温筒、发热体和坩埚等材料，推广碳/碳复合材料刹车片、高温紧固件等在运输装备、高温装备中的应用。

(3) 陶瓷基复合材料。进一步提高特种陶瓷基体和碳化硅、氮化硅、氧化铝等增强纤维，以及新型颗粒、晶须增强材料及陶瓷先驱体制备技术水平，加强在削切工具、耐磨器件和航空航天等领域的应用。

(4) 金属基复合材料。发展纤维增强铝基、钛基、镁基复合材料和金属层状复合材料，进一步实现材料轻量化、智能化、高性能化和多功能化，加快应用研究。

5. 前沿新材料

(1) 纳米材料。加强纳米技术研究，重点突破纳米材料及制品的制备与应用关键技术，积极开发纳米粉体、纳米碳管、富勒烯、石墨烯等材料，积极推进纳米材料在新能源、节能减排、环境治理、绿色印刷、功能涂层、电子信息和生物医用等领域的研究应用。

(2) 生物材料。积极开展聚乳酸等生物可降解材料研究，加快实现产业化，推进生物基高分子新材料和生物基绿色化学品产业发展。加强生物医用材料研究，提高材料生物相容性和化学稳定性，大力发展高性能、低成本生物医用高端材料和产品，推动医疗器械基础材料升级换代。

(3) 智能材料。加强基础材料研究，开发智能材料与结构制备加工技术，发展形状记忆合金、应变电阻合金、磁致伸缩材料、智能高分子材料和磁流变液体材料等。

(4) 超导材料。突破高度均匀合金的熔炼及超导线材制备技术，提高铌钛合金和铌锡合金等低温超导材料工程化制备技术水平，发展高温超导千米长线、高温超导薄膜材料规模化制备技术，满足核磁共振成像、超导电缆、无线通信等需求。

新材料产业的发展，应加强新材料学科建设，加大创新型人才培养力度，改革和完善企业分配和激励机制，完善创新型人才评价制度，建立面向新材料产业的人才服务体系。鼓励企业建立新材料工程技术研究中心、工程实验室、企业技术中心、技术开发中心，不断提高企业技术水平和研发能力。围绕材料换代升级，建立若干技术创新联盟和公共服务平台，组织实施重点新材料关键技术研发、产业创新发展、创新成果产业化、应用示范和创新能力建设等重大工程，发挥引领带动作用，促进新材料产业全面发展。

四、广东省新材料产业现状和发展趋势

（一）广东省新材料产业发展现状

作为经济大省，广东在经济快速发展的同时，也将新材料产业确定为"十二五"期间八大战略性新兴产业之一，并出台了《广东省新材料产业发展"十二五"专项规划》，引导全省新材料产业的发展。广东省既是新材料生产大省，也是新材料需求大省，具有良好的产业基础，技术水平与综合实力位居全国前列。在改性塑料、薄膜、涂料、化学建材等高分子材料，电子陶瓷及片式电子元器件，印刷电路板，铝、镁轻合金材料，新型建筑材料，新型二次电池材料，大功率 LED（发光二极管）芯片，OLED（有机发光二极管）等新型发光显示材料及器件等领域均处于国内领先地位。2012 年，广东省统计局建立了八大战略性新兴产业统计指标体系并试运行，根据统计结果，2012

年广东新材料产业实现工业总产值1339.09亿元，同比增长6.1%，实现工业增加值299.16亿元，同比增长7.9%，实现销售产值1293.8亿元，同比增长4.1%，实现主营业务收入1289.7亿元，同比增长0.8%，实现利润60.1亿元，上缴税收32.5亿元，产业总体规模位居全国前列。目前广东省规模以上新材料企业1800余家，其中高新技术企业600多家，约占全省高新技术企业总数的14%，其中新材料产品产值超亿元的企业300余家，行业从业人员约10万人。广东省新材料产业的若干重要门类如先进高分子材料、半导体照明材料、新能源电池材料等已初步形成了较为完整的产业链。新材料企业主要分布在广州、深圳、佛山和东莞4市，产业规模占全省60%以上。目前，已建成国家级新材料产业基地1个、国家火炬计划特色材料产业基地15个、省级新材料特色产业基地32个，初步形成了广州新材料产业国家高技术产业基地、深圳国家半导体照明基地、佛山光伏产业基地等一批特色鲜明、竞争力较强的新材料产业集聚区，并培育出一批处于国内领先地位的新材料龙头骨干企业。

1. 广州市

广州市重点发展有机高分子材料及制品、先进金属材料、无机非金属材料、复合材料、电子信息材料、生物医用材料、清洁新能源材料等新材料领域，已形成较完整的研发和产业体系。目前，广州市新材料产业规模占全省的1/4左右，新材料企业有400余家，新材料产品产值超亿元的企业有100多家，培育出金发科技、华南轮胎、联众、白云化工、冠昊生物、天赐高新等一批具有较强竞争力的新材料骨干企业。

2. 深圳市

深圳市重点发展电子信息材料、新能源材料、生物材料等支撑领域新材料，新型功能材料、功能结构一体化材料等优势领域新材料和超材料、纳米材料、超导材料新兴领域新材料。目前，深圳市新材料产业规模占全省的1/5左右，新材料领域高新技术企业有300余家，培育出比亚迪、贝特瑞、中金岭南、南玻、光启、格林美等一批处于国际国内领先地位的新材料龙头企业，建有全球首条超材料生产线（光启超材料生产线），未来前景乐观。

3. 佛山市

佛山市重点发展高端金属材料、新能源材料、电子信息材料、化工新材料、先进高分子材料等新材料领域，是全国最大的铝型材、建筑陶瓷材料、不锈钢、包装膜、偏光膜和功能膜生产基地，新材料产业特色明显、优势突出。目前，佛山市新材料产业规模占全省的1/6左右，规模以上新材料企业有400余家，培育出佛塑科技、联塑科技、邦普、奔朗、新劲刚、炜林纳、钜仕泰等一批特色鲜明的新材料小巨人企业。

4. 东莞市

东莞市重点发展电子信息材料、新能源材料、先进复合材料和生态环境材料等新材料领域，在新能源电池材料、镁合金、太阳能玻璃等领域优势突出。目前，东莞市新材料产业规模占全省的1/7左右，规模以上新材料企业200多家，培育出生益科技、杜邦电子、东莞新能源、贝特利、宜安电器、中成化工、杉杉电池材料等一批具有一定市场影响力的新材料优势企业。

（二）存在的主要问题

近年来，广东省新材料产业发展取得积极进展，产业发展初具规模，产业链条基本成型，产业集聚态势初步形成，自主创新能力基础较好，市场需求空间广阔，培育出一批处于国内领先地位的新材料龙头骨干企业。但从总体上看，广东省新材料产业还存在不少亟待加强和改进的地方。

1. 企业规模普遍偏小，产业缺乏统筹规划和政策引导

产值超过10亿元的企业较少，主要以中小企业为主，生产中低端产品的中小企业占据了大多数，综合竞争力不强，对地方经济和相关产业的辐射带动作用不明显。由于新材料企业规模偏小，与国内外相关的大企业，尤其是一些跨国公司直接开展竞争，往往缺乏足够的抗风险能力。新材料品牌优势不明显，优势企业较少，产品档次与附加值相对较低，缺少核心专利，国际竞争压力大。以电池企业为例，虽然广东新型电池产业发展迅猛，出现了比亚迪、比克等国际国内领先的龙头企业，以及贝特瑞等电池材料知名企业，但产业短板仍明显，表现为锂电池生产小厂林立，产品质量参差不齐，整个产业缺乏统一规划，大部分小厂商技术创新能力不强，产品同质化严重，甚至还有不少锂电池产自家庭作坊，环境保护问题较为严峻。

2. 产业链条短，产业综合配套能力不强

新材料企业总体上仍集中在相关产业链的中低附加值环节，后续加工能力和应用推广能力偏弱，产业综合配套能力不强。产业链的深度应用开发能力较差，普遍存在产业链条过短、位置过低的现象，在同一产业链上处于高端位置和拥有较高附加值的设备制造、模具制作及研发体系介入太少，很多领域甚至是空白。新材料产业主要是靠市场拉动发展起来的，在原材料领域不具备比较优势，因此原材料价格的波动将对企业生产运营产生较大影响。另外，由于材料的基础性，近几年不利的宏观经济形势，造成了其他行业对材料需求下降，也对新材料企业的发展产生了一定影响。

3. 产业集聚水平尚需提高

在规划和政策出台之前，新材料产业缺乏专门管理和服务，可以说走的是一条自由式发展道路。与生物产业相比，新材料企业布局比较分散，缺乏大型产业园区，难以形成和发挥新材料产业集聚效应。近年来，广东省加强规划建设新材料产业园区，但尚处于规划建设阶段，离真正发挥作用还有一定时间。与此同时，部分产业基地或园区内产业同质化竞争问题仍较突出，企业间专业化分工和差异化经营格局尚未形成，产业缺乏集聚，影响了产业协同发展，产业链需要进一步完善。配套企业能力不强，大多数企业处于独立完成生产制造的全过程，相互之间关联度不高、影响力小，影响了新材料产业的核心竞争力和整体实力的发挥。

4. 自主创新能力有待提升

新材料产业中前沿领域比重仍较低，产品跟踪仿制的多，前瞻性技术储备不足，集成创新能力薄弱，部分产品集中在各种初级矿产和低档加工产品方面，高性能和高附加值的材料产品品种少，深加工产品发展不足。关键核心技术和装备主要依赖进口，与装备制造企业的同步开发合作不多，特别是一些品种比较新、技术含量比较高的新材料产品应用推广缓慢。研发投入有待进一步提高，技术创新能力有待进一步增强，与医疗器械、生物制药行业相比，还存在一定差距。新材料产业民营企业居多，绝大多数企业缺少自主创新条件，如资金短缺、技术人才匮乏、发展规模有限等，即使有企业开展技术创新活动，但仍以内部研发和工艺创新改进为主，拥有的自主知识产权太少，企业研发投入普遍不足。与此同时，近两年新建的一批创新机构的创新载体作用还有待进一步发挥。

5. 人才、资金、生产场所等生产要素紧缺

人才资源较为紧缺，影响了广东新材料产业的长远发展。从人才培养来看，自身培养的材料技术人才难以支撑广东新材料产业的快速发展。从人才引进来看，近年来受较高生活成本和高房价的影响，国家统筹推进区域协调发展，城市间人才竞争激烈，广东对人才的吸引力严重下降。同时，在人才自身培养不足、引进难度加大和人才外移加剧的背景下，广东人才比较优势渐趋弱化，发展后劲不足。

与传统材料产业相比，新材料产品在研制、开发和产业化各阶段都需要大量的资金投入，同时新材料企业的无形资产比重较大，产品、技术、市场和财务有着较大的不确定性，目前新材料产业化项目的孵化、风险投资机制尚未建立，资金短缺难题难以得到快速解决。

随着新材料产业的不断发展壮大，企业开始不断扩大生产规模，对土地诉求有增大的趋势。目前，新材料企业正面临生产研发场地缺乏和不确定性的烦恼，场所问题已经成为制约新材料产业发展的主要因素之一，产业转移迹象较为明显，未来将影响产业发展水平。

（三）广东省新材料产业发展趋势

广东省出台了贯彻国务院《关于加快培育和发展战略性新兴产业的决定》的意见，发布实施《广东省新材料产业发展"十二五"专项规划》，确定了包括新材料在内的八大战略性新兴产业重点领域，在"十二五"期间，省财政集中投入220亿元支持战略性新兴产业发展，并在市场培育、标准制定、知识产权、人才培养和引进、财税支持、金融创新、土地供给等方面出台一系列重磅扶持政策，支持骨干企业发展壮大，推动产业基地扩容升级，促进产业链条延伸完善，建立战略性新兴产业重点项目审批"绿色通道"，加快项目审批事项办理进度。据粗略统计，广东省"十二五"期间新材料产业建设项目近60个，项目总投资近700亿元，涵盖特种金属材料、高分子材料及复合材料、无机非金属材料、超材料、纳米材料等领域，主要集中在广州、深圳、佛山。

广东省将推动建立和完善新材料行业管理体系，选择最有可能率先突破和做大做强的新材料领域予以重点推进，大力发展稀土及稀有金属功能材料、新型电子信息材料、先进电池材料、高性能膜材料等科技含量高、产业基础好、市场潜力大、带动作用强的细分产业，培育一批创新能力强、创业环境好的特色新材料产业基地，扶持一批具有国际竞争力的龙头企业和创新能力较强的成长性企业，为广东省高端装备制造、新能源汽车、半导体照明等其他战略性新兴产业发展提供基础支撑和保障，全面提升广东省新材料产业竞争力。

广东省新材料产业将突出做好"五个一"工程：

1. 完善一个统计认定制度

建立新材料产业专家库，在新材料领域选择30家左右的龙头企业作为重点联系企业，建立基本情况报送制度，开展日常运行监测与统计分析，编制新材料产业发展分析报告，为决策和管理提供基础依据。根据工信部工作部署，开展新材料企业、产品认定试点，明确新材料产业的边界与范围，为加强行业管理创造条件。

2. 制定一个发展指导目录

落实国家和省新材料产业"十二五"发展规划，制定新材料产业化发展指导目录，明确重点发展领域，引导投资方向。抓好工信部《新材料产业"十二五"发展规划》十大工程和400个重点产品的对接实施工作，合理选择广东省重点承接发展的工程和产品。

3. 建设一批产业基地

加快广州新材料、佛山新材料、汕头锆材料、韶关金属材料和清远光电子材料产业等省市共建战略性新兴产业（新材料）基地建设，继续推动新增认定一批新材料产业基地，推进省市共建战略性新兴产业基地建设，协调解决产业链关键配套问题，增强产业整体配套能力和竞争优势。

4. 组建一个产业联盟

在新材料领域选择有一定特点和潜力的行业（初定稀土稀有金属）组建跨领域、跨行业、跨地区产业联盟，推动政府、企业、科研机构和中介组织有效衔接和产业链全链条对接。

5. 扶持一批骨干企业和重点项目

整合国家、省、市、企资源，推动一批新材料重点工程和项目实现"产学研用"一体化发展，打造若干新材料细分领域领先优势基地。依托省战略性新兴产业政银企合作专项资金，集中扶持一批新材料骨干企业和重点项目，完善上下游配套产业，优化产业发展环境。依托"广货网上行"、"广东商贸城"等平台，帮助新材料产品开拓内需市场，组织新材料企业与下游应用企业的对接交流活动，促进新材料产品推广应用。

第二章 新材料产业标准化发展现状

一、标准化与技术应用、产业发展的关系

标准化是促进技术和产业发展的重要技术基础，标准是人们在其发展过程中积累起来的经验和知识的体现，也是其发展水平的基线或起点。它在技术与开发、科研与生产、市场与需求、供应与采办、政府与企业之间，发挥着"桥梁"与"纽带"作用。标准化对于促进行业的技术进步，节约利用资源，提高经济效益，推广科学技术成果，适应市场需求，提高产品的通用互换性具有重要意义。同时，技术和生产的发展变化，也推动了标准化活动的变化和发展，标准化在世界技术和经济活动中的地位日益重要。

（一）促进企业技术创新

标准化是新技术的载体，标准化与科技发展有着极为密切的关系。标准是依据科学、技术和经验的综合成果而制定的，它包含了许多成熟的先进技术，反映了具有市场潜力的主流技术，提供了大量的技术动向和数据，并与新技术的发展保持同步，所以，加强标准化工作对促进科技进步具有重要意义。

标准化能够促进企业提升技术与产品开发能力。具体而言，围绕提高企业自主开发能力的设计技术、制造技术、测试技术、计算机和软件技术、管理技术等都与标准化有关。标准化为技术改造（包括技术引进）提供了重要技术导向，新标准促进产品更新换代，企业新技术、新成果借助标准载体，可以加速技术传播，促进产品创新，促进新技术产业和新兴市场的形成。通常，技术改造是围绕产品及企业的开发能力而进行的。与产品直接相关的产品标准及其配套标准，为企业产品改造目标、装备和测试手段能力的提高及最终考核验收提供基本的技术依据。

（二）提高产品质量水平

产业发展必须有产品质量作为坚强后盾，标准定量地给出了衡量产品质量特性的各项要求以及相应的考核或评测方法。所以，标准是产品质量的准绳，是衡量产品质量的尺子，是检验工作的依据。在市场经济中，规范性文件（包括技术法规、标准、规范、规程、导则、规则、指南等）为进入市场的产品质量提供了科学的衡量依据。在市场中，不管是国有企业还是个体私营企业，不管是外资企业还是内资企业，它们的产品质量合格与否或能否进入市场，都使用同一把"尺子"——标准来进行"度量"，标准使大家都站在同一起跑线上参与市场竞争。

此外，规范性文件为市场中产品质量的监管及仲裁提供了依据。市场监管体系的技

术依据就是标准：第一，质量监督的抽样、试验和检查的程序及方法，必须依据标准；第二，合格判据，必须依据标准；第三，环境试验设备和测量设备等试验手段的配备，必须依据标准；第四，合格评估、鉴定和保证，必须按有关规范性文件的规定进行；第五，实验室的注册、认可和批准，也必须按有关规范性文件的规定办理。

（三）保证产品的通用互换

保证产品的通用互换性是技术标准的基本属性之一。对某些零件或部件的种类、规格，按照一定的标准加以精简统一，使之能在类似产品中实现通用互换，既保护了消费者的利益，又避免了社会财富和物质资源的浪费，是用户和制造商共同追求的理想目标，其经济效益和社会效益显而易见。

在实际生产中，通用化的目的是最大限度地扩大同一产品（包括元器件、部件、组件、最终产品）的使用范围，从而最大限度地减少产品（或零件）在设计和制造过程中的重复劳动。其效果体现在简化管理程序，缩短产品设计和试制周期，扩大生产批量，提高专业化生产水平和产品质量，方便顾客和维修，最终获得各种活劳动和物化劳动的节约。通用标准化的实施从产品开发设计开始，一是在对产品进行系列开发时，通过分析产品系列中零部件的共性与个性，从中找出具有共性的零部件，能够通用的尽量通用，这是系列内通用，是最基本和最常用的环节。如有可能，还可以发展系列间的产品和零部件通用。二是单独开发某一产品（非系列产品）时，也尽量采用已有的通用件。即使是新设计的零部件，也应充分考虑使其能为以后的新产品所采用，逐步发展成为通用件。三是在老产品改造时，根据生产、使用、维修过程中暴露出来的问题，对可以实现通用互换的零部件尽可能通用化，以继续降低生产成本，保证可靠性，焕发老产品的青春。

（四）应对技术性贸易壁垒

当今，世界经济的全球化格局正在形成，各国经济已从"互通有无"转向"互相依存"。在这一形势下，标准化、通用化的国际潮流成为对犬牙交错的国内外市场进行协调、沟通、信任、简化的有效手段。在国际贸易中，世界贸易组织已经形成了一套国际贸易规则，其中贸易技术壁垒协议对技术法规、标准、合格评定都做出了明确规定。如果各方都按规定执行同样的要求，就可以消除贸易中的技术壁垒；如果不按规定的要求执行，就可以设置贸易中的技术壁垒。因此，我们应当运用标准化手段，对国内与国外标准之间的差异进行分析和研究，认真比对各类技术指标及材料检测的试验方法和要求等差异，通过对自己的产品进行适应性改进来应对技术性贸易壁垒，规避市场风险，扩大国际贸易。

二、国内外新材料产业标准建设现状

根据《广东省新材料产业发展"十二五"专项规划》（粤经信材料〔2011〕666号），广东省现阶段重点发展先进金属材料、新型无机非金属材料、高性能有机高分子材料及复合材料、特种精细化工材料、新型稀土功能材料五大领域。2012年3月由广东省政府办公厅印发的《广东省战略性新兴产业发展"十二五"规划》，在新材料领域的分类中，增加了"前沿新型材料"一类。如果将稀土功能材料列入先进金属材料分类中，那么可将新材料种类分为先进金属材料、新型无机非金属材料、高性能有机高分子材料及复合材料、特种精细化工材料、前沿新型材料五大类。下面我们就主要介绍新材料领域中这五大分类的标准建设情况。

（一）先进金属材料

1. 钢铁与黑金属材料

钢铁和黑金属领域新材料的产生，大部分来源于钢铁和黑金属传统产业的制造和应用过程中，其标准化过程与传统材料的标准化融合在一起。

国际标准化组织ISO中，负责钢铁及黑金属相关标准制修订的标准化技术委员会主要是9个ISO/TC、30个SC。自1978年9月1日我国恢复在ISO席位以来，我国由冶金工业信息标准研究院负责归口管理并组织参加钢铁及其原材料工业方面的国际标准化技术委员会的标准制修订工作，其中TC5黑色金属管与管件技术委员会、TC17钢技术委员会等15个委员会共制定了1061个ISO标准及技术报告。我国的钢铁及黑金属材料标准化程度与国际水平基本相当。在我国国家和行业标准中，由国家发展和改革委员会（以下简称"国家发改委"）、铁道部、原冶金部等部门制订的各行业涉及钢铁的标准共849项，其中采标标准65项，涵盖GJB、HB、YB等多个行业标准。

2. 有色金属

与有色金属相关的先进金属材料是目前先进金属材料的重要组成部分。在标准化分工上，部分有色金属材料的标准化仍然与传统材料融合在一起，但与黑金属材料不同的是，很多先进有色金属材料已经能够在各自的领域成为主要的甚至是核心的材料。

在国际标准化领域，负责有色金属标准制修订的ISO标准化技术委员会主要包括ISO/TC26（铜及铜合金）、ISO/TC79（轻金属及其合金）、ISO/TC115（镍及镍合金）、ISO/TC18（锌及锌合金〈暂停〉）。ISO/TC79/SC5（镁及镁合金）已完成9项国际标准的制定，标准体系基本涵盖了国际范围内广泛生产和销售的镁及镁合金产品、主要检测方法的范围。特别是以河南宇航金属材料有限公司为首的多家国内企业，还以国家标准为蓝本，将我国的先进标准GB/T 3499转化为国际标准，并诞生了我国有色金属领域首例以我国为主制定的国际标准ISO8287—2011《原生镁锭》。ISO/TC26（铜及铜合金）国际标准化技术委员会成立于1947年，目前的秘书国是中国，其工作范围是铜及铜合金的非变形、变形和铸造产品的标准化工作，其中包括铜及铜合金的材料规范、尺寸及偏差、特性测试的方法等，自成立以来，共完成38项国际标准的制定，其中基础标准6项、产品标准1项，其余均为方法标准。

在我国，《有色金属工业"十二五"发展规划》明确提出："加强标准化建设——适应有色金属工业加快产品结构调整、发展新材料的需要，建立、修订、完善技术和产品标准。进一步做好能耗、安全生产、清洁生产标准的制定。制定再生有色金属能源消耗标准和环保标准。加大参与国际标准化工作的力度，实现国际国内标准接轨和双向转化。"推进有色金属行业标准化是落实"十二五"规划的重要任务。

全国有色金属标准化技术委员会于 1999 年成立。截止到 2012 年 10 月，我国拥有有色金属国家标准 1153 项、行业标准 1134 项，标准数量远超欧美等发达国家，成为名副其实的有色金属标准第一大国，同时我国着力推进采用国际标准和国外先进标准，将美国、德国、日本标准作为采标的重点对象，使我国有色金属标准在很短时间内缩小了与国际先进标准的差距。目前，我国国家标准和行业标准的采标率已分别达到 88% 和 83%。近十几年来，我国有色金属行业尤其是加工行业发展迅速，产业水平得到很大提升。在这一过程中，标准化起到了重要的保障和牵引作用，使产业的发展和标准的发展实现了无缝衔接。随着近年来建设环境友好型、资源节约型社会的要求逐步增强，我国尤为关注再生金属、能耗、安全、清洁生产等方面的标准。截至 2011 年 6 月，我国已发布再生金属标准 25 项、能源标准 82 项、安全生产标准 8 项、清洁生产标准 6 项，这些标准的发布实施，为有色金属工业的健康、可持续发展提供了重要保障。我国还积极加强标准修订工作力度，努力保证标准的适用性。截至 2011 年 6 月，2006 年后即五年标龄的标准达到 70% 以上，这意味着"十一五"期间每年有 300 项左右标准得以更新。广东省有色金属标准化工作经过多年努力，也取得了长足进步，与国际标准化程度同步甚至走在国家标准化的前列。

3. 新型稀土功能材料

稀土是 21 世纪重要的战略资源，不仅是重要的先进金属材料，也是形成以其他类型基础材料为主体的新型复合功能材料的重要组成部分。我国稀土资源占全球总储量的 53.5%，成为世界重要的稀土产出国。

在国际标准化组织 ISO 中，没有独立的稀土标准制修订委员会，与稀土相关的标准仅有 ISO/TC85/SC5（核能源循环）出台的 3 项检测标准。

在我国，稀土工业已经成为当前重点发展的产业之一。2011 年 5 月 10 日，《国务院关于促进稀土行业持续健康发展的若干意见》颁布，在大力强调保护环境和战略性资源的同时，把"稀土新材料对下游产业的支撑和保障作用得到明显发挥"作为目标之一。同时，《稀土工业污染物排放标准》自 2011 年 10 月 1 日起实施，作为"十二五"期间环保部发布的第一个国家污染物排放标准，该标准的制定和实施将有利于提高稀土产业准入门槛，加快转变稀土行业发展方式，推动稀土产业结构调整，促进稀土行业持续健康发展。在广东省，2012 年 2 月，经广东省政府批准，以广晟资产经营有限公司为主体组建成立广东省稀土产业集团。该集团与曾充当广东稀土资源整合唯一旗手角色的上市公司广晟有色金属股份有限公司同属广东省广晟资产经营有限公司的子公司。集团成立后动作频频，先后与韶关、河源、汕尾、茂名等多个地方政府签订稀土产业发展合作框架协议。

在标准制定方面，GB/T 28504.1—2012《掺稀土光纤第 1 部分：双包层掺镱光纤特性》是我国稀土光纤的首个国家标准。该标准主要涉及掺稀土光纤中双包层掺镱光纤，主要应用于具有广泛应用前景的光纤激光器，光纤激光器属于第三代激光器，对于光纤激光器的发展至关重要。2013 年 12 月 27 日，广东省稀土标准化技术委员会在江门市正式揭牌成立，由江门市科恒实业股份有限公司承担委员会秘书处工作。

（二）新型无机非金属材料

1. 新型节能和绿色建筑材料

欧美等发达国家一向作为节能的先锋力量，以自身高端技术为优势，不断推出与建筑节能有关的法规及标准。美国法制比较完善，政府一般以立法形式制定强制性的最低能源效率标准，从而推动各种新型节能和绿色建材的发展。如美国过去几年出台了《国际建筑节能法规 IECC》、《国际住宅法规 IRC》、《ANSI/ASHRAE/IESNA90.1 标准（除低层住宅之外的新建筑节能设计）》和《ASHRAE90.2 标准（新建低层住宅节能设计）》等多个法规标准来推动建筑节能。而具体到确立建筑行业标准的任务，则属于各州政府的职权，比如加利福尼亚、纽约等经济比较发达的州，其建筑节能标准比联邦政府的标准还要严格。美国目前应用最为广泛的建筑标识体系是由美国环保署（EPA，Environmental Protection Agency）在 1992 年推出的"能源之星"（Energy Star）体系。"能源之星"所能认证的产品多种多样，小至电灯泡，大至房屋。LEED（Leadership in Energy and Environ – mental Design）也是应用非常广泛的一个建筑标识体系，它是美国节能与生态环境建筑委员会为满足美国建筑市场对节能与生态环境建筑评定的要求，提高建筑环境和经济特性而制定的一套评定标准。LEED 目前在世界各国的各类建筑环保评估和绿色建筑评估标准中被认为是最完善、最有影响力的评估标准。为促进自愿性能耗标识产品的推广应用，美国的政府部门采取多种激励措施并积极发挥示范作用。经济激励是成功实施能效标准和标识特别是"能源之星"标识的关键性配套政策措施。美国各级政府和公用事业公司采取多种激励措施，对增强公众节能意识、推广节能产品（包括建筑）取得了非常显著的效果。

欧盟推动新型节能和绿色建材的发展也是通过立法、认证的方式。在提高能效方面，欧盟一直走在世界的前列。早在 2002 年，欧洲议会和欧盟理事会就在布鲁塞尔通过了《欧盟建筑能源性能指令〈2002/91/EC〉》，而欧盟也在 2011 年 3 月 9 日颁布了新的建筑产品法规（305/2011/EU – CPR）取代旧的建筑产品指令（89/106/EEC – CPD），并通告 CPR 于 2013 年 7 月进入强制执行阶段。CPR 要求任何以永久性方式构成建筑工程的任何产品，建筑工程包括建筑物和土建工程，如玻璃、混凝料、水泥、管道、屋顶材料、木板、吊顶、沥青混合料、地板、墙纸壁纸、建筑用颜料、下水道设备、砖块、门窗、结构金属产品、保温材料、防水材料、结构木料、交通信号指示等，都需要取得 CE 标志方可在欧盟市场上出售。

广东是我国的建材生产大省，从 20 世纪 80 年代后期开始，广东省建材产品在全国市场的占有率多年来居全国首位。新型节能建材是区别于传统的砖瓦、灰沙石等建材的建筑材料新品种，行业内对新型建筑材料的范围作了明确的界定，即新型建筑材料主要包括新型墙体材料、新型防水密封材料、新型保温隔热材料和装饰装修材料四大类。它生产耗能低，使用中的节能效果显著，而且还具有节土、节地、环保、利废、隔热保温、防火、轻质、减少运输费用、施工便捷、成本低廉等特点。目前国内关于新型节能和绿色建筑材料的标准约有 700 多项，个别标准已陈旧过时，新建立的标准大部分参照或采用 ISO 国际标准。

1997年，我国颁布了最早的与建筑节能相关的法律法规——《中华人民共和国节约能源法》与《中华人民共和国建筑法》，除了实施条例或实施办法外，我国还围绕推行新型建材和墙体改革制定了一系列国家与行业标准。"十一五"期间，国家大力制定标准初有成效，弥补了不少新型节能建筑材料的行业标准与国家标准的空缺，制定了如JGJ 144—2008《外墙外保温工程技术规程》、GB/T 25352—2010《隔热隔音材料耐烧穿试验方法》、GB 26540—2011《外墙外保温系统用钢丝网架模塑聚苯乙烯板》、JC/T 2122—2012《轻质混凝土吸声板》等标准，填补了建筑物保温、隔音吸音材料标准方面的空缺，对新型墙材及节能建材起到了良好的规范作用。另外，节能、超薄、安全玻璃也属新型节能和绿色建筑材料，我国已在2002年发布了GB/T 18915.2—2002《镀膜玻璃 第2部分：低辐射镀膜玻璃》以规范Low-E玻璃的产品标准，目前国产Low-E玻璃大多按照此推荐性国标生产，而出口欧洲的Low-E玻璃则要符合其强制性EN 1096—4：2004《建筑物用玻璃 涂层玻璃 第4部分：合格评价/产品标准》，取得相应的CE标志才可顺利出口。我国还发布了最新的浮法玻璃标准，如JC/T 2128—2012《超白浮法玻璃》、GB/T 29157—2012《浮法玻璃生产生命周期评价技术规范（产品种类规则）》、GB 26453—2011《平板玻璃工业大气污染物排放标准》等。

2. 高性能陶瓷材料

高性能陶瓷材料是新材料的重要组成部分，在国民经济中的能源、电子、航空航天、机械、汽车、冶金、石油化工和生物等领域有广阔的应用前景，是工业技术特别是尖端技术中不可缺少的关键材料。

美国先进陶瓷发展的重点为高温结构陶瓷，目前在航天技术、汽车、航空器、核工程、医疗设备及机械动力等方面已进入大范围使用阶段。日本近年来则一直将精细陶瓷看作决定未来竞争力前途的高科技产业，不遗余力地不断加大投资力度，其生产的先进陶瓷敏感元件已占据国际市场主要份额。此外，日本在开发陶瓷发动机方面也走在世界前列。欧盟各国也在功能陶瓷与高温结构陶瓷两方面不断加大投资力度，目前研究的重点为发电设备中应用的新型材料技术。欧美各国对陶瓷产品不断提高技术门槛，尤其是近年强化环保生态标准，对陶瓷制品原材料和成品中有毒物质的含量或释放量做出了严格限定，对加工生产环节中的能耗、自然资源使用量、废弃物的处理均提出严格要求。目前，全球各类高性能陶瓷及其产品的市场销售总额每年达数百亿美元，年增长率达8%。

我国现有陶瓷标准400多条，约有200条为2000年前制定的。随着科技的创新与节能减排的大环境推动，陶瓷产业注定要往复合型、轻薄型、电子型、生物型及节能方向发展，我国近年来也制定出台了有关标准。随着两个强制性国家标准GB 21252—2007《建筑卫生陶瓷单位产品能源消耗限额标准》与GB 25464—2010《陶瓷工业污染物排放标准》的实行，我国陶瓷企业开始了环保节能之路。根据国家级科研项目《大规格超薄建筑陶瓷砖产业化技术开发》推出的技术标准成果，应用标准JGJ/T 172—2012《建筑陶瓷薄板应用技术规程》和产品标准GB/T 23266—2009《陶瓷板》也已出台。

我国的特种陶瓷行业的标准化工作主要由全国工业陶瓷标准化技术委员会

(TC194）负责，范围包括工业陶瓷、结构陶瓷、特种陶瓷、红外陶瓷等专业领域的标准化工作，业务上与国际标准化组织 ISO/TC206 对口，秘书处设在山东工业陶瓷研究设计院。目前，全国工业陶瓷标准化技术委员会下设三个分技术委员会，即耐磨陶瓷衬板应用技术、结构陶瓷和功能陶瓷分技术委员会，功能陶瓷分技术委员会主要负责绝缘陶瓷、介电陶瓷（主要是电容器和微波陶瓷）、铁电陶瓷、压电陶瓷、热释电陶瓷、电致伸缩陶瓷、电光陶瓷、透明陶瓷、半导体（PTC、NTC）陶瓷和磁性陶瓷的标准修制定工作。由于我国是国际精细陶瓷标准化技术委员会创始成员国，并一直作为正式会员国参与国际精细陶瓷标准化技术委员会的工作，因此我国的精细陶瓷标准化工作同国际联系紧密，特别是在检测方法的标准化方面基本参照国际标准制定。截至2012年，全国工业陶瓷标准化技术委员会共制定标准44份，其中基础标准2份，检测方法标准25份（国家标准18份，行业标准7份），产品标准17份（国家标准1份，行业标准16份）。与日本和美国的特种陶瓷标准化技术委员会注重检测方法标准制定不同的是，我国的特种陶瓷标准化技术委员会还注重相关产品标准的制定，尤其是山东工业陶瓷研究设计院和中国科学院上海硅酸盐研究所在相关领域的标准化工作成绩突出，但与美国制定出60多个检测方法标准相比，我国还有很多工作要做。

3. 电子信息材料

当前电子信息正向着集成化、微型化和智能化方向发展，相应地要求电子元器件逐步向微型化、薄膜化、多功能、高效能、高可靠性和高稳定性方向发展。近年来，敏感元件及传感器片式化等无机非金属电子信息产品生产技术在世界各国得到迅速发展，美国、法国、德国、荷兰、日本等国均已实现产业化。由于产品技术含量高，国外在此技术领域对我们严格保密。目前，受到技术方面的制约，电子信息材料的国内外标准均呈现更新快、专利化的趋势。国内外均有一些基础性的电子信息材料基础标准，或与环保有关的标准，但其技术核心和产品标准均由企业自己掌握。目前，国内现有无机非金属电子信息材料标准近200份，多与国际标准接轨，然而近几年行业发展快，标准并未能跟上发展的步伐，需进一步贴近实际，更新老旧标准，提高标准要求。同时，与美国、日本比较，我国标准还有一定的差距。

（三）高性能有机高分子材料及复合材料

新材料领域的技术竞赛正在全球上演。各国政府或地区委员会，以及相关组织纷纷出台各种技术法规和标准，规范企业和产品市场。

传统高分子材料的应用广泛，标准和技术法规数量庞大。传统塑料经过改性后具有了新的性能或功能，也跻身新材料的行列，对应的技术法规或标准经过更新后，也成为新材料相关的技术法规或标准。因而，在高分子新材料领域的标准数量庞大，新材料的更新换代及其标准的更新一直在持续。近几年，多种高分子新材料的推出导致标准的更新速度加快，仅ISO组织2010—2012年间在高分子材料领域就有超过15条基础标准、50多条产品质量标准和60多条测试技术标准得到更新或制定。发达国家推出和更新标准的速度更快，如欧盟标准化委员会推出的不包括等同采用ISO或IEC标准的标准，2010年以后更新或制定高分子新材料基础标准10余条、产品质量标准50多条以及超过 30 条检测技术标准。美国在 2010—2012 年间共更新或推出了高分子新材料相关标准 60 余条，其中约 10 条来自非政府组织。日本也更新了近 20 条相关标准。以上统计数字都不包括各发达国家等同采用的国际标准数。

标准的更新，很多是以传统塑料标准为基础的标准修订，增加了经过技术升级或改性成为新材料以后的术语、制备方法、规格、测试方法等内容。新推出的新材料标准有 CEN/TR 15932—2010、CEN/TR 15932—2010、ASCE 52—10—2010、JIS C5101—26—2012 系列标准等。

我国高分子领域现行的国家标准有 700 多条，行业标准 1000 多条。其中 2000 年之前制定的现行标准有 70 余条，2000—2004 年五年间实施的标准 130 条左右，2005—2010 年五年间实施的标准近 400 条，2010—2012 年新实施的标准有 180 条左右，标准更新的速度充分说明了高分子领域推陈出新的速度。在更新过的标准中，只有传统高分子材料测试方法不属于高分子新材料标准。2006 年以后实施的标准中，传统高分子材料试验方法的修订标准不超过 50 条，即大部分标准都属于高分子新材料领域的标准。

与国际和国外先进标准相比，我国 2010—2012 年间的标准更新主要集中在产品质量标准的更新和制定上，测试方法类的标准比较少。在产品质量标准中，产品的类型与国际标准的类型差别较大。相对而言，我国 2010—2012 年的产品质量标准，比较侧重于推出新型材料以及新型材料产品标准，而国际上和发达国家 2010—2012 年推出的标准，类型比较广泛，但多数集中在传统的管材、板材、包装、胶黏剂等标准的更新上，新材料领域推出的新标准不多。发达国家新材料的标准更多地出现在企业或其他标准化组织的标准中。

（四）特种精细化工材料

1. 船舶产业链配套用精细化工材料

截至 2009 年 12 月，我国现行有效船舶工业标准共 2173 项，其中国家标准（GB）450 项、行业标准（CB）1723 项，专业覆盖船舶通用基础、船舶总体、船体结构、船舶舾装、船舶管系及附件、船舶主辅机及附件、船舶轴系及推进装置、船舶电气系统及设备、船舶导航与通信系统及设备、信息技术应用、船用材料、造船工艺、船舶修理、管理等多个领域，基本满足了同时期我国常规船舶设计、建造、维修和管理的需要。

目前，船舶工业对口的现行 ISO、IEC 国际标准已有 70% 被我国不同程度地转化，并基本实现了对国际标准最新版本的跟踪等同采用。与此同时，我国船舶工业还积极参照日本工业标准（JIS）、美国标准（ANSI）、法国标准（NF）、欧洲标准（EN）、美国材料与试验协会标准（ASTM）等国外先进标准制定我国标准，并在相关标准制定中不同程度地遵照或引用国际海事组织《1974 年国际海上人命安全公约》（SOLAS）和《73/78 国际防止船舶造成污染公约》（MARPOL）等公约规则、国际航道航行规则以及国际各大知名船级社规范中的技术要求，在较大程度上提高了我国船舶工业标准的技术水平和国际化程度。

2. 电子信息和能源产业配套用电子化学品

电子化学品所涉及的业务领域和技术范围十分广泛，国际和国内均有很多标准化组织从事该领域标准化工作，各标准化组织涵盖的领域和侧重的范围不尽相同。SEMI（国际半导体设备与材料协会）是一家全球高科技领域专业行业协会，创建于1970年，拥有会员公司2000多家。会员是从事半导体、平面显示、太阳能光伏、纳米科技、微电子机械系统等领域开发、生产和技术支持的公司。SEMI标准在国际上具有广泛的代表性和权威性，是世界范围内半导体设备和材料领域的事实工业标准，其标准化工作领域涉及设备/设备自动化、材料、气体、工艺化学品（高纯试剂）、封装、平板显示、微光刻、光伏、微电子机械系统等。截至2012年4月，SEMI标准中涉及电子化学品领域的标准共有228项。IEC/TC91国际电工委员会电子装联技术委员会成立于1990年，是国际上从事包括印制电路板在内的整个电子装联技术领域工作的标准化组织，其业务领域涉及印制电路板及其组装件设计、印制电路板、印制电路板基材、电子装联等。近年来，随着欧盟RoHS（《关于限制在电子电器设备中使用某些有害成分的指令》）等相关法规的出台，针对市场对绿色电子产品的需求，IEC/TC91重点开展了一批适应无铅、无卤要求的印制板及基材的标准化工作。IEC/TC91中涉及的电子化学品标准主要集中在印制电路板材料和电子组装件材料上。截至2012年，涉及该领域的标准共计44项。

SAC/TC203全国半导体设备和材料标准化技术委员会成立于1992年，前身是EMI中国标准化委员会，对口国际SEMI相关工作，所涉及业务领域基本与SEMI相同，涵盖半导体材料、光伏材料、平板显示材料、LED照明材料、电子气体、电子封装材料、工艺化学品、微光刻设备等。目前SAC/TC203下设五个分技术委员会和五个工作组，其中电子气体分技术委员会（TC203/SC1）负责电子工业用气体相关标准化工作；电子封装材料工作组（TC203/WG4）负责电子封装材料相关标准化工作；电子化学品标准工作组（TC203/WG3）负责除电子特种气体和电子封装材料以外的电子化学品领域标准工作，已形成标准体系框架，目前，SAC/TC203归口的电子化学品领域标准项目（包含现行标准和在研标准）共计98项。SAC/TC47全国印制电路标准化技术委员会，是IEC/TC91在国内的对口标准化组织，主要负责电子装联技术领域标准化工作，业务领域与IEC/TC91基本相同。目前，SAC/TC47归口的印制电路板材料及配套化学品标准（包括现行和在研标准）共计96项，其中，现行标准60项，在研标准36项（含26项修订标准）。

3. 航空航天产业链配套用精细化工材料

截至2008年，航空材料（含热工艺及理化测试技术）的国家军用标准和行业标准已有约1400项，其中GJB约300项，HB约1100项，在国防科技工业标准体系表中，航空材料及其相关标准部分，目前已有60%左右的项目已经制定成标准，标准的总体技术水平达到国际同类标准20世纪90年代末期水平，基本满足了现役、在研武器装备和主导产业的需要。

对于高温合金、钢铁、铝镁合金、钛合金等主要金属材料来说，其变形材料标准，包括板、棒、丝、带、管、异型材以及锻件等主要是以国军标（GJB）和国标（GB）为主，而铸件标准则主要以航空行业标准（HB）为主，且已基本上制定了相应的HB、GJB或GB。对于非金属材料来说，由于有相当一部分材料是由航空自行研制和生产的，因此相对来说HB较多，由民口部门生产和供货的材料，则仍是以GJB为主。目前在航空领域已定型生产的各型号中已经使用成熟的一般材料均已纳入标准，并已基本完成了由技术协议、企业标准向 GJB 和 HB 的转化。这些材料标准除个别自行研制的材料外，均参照或等效国外先进标准，并结合航空科研生产的实际情况而制定，标准的技术水平与国外同类先进标准水平相当。但鉴于国内现有的技术水平和设备条件，少数标准在某些技术指标上与国外先进标准相比还有一定差距。目前，大多数标准对已定型生产的各型号产品是有效和适用的，并且已成为各型号材料设计、生产、订货和验收的依据。

但是，对于近年来发展的一些在研型号上应用的新型高性能的材料，金属材料如超高强度耐蚀钢和高强度沉淀硬化钢、高强高纯铝合金和损伤容限型铝合金、高性能铝锂合金、损伤容限型钛合金等，非金属材料如吸波涂料、耐温耐介质性能更好的橡胶密封材料，复合材料如新型树脂基复合材料、陶瓷基复合材料、金属基复合材料等目前还没有纳入 GJB 或 HB，仍然使用临时技术协议或企业标准。

4. 汽车产业链配套用精细化工材料

我国汽车产业的标准化工作从 20 世纪 80 年代以前就开始了，不过由于观念的原因，80 年代以前汽车行业出台的国家标准是非常少的，随着对标准化工作的认识，汽车行业颁布的国家标准越来越多，累计出台的国标数目从 80 年代末期的 45 项，发展到 2006 年的 465 项，在 19 年的时间里，增长了近 10 倍，年均增长率达到了 13.85%。汽车工业采用国际标准率从 1990 年的 33.3% 发展到 2006 年的 52%。从 1990 年到 2006 年汽车产业的数据可以看出，我国汽车产业标准化工作还是得到了比较明显的发展，标准有效存量年均增长率为 10.43%，同期我国汽车产业实际工业增加值年均增长率为 16.62%。

5. 涂料

随着我国涂料产业升级及与国际标准的接轨，涂料行业相关标准的制定和执行，推动了行业的健康发展。2008 年 2 月 29 日，全国工业产品生产许可证办公室批准发布了《危险化学品涂料产品生产许可证实施细则》，该细则于发布之日起开始实施。细则规定在中华人民共和国境内生产、销售或者在经营活动中使用危险化学品涂料产品（含一级、二级易燃溶剂的危险化学品涂料产品，包括分装）必须于 2008 年 10 月底前完成生产企业 100% 取证任务。任何企业未取得生产许可证不得生产危险化学品涂料产品，任何单位和个人不得销售或者在经营活动中使用未取得生产许可证的危险化学品涂料产品。由国家质量监督检验检疫总局负责危险化学品涂料产品生产许可证统一管理工作。

2007 年 12 月 18 日，国家安全生产监督管理总局提出了《涂料生产企业安全技术规程（送审稿）》。该标准规定了涂料生产应采取的基本安全技术措施，包括总平面图布局规划、防火防爆、防雷防静电、电气安全、生产装置安全、防尘防毒、防噪声、防护用品、涂料生产作业安全和安全管理等方面内容，适用于在中华人民共和国境内从事溶剂型涂料、无溶剂涂料、水性涂料、固体粉末涂料等不同类型涂料（包括涂料用树脂、乳液）的生产企业，油墨、黏合剂、树脂生产企业亦可参照使用。

2007 年 9 月 10 日，行业内部公布了《涂料工业水污染物排放标准》（征求意见稿），此标准为强制性标准，已正式发布实施。自该标准实施之日起，涂料工业企业特有的生产工艺和装置的水污染物排放控制按该标准的规定执行，不再执行《污水综合排放标准》（GB 8978）中相关的排放限值。该标准适用于涂料工业企业的水污染物排放管理，涂料工业企业建设项目的环境影响评价、环境保护设施设计、竣工验收及其投产后的污染控制和管理，并对环境敏感地区的污染物排放限值做出了特别规定。

2008年，修订了GB 18581—2001《室内装饰装修材料 溶剂型木器涂料中有害物质限量》和GB 18582—2001《室内装饰装修材料 内墙涂料中有害物质限量》标准，新制定国标《室内装饰装修材料 水性木器涂料中有害物质限量》、《建筑用外墙涂料中有害物质限量》、《玩具用涂料中有害物质限量》。新标准均是对人体和环境有害物质容许量的要求，强调产品的环保性能。新标准提高了有害物质限量的要求，增加了消费者比较关注的苯类化合物的限量要求，更重要的是修改完善了相关的测试方法，尤其是对挥发性有机化合物的测试方法进行了大幅度修改，由目前总挥发物除水的方法改为用气相色谱直接测试，使其与目前国际国内通用的测试方法相吻合，以尽可能减少测试误差。

针对以钛白粉与氧化铁为代表的无机颜料行业，我国采取了一系列宏观调控和加快产业结构调整的措施：对新建钛白粉产能实行较为严格的准入制度；对无机颜料行业积极推行环境友好型清洁生产工艺的普及和政策扶植。通过"十一五"期间的积极努力，"十二五"期间颁布的标准及政策法规《清洁生产标准——钛白粉》、《清洁生产审核指南——钛白粉》、《清洁生产标准——氧化铁》、《清洁生产审核指南——氧化铁》、《钛白粉行业准入条件》、《无机颜料工业污染物排放标准——钛白粉、立德粉》、《无机颜料工业污染物排放标准——氧化铁系》等，将对行业的健康发展起到积极的推动作用。

6. 水处理剂

新技术、新产品的推广应用需要标准化。现代社会与工业的快速发展和水资源匮乏及污染加剧的严峻形势，都会极大地促进水处理化学品新品种、新技术的不断出现和产业规模的扩大。同时，新型水处理化学品的研究开发正趋于向高效、低毒、无公害方面发展，标准化工作必须紧跟发展趋势。

在缓蚀阻垢剂方面，有机磷和聚合物分散剂仍是目前广泛应用的品种，水处理剂分会在1999—2000年制定了AA-AMPS和PBTC的行业标准，在2004年完成了《二亚乙基三胺五亚甲基膦酸》的制标工作。另外，2005年开始制定《聚天冬氨酸》、《聚环氧琥珀酸》等标准。这些标准的制定将推动相关产品的应用。

在杀菌灭藻剂方面，近年来对氯气的限制，使得溴类化合物及二氧化氯等氯化性杀菌剂有了更大的发展空间，水处理剂分会根据市场需要，及时制定了《稳定性二氧化氯溶液》国家标准和《异噻唑啉酮衍生物》及《二氯异氰尿酸钠》行业标准。

在絮凝剂方面，高效、低毒或无毒的无机和有机高分子絮凝剂正逐步替代传统絮凝剂。近年来，随着水质污染状况加剧，用水质量标准提高，要求絮凝剂不仅有高效除垢功能，同时还应具有去除COD、磷氮以及杀菌灭藻、氧化还原多种功能。因此，无毒、高电荷、高分子量阳离子有机絮凝剂，天然高分子絮凝剂和微生物絮凝剂将是今后产业发展的重点和趋势。在这种形势下，水处理剂分会及时修订了《水处理剂聚氯化铝》、《水处理剂聚合硫酸铁》、《水处理剂硫酸铝》等强制性国家标准。

7. 油墨

在20世纪80年代，欧美国家率先倡导了绿色印刷的概念。欧盟、美国、日本等国家及地区早已有关于环保油墨相关的规定，如日本关于食品包装材料用印刷油墨的自主限制性规定、德国包装标准中对印刷油墨的合理性给予了规定。关于与食品接触的出口包装材料，欧盟的相关法令很多，聚氯乙烯（PVC）中氯乙烯单体，纸制品中的氯联苯（PCB），粘合剂、印刷油墨中的可溶、可挥发性物质和有害重金属等均被列为在食品、医药以及可能与儿童接触的产品包装中限制使用的材料。英国也已立法了环保油墨的标准"在食品包装袋印刷中禁止使用溶剂型油墨"等相关规定。日本印刷油墨行业协会则制定了不适合印刷食品包装材料物质的否定列表。此外，在欧美各国和日本等发达国家，除胶印油墨外，水墨正在逐步取代传统的溶剂型油墨。而衡量油墨环保的重要内容是有毒有害物质种类、含量和有机挥发物含量。

目前各国尤其是发达国家对有害重金属的迁移量进行了严格的限制，例如欧盟安全标准 EN 71—3：2000 *Safety of toys. Specification for migration of certain elements*、EN 71—7：2002 *Safety of toys. Finger paints. Requirements and test methods*；美国 ASTM F963—2008 *Standard Consumer Safety Specification for Toy Safety* 和欧盟 2009/48/EC 指令，对油墨中的重金属含量都有严格限制的标准和法规。欧盟 2009/48/EC 指令对迁移元素的限制增加到了 19 种，并且按照材料的干燥、液态、刮漆不同状态设定了不同的限量指标。我国目前的环保油墨标准对有毒有害物质的迁移的相关规定不管是在种类上，还是在限值指标上和该指令相比都存在比较大的差距。

（五）前沿新型材料

1. 纳米材料

据统计，我国目前与纳米材料相关的国家标准和行业标准共计 46 项。结合纳米材料的发展情况，目前比较紧缺的标准是：纳米金（或其他贵金属）粉、纳米稀土催化剂、纳米石墨烯。

市场上已经有纳米金粉等贵金属，纳米金是指金的微小颗粒，其直径为 1～100nm，具有高电子密度、介电特性和催化作用，能与多种生物大分子结合，且不影响其生物活性。由氯金酸通过还原法可以方便地制备各种不同粒径的纳米金，其颜色依直径大小而呈红色至紫色。纳米金的应用很广，但关于纳米金的标准还没有制订。作为前景明朗的前沿新型材料，纳米稀土催化剂和纳米石墨烯的标准也亟待制订。

2. 超材料

结合目前超材料的发展，比较紧缺的标准是：隐形材料的制备，特别是应用于军事上的隐形材料的制备；运用到医学上的"超材料"管道；超材料平板卫星天线等。但作为一种新兴材料，国内外还未见标准或技术法规。我国已于 2013 年底在深圳成立了全国电磁超材料标准化技术委员会和技术联盟，预计不远的将来会在这一领域有所突破。

3. 智能材料

智能材料是一种能感知外部刺激，能够判断并适当处理且本身可执行的新型功能材料，包括压敏、磁敏、光敏、气敏、声敏、色敏、热（温）敏、湿敏、电磁波敏感材料和形状记忆材料。材料范围覆盖金属材料、无机材料、有机材料等领域，是未来打造智能生活的重要原材料。常见的压敏、磁敏材料已有不少产品及其标准问世。但产业整体发展良莠不齐，需要进一步以标准化规范。同时，大量高技术含量的智能材料仍处于研发和标准缺失状态，需要为已经产业化和即将产业化的产品制修订大量的标准。

4. 光电材料

光电材料是指用于制造各种光电设备（主要包括各种主被动光电传感器、光信息处理和存储装置及光通信等）的材料，主要包括红外材料、激光材料、光纤材料、非线性光学材料等，是目前和今后一段时间新材料领域最热门的材料之一。光电材料包括无机光电材料和有机光电材料及其附属材料。这一领域目前已经成立了多个国家TC和省级TC，相关标准的出台速度较快，预期可以在较短的时间内实现产业覆盖，并赶超国际先进水平。

5. 新能源材料

新能源材料是广东省"十二五"规划中提出的重点发展的方向之一，也是未来一段时间国际能源竞争的关键。新能源材料包括太阳能、风能、生物能、化学能等与煤、石油、天然气等传统能源相区别的新型可再生能源。目前，国家和省级太阳能标准化技术委员会已于一年前成立，正在酝酿产业升级。化学能如新型电池材料，处于研发阶段的产品种类繁多，已有小部分产业化以及标准问世，如GB/T 29840—2013《全钒液流电池》、GB/T 10077—2008《锂原电池分类、型号命名及基本特性》、GB/T 12725—2011《碱性铁镍蓄电池通用规范》、GB/T 20042.1—2005《质子交换膜燃料电池 术语》、GB/T 20042《质子交换膜燃料电池》系列标准等十余项国家标准。但仍有部分产品，如锂流电池等，未见有标准。对于已经出台的标准，标准化的推广和对相关企业的政策引导和推动，还需要进一步加强。

第三章 新材料产业标准体系

一、新材料产业标准体系概述

标准化是引导新材料产业发展的重要手段之一。技术标准战略是产业转型升级必备的配套战略，是促进技术发展、保障产业健康的重要条件。同时，标准化对引进新技术，保障新技术快速应用同样有重要的作用。

1. 通过标准化带动产业技术发展和市场拓展

一方面，目前我国的标准制修订速度和频率，与新材料的更新换代速度不相适应。最简单直接的以标准化带动技术进步的方法，即通过对国际先进新材料标准进行系统研究，将相关的技术指标进行比对，然后逐渐实现与国际标准的对接，以完善新材料的标准体系；通过对国外先进技术和标准的深入研究，对新材料企业在产品研发方面提供技术参数的指导。

另一方面，发达国家的新材料发展速度是远远高于其标准化速度的。因而，除在已有标准领域赶上发达国家先进水平外，研究科研技术领域的新材料发展进度，与产业结合，制定具有我国特色的、具备更高技术要求的技术标准，抢占国际标准化先机，为我国新材料产业拓展国际市场埋下伏笔，也是保障新材料产业发展的重要步骤。

2. 通过标准化规范产业发展

我国新材料企业规模大多较小，甚至有的材料生产前期投入不大，或者有传统产业产品借助新材料的噱头拓展市场，导致目前已经出现了部分新材料产品质量良莠不齐、低质量产品充斥市场的现象。由于缺乏相应材料或产品标准，消费者对产品质量难以确定，影响了优质新材料产品的市场和新材料产业的发展。因此，有标可依是抓好新材料产业发展源头的重要举措。

3. 科技服务业的标准化促进产业发展

虽然科技部和科技厅出台了多种政策鼓励企业转型升级，例如组建高新示范区、建立产业联盟、创建科技创新型企业、为企业派驻科技特派员、成立中小企业创新资金等，对以新材料为主的高新技术企业的发展起到了一定作用，但新材料产业的发展现状说明，科技服务的力量还不够，我国现在科技服务业种类较多但产业不发达，市场范围有限。因此，必须通过标准化规范和引导各层级科技服务业，尤其是第三方服务机构的服务项目，培养服务机构的市场公信力，推动科技服务业为新材料发展发挥作用。

我国正处于产业升级的大变革时期，社会各界都在为产业的转型升级献计献策。新材料产业的发展是各行业抓住转型升级核心的重要突破口，也是掌握未来科技主导权的重要筹码。我们期待通过标准化，突破新材料产业快速发展瓶颈，实现产业转型升级。

建设新材料产业标准体系需遵循以下基本原则：

（1）坚持政府引导与企业自愿相结合。通过政府引导，使新材料产业标准体系建设逐步从"自上而下"的政府引导过渡到"自下而上"的企业需求，使标准化工作成为企业提高核心竞争力的内在动力。

（2）坚持政策激励与技术服务相结合。制定完善的政策激励措施，强化技术辅助作用，全面提高标准技术机构的服务能力，积极鼓励企业将自主知识产权成果转化为技术标准。

（3）坚持突出重点与分类指导相结合。新材料产业覆盖面广，涉及产品领域多。新材料标准规划依据政策要求和产业发展现状，制定产业优先次序，提高标准技术服务的针对性，突出特色，分类指导，全面推进。

（4）坚持协同发展与共同进步相结合。鼓励企业制定高于行业标准、国家标准或国际标准的企业标准或联盟标准。发挥龙头骨干企业的辐射带动作用，加快推动产业集聚发展，相互借鉴，形成行业合力，使标准体系建设成为推动各行业共同发展的内在动力。

二、新材料产业标准体系框架

大多数新材料是在传统材料基础上的提升、创新和衍生，大多数传统材料经过改造或改性都有可能成为新材料，因而新材料的分类应以传统材料分类为基础，增加不能准确纳入传统材料分类中的新材料特色种类。

传统材料按照物理化学性质，分为金属材料、无机非金属材料、有机高分子材料和精细化工材料。随着时代和科技的发展，复合材料也成为一类重要的分支。按照用途来分，材料又可以分为结构材料和功能材料，更细致的按照应用领域的分类方法，材料可分为电子材料、航空航天材料、核材料、建筑材料、能源材料、生物材料等。

以传统材料为基础的先进金属材料、新型无机非金属材料、高性能有机高分子材料和特种精细化工材料均是新材料的重要组成部分。每一个分类中产生的新材料数量繁多，性能特征迥异，功能多样，或特征和功能交叉。在现阶段对新材料产品的普遍认知中，每一类具有特殊特征或功能的新型材料均被认作一类新型材料，因而材料种类数量巨大，且随着时代的变迁，材料种类尤其是功能材料的种类呈现此消彼长的发展过程。如某材料的光性能，在一个时代内可能使其成为重要的光材料，但新的技术或材料取代了其光材料的地位，使其有可能长期退出光材料的历史舞台，也可能在很长时间以后经过技术改造重返光材料市场。因此，在进一步分类中，应尽量囊括大部分有能力纳入新材料范畴的材料类型，并能够为未来新材料的增减提供窗口。新材料的来源不外乎传统工程材料性能的提升和其他功能的增加，因而可在传统材料分类的基础上，按照新材料来源分为高性能工程材料和功能材料，在每个分类下按需增减材料项。这种分类方式，既能够保证长短期新材料的容纳能力，将大部分新材料产品纳入一个有机的系统，又能够适度简化分类，提高系统的实用性。该分类方法对于先进金属材料、新型无机非金属材料和高性能有机高分子材料都有良好的适用性。

在传统材料类型本身非常多（超过13种）的精细化工材料领域，高性能工程材料和功能新材料的种类和数量非常巨大，且精细化工材料的分类不限于工程材料和功能材料。超过13类的传统精细化工材料在新材料领域的发展速度并不均衡。如改性剂、粘合剂等类新材料频出，而纸浆、日化等领域新材料种类增长速度目前相对缓慢。在精细化工材料领域，新材料的出现速度和材料数量与其产业发展速度密切相关，且伴随产业发展的进度消长。因而，精细化工领域的新材料，更应该从产业发展的角度去认知，成为支撑各产业新材料和新技术发展的"螺丝钉"。精细化工领域新材料的分类，应以产业领域来划分，并成为一个开放的、能够增减其他产业的分类方式。

除传统材料的改性材料外，新材料还有一个重要分类，即不能被传统材料覆盖的新兴材料。新兴材料的兴起和退出，与时代发展的需求相适应，可能成为成熟的材料纳入传统材料领域，也有可能长期地退出历史舞台。因此，我们将其称为前沿新型材料，并将其作为一个长期开放的系统，增加具有长短期发展前景、暂时不能被传统材料容纳的新材料，剔除在进入传统材料之前就可能长期退出历史舞台的材料。

各种类型的复合材料是新材料的一个重要组成部分。在新材料以及传统材料中，复合材料的比例相当高。如将复合材料作为一个单独的新材料分支，将可能囊括其他类型新材料中的很多材料，造成较严重的分类交叉和重叠。而材料的复合，本身可以理解为是对一种或数种材料性能的提升或新功能的增加。因此，我们将复合材料融入传统材料分类或前沿新型材料中，以复合材料中的主体或核心材料决定其分类，以其新兴材料特征决定其前沿新型材料的位置。

综上所述，我们可将新材料分为五个大类，即先进金属材料、新型无机非金属材料、高性能有机高分子材料、特种精细化工材料和前沿新型材料（见图3-1）。

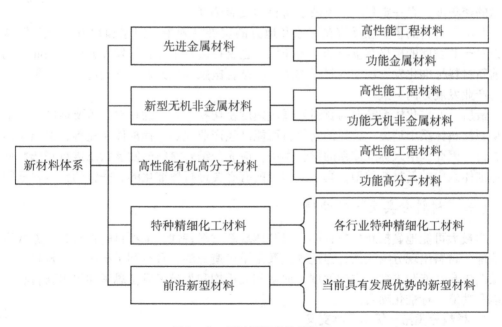

图3-1 新材料标准体系框架

广东省新材料产业标准体系规划与路线图

三、新材料产业标准体系编制说明

（一）标准类型

新材料标准化的主要任务是引领新材料产业化、规范和加快科技成果转化，促进产业发展。作为新兴产业，规范性基础标准、测试方法标准应为最活跃的领域；安全性标准作为基础保障，应紧随材料发展脚步；材料技术标准和应用技术标准是材料发展基本成熟的必然表现；设备技术标准贯穿材料进步的始末，是新材料进步的支撑，在某些新材料领域具有关键的作用。因此，这六个标准类型均应是新材料标准体系的重要组成部分。

（二）材料类型

新材料的产生、退出，以及重返历史舞台，是新材料发展和进步的一般过程。每一个历史时期均有不同种类的新材料问世或暂时离开。因而，在新材料体系框架下，材料类型是不断变化和更新的。材料发展的成熟程度不同，标准化的作用也各不相同。制定新材料标准体系，首先应该明确当前的新材料类型有哪些，暂时停留在探索检测方法阶段的材料类型有哪些，能够达到制定材料技术标准和应用技术标准的材料类型有哪些，以及产业或安全规范性标准有哪些。

首先，纳入新材料标准体系的标准类型，无论是传统材料、改性材料还是新型材料，都应该是活跃在科学研究前沿的材料，包括制造研究、工艺研究、产业化研究、应用研究、规范性研究等。因此，要全面了解新材料的发展现状，应从科研文献中发掘。文献的密集度，在一定程度上反映了材料的发展热度。

其次，材料的重要性反应在国家和地方的发展规划中。国家和地方的产业发展规划，对产业发展的格局有重要的影响作用，也直接影响了材料的发展方向。因此，列入当前新材料标准化发展规划的材料类型，应结合国家和地方发展规划进行适当裁减，使其与产业发展方向一致。

最后，标准化体系需要与材料发展成熟度密切相关。有的材料在需要标准化之前已经从新材料体系中消失；曾经的新材料可能已经产业成熟，标准体系完善，退出了新材料类目。因此，纳入标准体系的材料类型，应充分结合材料的发展状态进行筛选，使纳入标准体系中的新材料类型，真正成为当前有必要进行标准化的、完整的新材料地图。

（三）材料分类交叉的处理

为最大可能地囊括新材料种类，以及体现新材料特性，本项目的材料分类方式可能导致部分材料出现分类交叉，但这种交叉是不可避免的，且有利于激励同一材料在不同领域向更高性能和多功能方向发展，促使相关机构和人员多方位思考和提出新材料的高性能和功能性标准化项目。

1. 材料分类第一级别分类交叉

材料的微观化发展，以及大量复合材料的产生使得不同种类材料之间的界限越来越模糊，部分新型材料存在分类交叉。尤其是特种精细化工材料、前沿新型材料与前三种传统材料分类之间的交叉。如包含稀土元素的精细化工产品、含有多种材料类型的新能源材料等。本体系采用优先纳入先进金属材料、新型无机非金属材料和高性能有机高分子材料，不能纳入前三类材料的、有特殊发展需求的材料纳入前沿新型材料，特种精细化工材料排最后的排序方式，按照决定材料高性能和功能性的核心材料的类型，决定材料的名录。如包含稀土元素的精细化工产品纳入先进金属材料分类中，与新能源相关的复合材料纳入前沿新型材料中。

有的文献将光电材料列入前沿新型材料中。由于光电材料的基础材料种类较多，且分散在各个分类中，从材料分类的角度来看，如将光电材料作为独立分支，其中将需要再次细分为与第一级分类相似的子类目，分类方法将更为复杂。因光电材料可能包括或属于无机材料、有机材料、精细化工材料、金属材料等各个分类，本体系中将光电材料分解在其他类型材料的光学、电磁学材料二级分类中。

2. 材料分类第二级别分类交叉

对于具有多个功能的材料，按照其性能和功能性分类必然带来分类交叉。本项目的分类原则为，按照其核心功能进行分类。如具有多方面的发展前景，也可以使相同材料出现在不同的功能分类中，以不同的标准名称体现不同的材料功能特性，以促进单一材料多功能性的发展。这也是很多企业在面对新材料发展方向的选择时，需要进行的思路引导。

3. 标准类型分类交叉

本项目有通用基础标准、设备技术标准、安全技术标准、测试方法标准、材料技术标准、应用技术标准六个种类的标准分类。通用基础标准体现同类材料共用的术语、设计规程等方面的内容；设备技术标准中列入与材料生产、加工、应用密切相关的，难以通过其他标准体系实现的标准项目；安全技术标准中列入与材料生产、加工、应用密切相关的安全操作指引或材料性能指标；测试方法标准相对比较明确，列入的是各种性能、功能指标测试方法的标准项目；材料技术标准中列入与材料性能直接相关的材料性能指标；应用技术标准中主要是难以在其他标准体系中体现的新材料应用产品标准项目。

四、新材料产业标准体系明细表（见表3-1）

表3-1 新材料标准化发展阶段

序号	新材料种类	新材料类目	标准化发展阶段
先进金属材料			
1	新型黑金属材料	短流程薄板坯连铸连轧产品	依赖传统钢材产业发展，新产品问世和应用速度快，有少量产品标准，大部分尚处于标准缺乏阶段
2		高强度合金钢	
3		耐磨合金钢	
4		铁基非晶合金带材	

续表 3-1

序号	新材料种类	新材料类目	标准化发展阶段
5		高性能轻量化汽车覆盖件钢	
6		汽车用高强、高韧金属材料	
7		超高硬高韧可锻喷射成形高速钢	
8		汽车用的细晶 TRIP 钢	
9		特种用途轻质金属基复合材料	
10		船用钢材	
11		高性能精密合金板	
12		高性能冷压板	
13		高性能棒、线材	
14		金属蜂窝材料	
15		高性能不锈钢制品	
16		陶瓷改性金属复合材料	
17		金属屋面系统用新型黑金属材料（不锈钢等）	
18		石油天然气输送钢管	
19		3兆瓦以上大型和特大型风力发电机组用风电齿轮箱、主轴、轴承材料	
20		能源、桥梁、交通运输、军事等重大工程需要的高性能特种钢铁材料	
21	新型有色金属材料	高性能铝合金	以传统产业为基础发展，新产品更新和应用速度快，标准化更新速度需要加快
22		轨道交通用大规格工业铝型材	
23		特种用途轻质金属基复合材料	
24		金属屋面系统用新型有色金属材料（钛锌板、铝锰板、铝镁板、铜板等）	
25		轻质钛铝合金以及 Y 或 Nb 的改性合金	
26		高精度铝化成箔、亲水箔、电子铝箔	
27		SiCp/Al 复合耐磨材料	
28		高纯阴极铜	市场上有产品，缺乏相应标准
29		高性能铜合金	
30		超薄电解铜箔	

续表 3-1

序号	新材料种类	新材料类目	标准化发展阶段
31		高导热铜合金引线框架、键合丝	
32		高强高导、绿色无铅新型铜合金接触导线	
33		高性能镁合金	
34		生物相容镁合金	
35		高性能锌合金	
36		单晶高温合金	
37		钨基合金材料	
38		铜铟镓硒、铜铟硫、碲化镉等新型薄膜光伏材料	
39		核级海绵锆	
40		银铟镉控制棒	
41	新型稀贵金属材料	高比容钽粉、高效贵金属催化材料	市场上有产品，产品规模不大，均缺乏相应标准
42		稀有金属超细纳米晶、特粗晶粒	
43		稀贵金属钎焊材料、铟锡氧化物（ITO）靶材	
44		钼电极、高品质钼丝、高精度钨窄带、钨钼大型板材和制件、高纯铼及合金制品	
45		高纯稀有金属及靶材	
46		核电站用锆基非晶合金	
47		稀土基荧光粉	
48		稀土发光材料（有机发光二极管用有机稀土发光材料、金属铱电致磷光材料、含钌配合物电致发光材料、DMIT 金属有机配合物电致发光材料、3D 显示用荧光粉、各色荧光粉等）	已有产品和相关标准，标准更新速度在加快
49	新型稀土材料	稀土改性材料（聚氯乙烯加工助剂、无机粉体加工助剂、聚氯乙烯用稀土/钙/锌多功能复合热稳定剂等）	
50		稀土催化材料（高储氧催化剂、石油裂化催化剂等）	市场上已有产品，标准尚缺乏
51		稀土抛光材料（氧化铈基稀土抛光粉、氧化铈基稀土抛光液等）	

续表 3-1

序号	新材料种类	新材料类目	标准化发展阶段
52		稀土基金属光纤激光器	产品处于研发和小试阶段，标准尚缺乏
53		稀土基电致发光材料	
54		稀土基光致发光材料	
55		稀土基永磁材料	
56		超级电容器	
57		磁致冷材料	
58		稀土磁致冷新材料	
59		超磁致伸缩材料	
60		稀土磁性材料（烧结钕铁硼磁体、粘结钕铁硼磁体、烧结钐铁氮、烧结铈铁硼磁体等）	
61		稀土储氢材料（动力电池用稀土储氢合金、低自放电型稀土储氢合金、高容量型稀土储氢合金等）	
62	功能金属材料	电磁屏蔽材料	有产品，但生产规模不大，标准化速度正在加快
63		半金属 Fe3O4 电磁屏蔽材料及其改性材料	
64		金属—织物复合屏蔽材料	
65		TiB$_2$/Si-Al 电子封装复合材	
66		非晶纳米晶合金材料	
67		高磁导率软磁材料	
68		高磁感取向硅钢	
69		高导电率金属材料及相关型材	
70		新 Fe-Al 系磁性材料	
71		过渡金属光纤激光器	
72		高性能铁氧体磁性材料	
73		巨磁电阻	
74		永磁材料	
75		高纯金属有机源（MO 源）材料	
76		钴配位金属材料	
77		金属—有机多孔材料	

续表 3-1

序号	新材料种类	新材料类目	标准化发展阶段
78		金属—有机骨架材料	
79		高温金属烧结多孔材料	
80		金属量子线材料	
81		高纯和低偏析材料	
82		储氢材料	
83		储 CO_2 材料	
84		位错型阻尼合金（镁铝合金、镁铝硅合金等）	
85		孪晶型阻尼合金（锰铜合金）	研发和初试阶段产品
86		铁磁型阻尼合金（铁铬硅合金、铁铬锰合金、铁铬钼合金、铁—镓合金等）	
87		超塑性阻尼合金（锌铝合金）	
88		非晶态材料	
89		准晶材料	
90		微晶材料	
91		高效散热材料	
92		低热膨胀材料（ZrV_2O_7）及其电子封装材料	
93		铁铬铝金属纤维多孔材	产品已走向市场，标准化速度正在加快
94		耐高温金属涂层材料	
95		耐腐蚀涂层材料	
新型无机非金属材料			
96		新型结构陶瓷材料	
97		聚二甲基硅氧烷（PDMS）改性陶瓷	以传统陶瓷产业为支撑发展，新材料产生速度和应用速度快，标准数量丰富，但界定高性能和新性能的标准缺乏
98		金属陶瓷	
99	新型陶瓷材料	纳米陶瓷	
100		SiC 改性复合材料	
101		超硬陶瓷	
102		光学透明陶瓷	有产品，但生产规模不大，标准缺乏
103		激光透明陶瓷	

续表 3-1

序号	新材料种类	新材料类目	标准化发展阶段
104		电光透明陶瓷	
105		其他光信息陶瓷	
106		电子功能陶瓷	
107		闪烁陶瓷	
108		多孔陶瓷	
109		钢化玻璃	
110		铅硅酸盐玻璃	以传统玻璃产业为支撑发展，新材料产生速度和应用速度快，标准数量丰富，但界定高性能和新性能的标准缺乏
111		铝硅酸盐玻璃	
112		硼硅酸盐玻璃	
113		钾钙玻璃	
114		光学防护玻璃	
115		防辐射玻璃	
116	新型玻璃材料	微晶玻璃	
117		生化玻璃	
118		液晶显示用彩色滤光片	
119		电磁玻璃	
120		激光玻璃	有产品，但生产规模不大，标准缺乏
121		压电玻璃	
122		萤石玻璃	
123		多孔玻璃	
124		其他功能玻璃	
125		纤维水泥	
126		膨胀水泥	
127		高贝利特水泥	以传统水泥产业为支撑发展，有新材料产生，应用速度快，但标准覆盖面不够，且界定高性能和新性能的标准缺乏
128	新型水泥材料	土聚水泥（地质聚合物）	
129		水泥石膏材料	
130		氯氧镁水泥胶凝材料	
131		高性能成分调节改性水泥	

续表 3-1

序号	新材料种类	新材料类目	标准化发展阶段
132		MDF 水泥材料	
133		防腐蚀聚合物改性水泥材料	
134		含均匀分散超细颗粒致密体系水泥	
135		弹性聚合物水泥材料	
136		太阳能热电站用储热水泥	
137		耐寒水泥材料	
138		多孔水泥/发泡水泥	
139		新型抗震水泥	
140		芳纶纤维/水泥复合材料	
141		磷酸盐水泥材料	
142		高胶凝性高钙水泥材料	
143		高早强性能水泥材料	
144		高混合材掺量水泥	
145		自诊断机敏水泥材料（光纤传感，碳纤维复合）	
146		自调节机敏水泥材料	
147		自修复机敏水泥材料	有产品问世，但尚未规模化生产，发达国家已有先进标准，我国标准尚缺乏
148		温度自监控水泥材料	
149		自增强机敏水泥材料	
150		压电水泥材料	
151		淤泥基水泥材料/生态水泥	
152	无机纤维	氧化锆纤维	有材料和产品，标准化速度正在加快
153		氧化铝纤维	
154		含硼纤维	
155		碳化硅纤维	
156	无机涂层材料	混凝土表面用耐腐蚀涂层	各类产品丰富，但标准化水平较低，难以界定高质量新材料和新产品
157		铝合金表面用耐腐蚀涂层	
158		石质表面用耐腐蚀涂层	
159		电子行业用高导热耐腐蚀涂层	

续表 3-1

序号	新材料种类	新材料类目	标准化发展阶段
160		金属表面隔热保温陶瓷涂料	
161		耐高温陶瓷涂料	
162		耐高温耐腐蚀微晶玻璃涂层	
163		硅基耐高温涂层	
164		磷基耐高温涂层	
165	耐火材料	刚玉质耐火材料	有新产品，部分产品已有成熟的产品和国内外标，新产品开发力度不大，新产品涌出速度慢
166		硅质耐火材料	
167		镁质耐火材料	
168		铬质耐火材料	
169		锆质耐火材料	
170		碳复合耐火材料	
171		镁质耐火材料	
172		钙质耐火材料	
173		特种耐火材料（La 质，Be 质）	
174	功能材料	B-C-N 系材料（富硼氮化硼，立方氮碳化硼，氮化碳 $\beta\text{-}C_3N_4$，类金刚石 DLC、a-C: H 膜，碳化硼 B_4C，纳米金刚石）	新产品丰富，有相应标准但覆盖面还不够，对新产品的区分和界定不够
175		立方氮化硼 c-BN 单晶产品系列	
176		超硬材料芯片划片工具	
177		超硬材料薄壁钻头/超硬材料内圆锯片	
178		晶圆倒角机	
179		超硬材料杯形砂轮（晶锭磨外圆工具）	
180		超硬材料晶片减薄工具	
181		超硬材料刀具	
182		超硬材料砂带	
183		超硬材料砂轮	
184		超硬材料平面磨削工具	
185		超硬材料线锯	

续表 3-1

序号	新材料种类	新材料类目	标准化发展阶段
186		超硬材料带锯	
187		超硬材料打孔机	
188		化学机械抛光（CMP）修整器	
189		超硬材料钎焊技术	
190		超硬材料金属结合剂—钴	
191		超硬材料电镀技术	
192		超硬材料陶瓷结合剂	
193		超硬材料用其他焊接技术	
194		超硬材料用其他结合剂	
195		多组分光纤	
196		单晶光纤	
197		红外光纤	
198		液芯光纤	
199		TiO_2 和 ZnS 涂层导光材料	有产品，新材料产品生产规模不大，部分有标准，但覆盖面不够
200		ZrO_2—SiO_2 涂层导光材料	
201		光纤光栅	
202		光防护材料	
203		GaN 基光学材料	
204		氟化钡光学材料	
205		偏硼酸钡光学材料	
高性能有机高分子材料			
206		碳纤维增强高分子材料	
207		耐老化高分子结构材料	各类材料和标准类型丰富
208		建筑、船用高效密封高分子材料	
209	工程材料	船用高分子结构材料	
210		航空用特种工程材料	
211		高性能固体润滑材料	国外有成熟的产品和标准，国内有产品和部分标准
212		新型高分子注浆材料	
213		新型高分子托辊材料	

续表 3-1

序号	新材料种类	新材料类目	标准化发展阶段
214	导光材料	CdS 改性光学材料	实验室产品，没有具体针对材料的标准
215		KBr、CsI 改性极远红外透过材料	
216		SiO_2 改性有机光学材料	
217		TiO_2 改性有机光学材料	
218		AL_2O_3 改性有机光学材料	
219		ZrO_2 改性有机光学材料	
220		CdHgTe 纳米晶改性有机光学材料	
221		二芳基乙烯、螺吡喃、螺噁嗪、俘精酸酐、偶氮类系材料、聚苯基喹噁啉、其他 OLED 材料	
222		稀土高分子发光材料	
223		卟啉类二阶非线性光学材料	
224		变色高分子材料及制品	
225		透明高分子硬质材料	有产品和部分有标准，但缺乏对高质量产品的标准
226		透明高分子凝胶材料（角膜接触镜片）	
227		光波转换材料（太阳能电池用、农用薄膜用等）	
228	电致发光材料	稀土激活电致发光高分子材料	国外有市场化产品，国内产品尚未成熟，没有相关标准
229		聚苯撑乙烯类（PPVs）电致发光高分子材料	
230		聚芴类（PF）电致发光高分子材料	
231		聚噻吩类（PT）电致发光高分子材料	
232		聚对苯类（PPP）电致发光高分子材料	
233		聚乙炔类（PA）电致发光高分子材料	
234		聚苯基喹噁啉类（PPQ）电致发光高分子材料	
235	光存储材料	偶氮类光存储材料	实验室产品，没有具体针对材料的标准
236	其他光学高分子材料	高分子光引发剂	
237		光致形变材料	
238	热学材料	新型保温材料	现有产品丰富，对高性能和高质量的标准缺乏
239		新型耐高温材料	
240		新型绝热材料	

续表 3-1

序号	新材料种类	新材料类目	标准化发展阶段
241		绝缘导热材料（特别是 LED 封装用高导热高分子材料、LED 封装用硅基高分子材料）	
242		非绝缘导热材料	
243		耐寒高分子材料	
244	电学材料	高分子电学隐身材料	有产品，产业规模不大，部分产品有标准，标准覆盖度不高
245		高分子电磁屏蔽材料	
246		高分子抗静电涂料	
247		超导高分子材料	
248		高分子导体	
249		高分子电极	
250		高分子电子传感器	
251		导电纤维	
252		聚合物导电泡沫材料	
253		聚乙炔导电材料	实验室产品，没有具体针对材料的标准
254		聚苯乙炔导电材料	
255		聚吡咯导电材料	
256		聚噻吩导电材料	
257		聚亚苯基导电材料	
258		聚苯胺导电材料	
259		有机半导体材料（萘、蒽、聚丙烯腈、酞菁和一些芳香族化合物）	
260	高分子薄膜材料	气体分离膜	现有产品丰富，对高性能和高质量的标准缺乏
261		液固分离膜	
262		离子分离膜（各类电池用膈膜）	
263		电透析膜	
264		液体膜	
265		富氧膜	
266		纳滤膜	
267		液流电池用质子传导膜	

续表 3-1

序号	新材料种类	新材料类目	标准化发展阶段
268		智能响应高分子膜（温度响应、PH 响应、分子识别、电场响应、光响应、压力响应、湿度响应等）	
269		铁红丙烯酸底漆	
270		富锌涂料	
271		金属防腐高分子蚀涂层	
272		水泥防水高分子涂层	
273		改性沥青防水涂层	
274	高分子涂覆材料	其他防水涂层	
275		航空器用特种防护涂层	
276		新型（电学、磁学）保温涂层	
277		燃料电池用金属双极板高分子涂层	
278		高分子涂覆织物	
279		抗藻高分子涂层	
280		防霉抗菌高分子涂层	
281		可生物降解高吸水高分子材料	有产品上市，但产能规模不大，没有相关标准
282		地面铺覆用吸水高分子材料	
283		有机调湿材料	
284	吸附材料	海上用高效吸油高分子材料	
285		液体中用高分子阻尼材料	市场上还没有产品，实验室已有成熟产品，没有相关标准
286		空气中用高分子阻尼材料	
287		固体中用高分子阻尼材料	
288		航空用高分子阻尼材料	
289		防水材料	新材料产品丰富，但标准缺乏，难以判定其高质量等级
290	阻隔防护材料	声波反射材料	
291		电磁波反射材料	
292		耐化学品高分子材料	
293		生物降解高分子材料	国内均已有相关产品和部分标准，但标准覆盖面还不够，且对于高质量产品的标准缺乏
294	环境保护高分子材料	光降解高分子材料	
295		可降解高分子制品	

续表 3-1

序号	新材料种类	新材料类目	标准化发展阶段
296		水性涂料（聚氨酯、丙烯酸等）	
297		季铵盐型抗菌材料	
298		以高分子为基体的复合抗菌除臭材料	
299		防霉抗菌高分子材料	
300		废弃高分子材料的二次利用	
301	药物辅助高分子材料	可降解药物缓释用高分子材料	
302		可降解颗粒型药物缓释高分子材料	
303		可降解水凝胶型药物缓释高分子材料	
304		可降解微胶囊型药物缓释高分子材料	
305		可降解纤维型药物缓释高分子材料	
306	生物相容高分子材料	高性能组织工程材料（用于血管等生物系统）	国外有成熟产品和标准，国内有产品，但量不大，国内标准缺乏
307		椎体替代材料	
308		组织生长诱导型高性能组织工程材料	
309		泌尿系统可生物降解支架材料	
310		消化道可生物降解支架材料	
311		新型心脏组织支架材料	
312		高分子水凝胶支架	
313		高性能手术缝合线	
314		组织替代材料	
315		防粘连膜材料	
316		仿生人工骨修复材料	
317		纳米羟基磷灰石复合支架材料	
318		高分子口腔填充材料	
319		引导组织再生膜材料（用于牙周组织等）	
320		纤维增强材料（碳纤维、生物陶瓷纤维、有机纤维、金属纤维）	
321		胶原和明胶	
322		聚羟基烷基酸酯	

续表 3-1

序号	新材料种类	新材料类目	标准化发展阶段
323		壳聚糖和甲壳素	
324		高分子止血材料	
325		高分子抗凝血材料	
326		高分子抗菌材料	
327		生物传感器	
328		改性明胶材料	
329		生物纳米纤维素材料	
330	其他新型高分子材料	自愈合高分子材料	研究领域，有小规模产品，无相关标准
331		新型印刷材料	有新印刷材料，但标准覆盖面不够
特种精细化工材料			
332		印楝素及印楝杀虫剂及其安全性	
333		杂（芳）环丙烯腈类农药	
334		含氟农药	
335	农药	新型杀虫剂（包括杀螨剂）	
336		新型除草剂	
337		新型杀菌剂	
338		农药安全性要求	
339		紫外吸收染料	不断有新材料问世，相应的标准会出台实施，但没有界定材料高性能或新功能的标准
340		激光防护用近红外吸收染料	
341		激光染料（PSPI，DEASPI 和 HEASPI 等）	
342		染料激光器	
343	染料	染料光敏化剂	
344		磷光染料	
345		新型黄色铱配合物磷光染料	
346		环保生态染料	
347		高性能活性染料	
348		高性能分散染料	

续表 3-1

序号	新材料种类	新材料类目	标准化发展阶段
349		特种纤维专用染料	
350		新型硫化染料	
351		新型酸性染料	
352		新型碱性染料	
353		新型喷墨印花用墨水材料	
354		纺织印染助剂	
355	涂料	环保涂料	各类新产品问世速度快，新产品产业化速度快，不断有相应标准实施
356		海洋涂料	
357		船舶涂料	
358		保温涂料	
359		电磁屏蔽涂料	
360		可剥离涂料	
361		纳米涂料	
362		粉状建筑涂料	
363		储能发光涂料	
364		弹性外墙涂料	
365		陶瓷涂料	
366		绝缘涂料	
367		新型柔感涂料	
368		特殊产品专用涂料	
369	油墨	水性油墨	已有两项行业标准，新产品不断问世
370		环保油墨	
371		大豆油墨（美国有标准和相应的认证）	国外有成熟产品和标准，国内尚无产品和标准
372		UV 刮刮奖油墨	
373		UV 弹性油墨	
374		UV 防伪油墨	各类产品丰富，无高质量、高功能产品的针对性标准
375		UV 皱纹油墨	
376		UV 减感油墨	

续表 3-1

序号	新材料种类	新材料类目	标准化发展阶段
377		UV 香味缓释油墨	有产品但无相关标准
378		UV 印刷电路板油墨	
379		可食用油墨	
380		隐形油墨（红外或紫外条件显色）	
381		电子行业专用油墨	
382		其他行业或产品专用油墨	
383	电子信息行业用精细化工材料	大规模集成电路用超净高纯试剂（异丙醚、乙二醇丁醚等 MOS 试剂）	国外有产品及相关标准，国内尚无相关产品和标准
384		平板显示材料用超净高纯试剂	
385		高分辨率感光干膜	有产品，无相关标准，产业化规模不大，处于小试阶段
386		感光聚酰亚胺	
387		平板显示专用光刻浆料	
388		液态感光成像阻焊剂	
389		光致抗蚀剂	
390		显像管用碳酸钾、氟化物、助焊剂、石墨乳	各类产品丰富，无高质量、高功能产品的针对性标准
391		电子墨水	
392		导电胶	
393		电解液	
394		电子封装精细化工材料	
395		LED 封装精细化工材料	
396	各类添加剂	食品添加剂（如生物法番茄红素、D-壳聚糖、糖醇类添加剂等天然产物添加剂等）	各类产品丰富，无高质量、高功能产品的针对性标准
397		饲料添加剂（单糖或多糖类饲料添加剂、饲料抗氧剂）	
398		石油添加剂	
399		混凝土添加剂	
400	各类反应加工助剂	增塑剂改性助剂	
401		抗氧剂改性助剂	
402		抗冲击性改性助剂	

续表 3-1

序号	新材料种类	新材料类目	标准化发展阶段
403		光稳定剂改性助剂	
404		成核剂	
405		降解助剂	
406		阻燃助剂	
407		其他功能助剂（透明剂、抗菌剂、永久抗静电剂、稀土稳定剂、抗海剂等）	
408		磁性纳米催化剂（氢化反应、酯化反应、C-C 偶联反应等，如合成丁酸丁酯用磁性 SO_2-4-ZrO_2 固体超强酸催化剂、磁性固体酸 ZrO_2/Fe_3O_4 催化合成尼泊金丁酯）	实验室应用，没有产业化，也没有相关标准
409		石油炼制脱钙剂	
410		石油炼制脱硫剂	
411		石油炼制阻垢剂	
412		Fcc 金属钝化剂	
413		铸造涂料	各类产品丰富，无高质量、高功能产品的针对性标准
414		铸造涂料助剂	
415		精密铸造用铸造蜡	
416		矿物浮选剂 新型捕收剂	
417		矿物浮选剂 新型起泡剂	
418		矿物浮选剂 新型调整剂	
419		环保型表面活性剂	
420		淀粉基表面活性剂	
421		氨基酸表面活性剂	
422	表面活性剂	双子表面活性剂	各类产品丰富，无高质量、高功能产品的针对性标准
423		功能型表面活性剂	
424		氟基表面改性剂	
425		硅基表面改性剂	
426		金属表面处理剂	

续表 3-1

序号	新材料种类	新材料类目	标准化发展阶段
427	净化、吸附材料	二氧化碳富吸材料	有产品问世，但规模不大，无相关标准
428		甲烷存储吸附剂	有研究产物但尚无市场化产品
429		汽油脱硫剂（特种分子筛、特种介孔材料）	各类产品较多，也有相关标准，但没有高质量产品标准，难以辨别质量等级
430		化工废水处理剂	有研究产物但尚无市场化产品
431		纤维吸附材料	
432		低浓度一氧化氮吸附剂	
433		煤层气中甲烷和氮气分离材料	研发阶段，技术还未成熟，国外有产品技术，国内外均无标准
434		煤层气中脱氧分离材料	
435		有序大孔材料	有多种产品和相关标准，但新材料改性材料有产品无标准
436		木醋液	国内外均有成熟产品，但无标准
437		水处理 缓蚀剂	只有1993年的行业标准，新材料有产品无标准
438		水处理 阻垢分散剂	
439		水处理 杀菌灭藻剂	目前有产品但没有标准，难以判断材料性能等级
440		水处理 絮凝剂	
441		水处理 净化剂	
442		水处理 清洗剂	
443		水处理 预膜剂	
444	化妆品和盥洗用品	药物化妆品	
445		防晒化妆品	
446		含天然提取物化妆品	
447		化妆品中生物活性助剂的添加及其安全性试验	
448		化妆产品中的包覆技术	目前有研究文献和相关产品，但没有相关标准，难以判定材料性能级别

续表 3-1

序号	新材料种类	新材料类目	标准化发展阶段
449		天然香料及其提取技术	已有天然香辛料分类的国家标准，但没有其他天然香料材料标准
450		新型香料	国内各类标准较多，没有高质量新材料标准和分辨方法
451	汽车制造用精细化工材料	造纸用淀粉	国内外各类标准较多，品质差异大，没有高质量材料标准
452		造纸用矿物填料	
453		造纸用颜料	
454		新型合成制动液及其添加剂	国外有成熟产品及标准，国内产品丰富，但国家和行业标准都缺乏，难以判断是否高效新材料
455		新型汽车自动传动液及其添加剂	
456		汽车冷却系统用化学品（堵漏剂、清洗剂）	国内各类产品丰富，但品质差异大，相关标准缺乏，难以分辨高效质量新产品
457		汽车润滑系统用化学品（抗磨剂、修复剂、保护剂）	
458		排放系统用化学品（尾气处理剂等）	国外有先进产品，国内有产品问世，但无相关标准
459		玻璃防雾剂	国内各类产品丰富，但品质差异大，相关标准缺乏，难以分辨高效质量新产品
460		车身用化学品（车身漆面研磨抛光剂、增亮剂、车身修补剂、轮毂清洗剂、轮胎护理剂）	
461	航空制造领域用精细化工材料	炭/炭复合航空器刹车材料	国外有先进标准，国内暂无标准
462		航空航天用高密度燃料	
463		航空机械用润滑油	
464	航海制造领域用精细化工材料	船舶免拆整体清洗剂	国外有成熟产品，有先进标准，国内标准中有液压油或清洁油清洗导则标准，但没有整体清洗清洗剂标准，国内目前已经出现类似产品和专业公司
465		船舶用新型防污涂料与防污剂	国外有成熟产品，有先进标准，国内有类似产品及其检测方法标准，但没有材料和应用标准

续表 3-1

序号	新材料种类	新材料类目	标准化发展阶段
前沿新型材料			
466	纳米材料	纳米材料相关产品	部分概念产品已走向市场，国际国内均已有通用基础标准、安全技术标准等，但材料技术标准和应用产品相关标准缺乏
467	超材料	电磁超材料（隐身材料、左手材料、光子材料、超磁性材料等）	小规模生产，标准化进程正在加快，引领国际标准
468	石墨烯材料	石墨烯相关产品	小规模生产，部分产品已在国内问世，标准化进程正在加快，引领国际标准
469	智能材料	磁致伸缩材料	已有相关产品问世，标准化程度尚低
470		形状记忆材料	医药领域产品已在用，价格昂贵，产量和市场化程度受限，医药领域产品已有相关国际国内标准，其他领域产品还未见市场
471		热敏、温敏、光敏、气敏、色敏、声敏、磁敏、压敏材料	各类产品层出不穷，已有不少标准问世，但标准化程度仍不能满足产业发展的需要
472	新能源材料	锂离子电池	已有各类标准问世，产品已经全面市场化，但市场规范性标准仍缺乏，性能仍存在缺陷，未来被新型能源材料取代的可能性大
473		太阳能电池	各类标准层出不穷，产业化进程正在加快
474		燃料电池	已有国家标准，但产业还不成熟
475		液流电池	已有国家标准，但数量有限，国际标准、国外先进标准没有查到

续表 3-1

序号	新材料种类	新材料类目	标准化发展阶段
476		其他电池	各类新型电池材料层出不穷，有的在成熟前就已退出历史舞台
477	生物基材料	生物基材料相关产品	全球发展热点，部分产品已经实现产业化，但标准化程度较低，各国对相关技术保密程度高

五、新材料标准体系统计与分析

新材料标准类目中列出了477项新材料项目，其标准化发展进度各不相同。表3-2中显示了新材料类目的统计情况。

表3-2 新材料体系材料类型统计表

统计类型	统计数量	百分比	统计类型	统计数量	百分比
先进金属材料	95	20.0%	实验室阶段材料	89	18.6%
新型无机非金属材料	110	23.0%	小规模产业化材料	164	34.4%
高性能有机高分子材料	126	26.4%	中试产业化材料	70	14.7%
特种精细化工材料	134	28.1%	需要市场化规范材料	154	32.3%
前沿新型材料	12	2.5%	统计类型	统计数量	百分比
			工程改性材料	89	18.7%
			功能改性材料	376	78.8%
			新型材料	12	2.5%

400余项材料的标准化项目可能会达到数千项。为确保科学有效的推进标准化进程，根据国家和地方规划重点，以及产业发展进度，应对现有新材料进行重要性分析，提出继续实施标准化项目的优先次序。依据表3-3、表3-4和表3-5的分析，经过适当调整，制定适用于本省的标准化体系规划。

表3-3 先进金属材料重要性分析

		特种金属功能材料								工程材料			
		稀土金属	稀有金属	电磁学材料	吸附或阻尼材料	金属薄膜材料	金属粉体材料	高纯金属材料	医用金属材料	高端结构钢材	轻合金材料	总计	排名
特种金属功能材料	稀土金属	1	2	2	1	1	1	1	2	1	1	13	2
	稀有金属	0	1	1	1	0	0	0	1	0	0	4	9
	电磁学材料	0	1	1	0	0	0	0	1	1	1	5	8
	吸附或阻尼材料	1	1	2	1	0	1	1	1	1	1	10	7
	金属薄膜材料	1	2	2	2	1	1	0	2	0	0	11	6
	金属粉体材料	1	2	2	1	1	1	0	2	1	1	12	5
	高纯金属材料	1	2	2	1	2	2	1	2	1	1	15	1
	医用金属材料	0	1	1	1	0	0	0	1	0	0	4	9
工程材料	高端结构钢材	1	1	1	1	2	1	1	2	1	1	13	2
	轻合金材料	1	2	1	1	2	1	1	2	1	1	13	2

表3-4 新型无机非金属材料重要性分析

		工程材料						功能材料						
		陶瓷材料	水泥材料	玻璃材料	人造石材	无机纤维	无机涂层	耐火材料	超硬材料	光学材料	电磁学材料	气凝胶	医用材料	总计	排名
工程材料	陶瓷材料	1	2	1	2	1	2	1	1	0	0	1	0	12	7
	水泥材料	0	1	0	2	0	1	0	0	0	0	1	0	5	11
	玻璃材料	1	2	1	2	1	1	1	0	1	1	1	2	14	4
	人造石材	0	0	0	1	1	1	1	0	0	0	0	0	4	12
	无机纤维	1	2	1	1	1	1	1	1	1	0	0	1	11	8
	无机涂层	0	2	1	1	1	1	1	1	0	0	0	1	9	10
	耐火材料	1	2	1	2	0	1	1	1	0	1	0	1	11	8
功能材料	超硬材料	1	2	2	2	1	1	1	1	1	1	1	2	16	2
	光学材料	2	2	1	2	1	1	1	1	1	1	1	2	16	2
	电磁学材料	2	2	1	2	2	2	2	1	1	1	2	1	20	1
	气凝胶	1	1	1	2	2	2	1	1	1	0	1	0	13	5
	医用材料	2	2	0	2	1	1	1	0	0	1	2	1	13	5

表3-5 高性能有机高分子材料重要性分析

		工程材料				功能材料												总计	排名
		合成树脂	特种橡胶	合成纤维	工程塑料	光学材料	电学材料	热力学材料	阻燃材料	薄膜材料	涂覆材料	吸附材料	阻隔材料	环境材料	耐腐蚀材料	封装材料	木塑材料	医用材料		
工程材料	合成树脂	1	2	2	1	0	0	1	1	2	1	1	1	1	2	2	1	1	20	4
	特种橡胶	0	1	1	1	0	0	0	0	1	2	1	1	1	2	1	1	1	14	14
	合成纤维	1	1	1	1	0	0	1	1	0	0	1	1	0	0	1	1	1	11	17
	工程塑料	1	1	1	1	1	1	1	1	1	1	1	1	1	1	1	1	1	17	7
功能材料	光学材料	2	2	2	1	1	1	1	1	1	1	1	1	1	1	2	2	1	22	2
	电学材料	2	2	2	1	1	1	2	2	1	2	1	2	1	1	1	1	1	24	1
	热力学材料	1	2	1	1	1	0	1	1	2	1	1	1	1	1	1	1	1	18	6
	阻燃材料	1	2	1	1	1	0	1	1	2	1	2	1	1	1	2	1	1	20	4
	薄膜材料	0	1	2	1	1	1	0	0	1	1	2	1	1	1	2	1	1	17	7
	涂覆材料	1	0	2	1	1	0	1	1	1	1	1	1	0	1	1	1	1	15	12
	吸附材料	1	1	1	1	1	1	1	0	0	1	1	1	0	1	1	0	0	12	16
	阻隔材料	1	1	1	1	1	0	1	1	1	1	1	1	1	1	1	1	1	16	9
	环境材料	1	1	2	1	1	1	1	1	2	2	1	1	1	1	1	2	2	22	2
	耐腐蚀材料	1	0	2	1	1	1	1	1	1	1	1	1	1	1	1	2	1	16	9
	封装材料	0	1	1	1	1	1	1	0	1	1	1	1	1	1	1	1	1	15	12
	木塑材料	1	1	1	1	0	1	1	0	1	2	1	2	0	0	1	1	1	14	14
	医用材料	1	1	1	1	0	1	1	1	1	2	1	0	1	1	1	1	1	16	9

相对于金属、无机非金属和高分子材料,作为"螺丝钉"作用存在的、以产业领域划分的精细化工材料,其重要性更多地取决于国家和地方的产业政策导向,以及国家和地方的经济特色。材料的特点在一定程度上虽也决定其发展的重要性,但发展潜力更大程度受政策的影响,因而在此处不再进行重要性的比对。同样,前沿新型材料领域,入选的前沿新型材料都是具有较强发展优势的材料类型,均是重要的新材料类型。

第四章　广东省新材料产业标准体系规划

一、广东省新材料产业标准体系概述

按照《广东省新材料产业发展"十二五"专项规划》的意见，结合广东省新材料产业发展现状和发展趋势，在"十二五"后期以及"十三五"时期，逐步形成"政府有效引导、行业紧密协调、企业积极运作"的产业发展模式，加强产学研的结合，加快新材料产业的科技成果转化速度。围绕国家和广东省新材料产业及战略性新兴产业规划，制定《广东省新材料产业标准化发展规划与路线图》。《广东省新材料产业标准化发展规划和路线图》鼓励企事业单位、高校、科研院所致力于关键领域的技术标准研究，出台适应广东省产业结构发展、具有广东省特色的地方新材料标准及国家标准，制定严于国家标准的企业标准；科学设立一批新材料产业标准化技术分委员会，形成有效的标准化持续发展和运行机制；建立和应用科技成果转化机制，推动前沿新型材料的科技成果转化，建立一批标准化示范区或示范基地，推动已投入生产的新材料产业的标准化进程；引导企业提高技术水平，参与国际标准的制修订，关注国外技术法规和标准化动态，逐步消除对外贸易中的技术贸易壁垒，提高省内乃至全国企业的国际竞争力；引导和服务一批新材料龙头企业，达到示范带动、整体推进的效果；建立广东省"十二五"新材料产业标准数据库，为全省实施技术标准战略提供服务平台；创新人才培育机制，充实人才队伍，分层次地建立标准化专家数据库，培养一批熟悉国际规则的国际标准化人才。争取实现以新材料标准体系为导向，提高广东省新材料相关产业发展速度的目标。

二、广东省新材料产业标准体系框架

根据《广东省新材料产业发展"十二五"专项规划》，广东省现阶段重点发展先进金属材料、新型无机非金属材料、高性能有机高分子材料及复合材料、特种精细化工材料、新型稀土功能材料五大领域。2012年3月由广东省政府办公厅印发的《广东省战略性新兴产业发展"十二五"规划》在新材料领域的分类中，增加了"前沿新型材料"一类。

广东省具有以电子信息、电气机械、石油化工、纺织服装、食品饮料、建材、造纸、医药、汽车九大产业为支柱的产业结构特点。该产业结构特点决定了广东省的新材料体系，是以新型无机非金属材料和高性能有机高分子材料为主体、特种精细化工材料和前沿新型材料为特长、先进金属材料为辅助的材料体系。在具体材料分类上，新型无机非金属材料和高性能有机高分子材料中的工程材料和功能材料均为主要类目，特种精细化工材料以电子信息、石油化工、造纸等与省内产业重点相适应的产业领域为体系重点，前沿新型材料的研发和产业化，以适应全省现有科研成果和产业化现状为原则进行选择和纳入（见图4-1）。

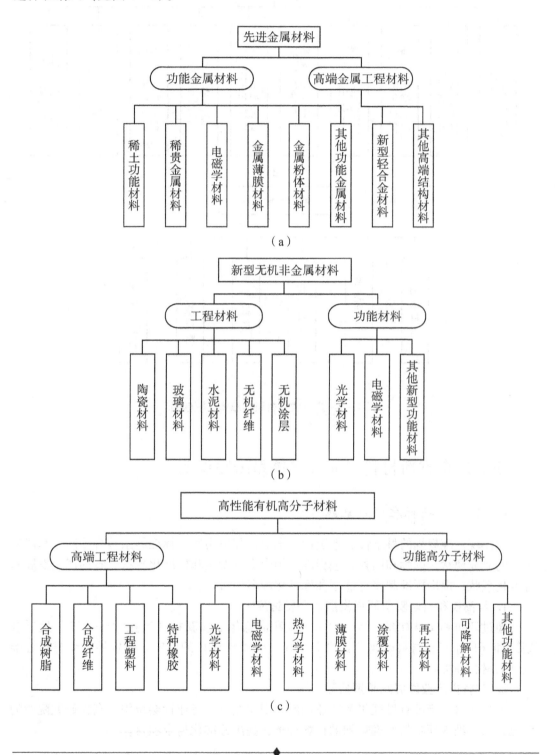

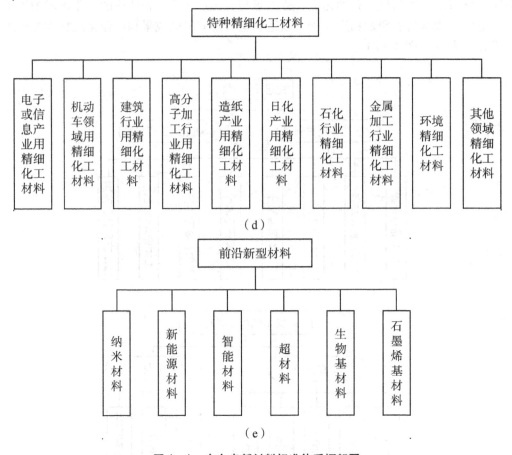

图 4-1 广东省新材料标准体系框架图

三、广东省新材料产业标准体系编写说明

(一) 预立项标准项目来源

为体现标准规划的科学性、系统性、全面性和适用性，标准体系结合了高校和研究机构的研究现状、国际和国外先进标准、国内产业发展和标准化现状、省内产业发展和标准化现状，提出标准制修订计划和标准化配套项目。

1. 与高校和科研院所研究发展水平相适应

通过调研和文献查询，结合国家工业和信息化部《新材料产业"十二五"发展规划》和《广东省新材料产业发展"十二五"专项规划》的内容，制定纳入新材料标准规划的材料种类。

2. 与省内产业发展水平适应

通过新材料标准意见征集和产业调研，根据企业、行业社会组织、高校研究院所的意见，修正纳入新材料标准规划的材料种类，提出标准化需求项目。

3. 与国际、国外标准化发展水平接轨

通过 ISO、IEC、ASTM、DIN、JIS 官方网站，查询与新材料相关的标准项目。国际和国外标准制修订中，并没有单独提出"新材料"标准化类目，大多数新材料相关的标准项目"淹没"在众多传统材料标准体系中。为保证查询结果的完整全面，本项目的查询关键词涉及传统材料和新材料的各个分支，从传统材料标准中逐个筛选出具有新材料特性的材料相关标准，使新材料的标准体系找到与国际、国外标准的对接和对比的依据，并进行了比对研究，摘出适用于广东省新材料产业发展的成熟的国际和国外先进标准。此类标准主要体现在通用基础标准和检测方法标准中。

4. 作为国内和行业内标准化的补充

按照标准类型分类，查询了国家标准和相关行业标准的标准项目，并与国际、国外先进标准进行了比对，得出广东省目前需要制定的标准项目，结合省内产业发展现状，提出标准制修订计划。

（二）标准项目优先级

广东省新材料标准体系规划预立项标准近 300 项，为保证标准项目有重点、有序地开展，规划中设置了标准预立项项目的优先等级。

优先等级共设三级，分别以"＊"号的个数表示。

（1）"＊＊＊"表示国家规划重点或省内规划重点，且有广东省企业申报承担。

（2）"＊＊"表示国家规划重点或省内规划重点，暂无企业申报，但省内有产且具备完成项目能力的项目，或在国家或省级规划重点范围内，采用国际、国外先进标准的项目。

（3）"＊"表示不在国家规划或省内规划重点范围内的企业申报项目，或采用国际、国外先进标准的项目。

（三）标准项目选择过程

广东省新材料标准体系的标准项目选取原则为"规划重点、产业需求、标准适用、地方性补充"。选取的过程经历了以下步骤：

（1）对照工信部《新材料产业"十二五"重点产品目录》，找到和标明"国家规划重点"。

（2）对照《广东省新材料产业发展"十二五"专项规划》，找到和标明"省级规划重点"。

（3）对照收集到的企业申报项目（其中部分申报项目在筛选中被淘汰，或名称发生变更，或成为系列标准的支撑部分），找到和标明"企业申报"。

（4）对于暂时没有企业申报的国家或省级规划重点，经网络和文献查阅、实地调研，确定生产企业及其生产状况，标明"省内有产"。

（5）对于暂时没有企业申报的前沿新型材料，经文献查阅，确定现在科研发展状况，经高校和科研院所调研，确定产业化进程和标准化需求，标明"引领标准"。

（6）需要采用的国际、国外先进标准，标明采用标准的来源。

（7）与国家标准、行业标准中新材料相关标准进行比对，删除没有必要制定地方标准的项目。

（8）召开专家讨论会和行业讨论会，对拟定项目进行再次筛选和修正。

（9）删除已经实施或在研的标准项目。

四、广东省新材料产业标准体系的任务

1. 先进金属材料

功能金属材料主要集中于稀土金属、稀有金属及其复合材料。功能金属材料，如半导体材料、靶材、储能材料、新型铜合金、金属粉体材料、新型耐磨涂层与薄膜、耐腐蚀涂层、耐高温表面涂层、高精度铝化成箔、亲水箔、电子铝箔、高性能铜箔、钨基合金、高纯和低偏析材料、快速凝固金属与合金（非晶态、准晶、微晶材料）、固相连续复合层状金属、核级海绵锆等材料均为具有优异功能特性的金属材料。

高性能特种钢铁材料包括高强、耐蚀、耐候、耐磨合金钢，天然气输送钢管，高性能轻量化汽车覆盖件钢，汽车用高强、高韧金属材料，3兆瓦以上大型和特大型风力发电机组用风电齿轮箱、主轴、轴承材料，国家能源、桥梁、交通运输、军事等重大工程需要的高性能特种钢铁材料和板、管、线型材、大型构件等。

高端有色轻合金材料，如轨道交通用大规格工业铝型材、高性能铝合金、高性能镁合金、钛合金、特种用途轻质金属基复合材料、颗粒或纤维增强金属基复合材料等高性能特殊功能金属材料，以及满足汽车、航空航天、生物医药等领域的特殊轻质材料。

2. 新型无机非金属材料

广东省的陶瓷、水泥、玻璃和石材，尤其是陶瓷和石材产业较为集中，有利于新材料产品的研发和快速应用。高性能改性陶瓷、改性水泥、改性玻璃和合成石材是新型无机非金属材料的重要组成部分。改性材料的发展大多有传统产业和供应链的支撑，发展较为稳健。无机纤维、无机涂层、耐火材料和抗震材料等，以其特种专用高性能在无机非金属工程材料领域占据一席之地。功能材料领域如光学材料、超硬材料和电磁学材料，均为近几年发展起来的具有良好发展前景的新型材料。

新型节能和绿色建筑材料是标准体系规划重点。包括大尺寸玻璃基板，具有轻质、高强、隔热、保温等特性的新型建筑材料，隔音和吸音材料，环保涂层材料，高效密封材料，低辐射节能玻璃，高性能车用玻璃，超薄、超厚、超白等优质浮法玻璃，玻璃镀膜的镀层材料，镀膜玻璃，智能调温、调湿、预警的智能建筑材料，高性能混凝土等。

广东省是陶瓷材料生产大省。陶瓷新材料发展重点包括节能环保陶瓷、新能源陶瓷、新型陶瓷色料、高强高韧结构陶瓷材料、特种用途的高性能陶瓷基复合材料、超薄建筑陶瓷材料、纤维和纳米颗粒增强材料、污水处理与过滤材料、自洁材料、抗菌材料、陶瓷过滤膜、陶瓷膜、超薄建筑陶瓷、高性能结构陶瓷、医用高性能硬组织植入材料、导电无机非金属材料、水泥基磁性材料和电磁屏蔽材料等。

电子信息是广东省的支柱产业，与之相关的无机非金属材料为规划重点，包括片式无源电子元件用陶瓷材料、电子敏感陶瓷材料、磁控溅射用靶材、高压高功率电力电子

元件用陶瓷材料、电子浆料、电子工业用功能玻璃、电子陶瓷用高性能化合物粉体和氧化物粉体，以及电子用陶瓷粉体及其器件材料。

3. 高性能有机高分子材料

高性能有机高分子材料及复合材料产业的特点是新材料问世迅速快，产业化迅速，ISO、IEC、ASTM、JIS、DIN 等国际标准和国外先进标准出台响应时间短。近十年内 ISO 和 ASTM 出台的新型材料标准中，很大一部分在我国标准体系中为空白。部分材料有标准，但更新速度较慢，远远不能满足新材料产业发展的需要。因此，在这一领域，依据广东省产业发展现状，首先从采用国际、国外先进标准开始，逐步发展到制定适合广东省产业发展需求、引领国际产业潮流的新材料标准，并进一步完善标准体系。

这一领域标准化任务包括合成树脂、高档合成纤维、塑料合金、先进复合材料、多功能材料、生物材料、多用途专用料、橡胶与塑料制品产业、耐高温尼龙、LED 封装有机硅树脂、电子级环氧树脂与电子用聚酰亚胺树脂（PI）、高性能聚丙烯、特种合成橡胶、高性能合成纤维、先进复合材料、阻燃材料、热收缩材料、新型热塑性弹性体、高性能热熔胶、硅酮密封胶、电池隔膜材料、双轴拉伸聚乙烯薄膜、以塑代钢材料、轻量化材料、钢塑复合材料、ABS（工程塑料）、PMMA（有机玻璃）、聚醚醚酮、液晶聚合物、聚碳酸酯、MDI 聚氨酯、生物降解材料、聚丙烯酸类材料、高性能碳纤维、特种玻璃纤维产业、纳米材料和功能填料、医用药用材料、有机发光材料、电池专用胶粘带、特种专用料、废弃高分子材料高附加值再生利用材料。

4. 特种精细化工材料

特种精细化工材料领域的分类较多，传统材料数量庞大。特种精细化工材料规划的重点是电子和 LED 封装材料、超净高纯试剂、光刻胶配套试剂、蚀刻溶剂、高分辨率感光干膜、导电胶、电解液等电子信息和能源产业配套用电子化学品，高性能、环境友好的涂料、粘合剂和油墨，高效、多功能、安全的食品、化学工业和高分子材料加工助剂，大力扶持精细功能粉体、新型催化剂、新型环境友好表面活性剂、以硅和氟为基础合成的表面改性剂、二氧化碳大规模富集吸附材料、分离材料、高效水处理剂，以及汽车、船舶和航空航天产业链配套用精细化工材料及配套材料。

5. 前沿新型材料

纳米材料、智能材料均属于跨材料学科的前沿新型材料，是国家工信部、广东省"十二五"规划中均提出重点发展的产业领域。新能源材料、超材料、石墨烯材料和生物基材料是正在成长中的高科技新材料。这六个领域已有部分纳入到相关产业的标准化规划和路线图，如深圳市标准化研究院制定的《广东省电动汽车产业标准体系规划与路线图（2011—2015 年）》；部分产业已成立专业标准化委员会，如广东省太阳能光伏能源系统标准化技术委员会、广东省 LED 光源标准化技术委员会和广东省动力电池标准化技术委员会。在全国标准化技术委员会中，与前沿新型材料关系密切的有全国纳米技术标准化技术委员会、全国电磁超材料技术及制品标准化技术委员会、全国太阳能标准化技术委员会、全国太阳光伏能源系统标准化技术委员会、全国燃料电池及液流电池标准化技术委员会、全国生物基材料及降解制品标准化技术委员会等。

伴随着标准技术委员会的建立，我国及广东省在纳米材料、新能源材料和生物基材料领域有少量标准出台，领先于国际、国外水平；超材料、石墨烯材料和智能材料领域，随着标准技术委员会的建成，不少标准项目已在制定过程中。在产业方面，纳米材料和智能材料的生产企业相对众多，但规模都较小。市面上该类材料品种繁多，但质量水平参差不齐，由于标准的缺乏，导致对其功能性和有效性无法判别。超材料和石墨烯产业更需通过标准来规范和引导产业发展。这六类前沿新型材料均是标准体系发展重点。与同时进行的国家和行业标准相比，广东省地方标准的制定更侧重于与广东省产业相关的产品标准的制定。

五、广东省新材料产业标准体系标准制修订建议（见表4-1）

表4-1 广东省新材料产业预立项标准建议表

序号	材料分类	标准分类	预立项标准	标准来源	优先级	标准立项方式
先进金属材料						
1	稀土功能材料	测试方法标准	稀土磁体材料——磁性在高温下的稳定性试验方法	国家规划重点，IEC/TR 62518 ed1.0—2009	＊＊	单个标准直接采用
2		材料技术标准	稀土磁性材料	多个材料是国家规划重点，省内有产（梅州、广州、江门）；"稀土钴永磁材料"已有国家标准，其他磁性材料还没有标准	＊＊	系列标准
3			稀土发光材料	多个种类是国家规划重点（8），省内有产；部分种有类有企业申报；部分种类是省内规划重点。已有"稀土长余辉荧光粉"国家标准	＊＊＊	系列标准
4			稀土储氢材料	多个种类是国家规划重点（11，12，13），省内有产（中山）；有一个测试方法国家标准 GB/T29918—2013	＊＊	系列标准
5			稀土催化材料	多个种类是国家规划重点（14，15，16），省内有产（惠州）	＊＊	系列标准

续表 4-1

序号	材料分类	标准分类	预立项标准	标准来源	优先级	标准立项方式
6			稀土抛光材料	多个种类是国家规划重点（20，22），省内有产（惠州，东莞）；"稀土抛光粉"有国家标准，抛光粉测试方法标准有多项；可制定细化的具体抛光材料的产品标准	**	系列标准
7		应用技术标准	稀土功能材料制品	企业申报多项	*	系列标准
8			工作场所中铍含量的试验方法	ASTM D7202—11	*	单个标准直接采用
9		测试方法标准	锆、铪及其合金的蒸汽环境耐腐蚀试验方法	ASTM G2/G2M—06（2011）	*	单个标准直接采用
10			用钚（Ⅲ）二极管阵列光学试验鉴定钚的试验方法	ASTM C1307—02（2008）	*	单个标准直接采用
11			用热电离质谱分光计测定铀或钚同位素的试验方法	ASTM C1672—07	*	单个标准直接采用
12	稀贵金属材料		铌铪合金	ASTM B654/B654M—10；ASTM B655/B655M—10	*	单个标准修改采用
13			铪及铪合金	ASTM B776—12	*	单个标准直接采用
14		材料技术标准	高性能钨基合金材料	ASTM B777—07（2013），省内规划重点，部分高性能新材料还没有标准	**	系列标准部分直接采用，部分申报
15			核级海绵锆	国家规划重点，省内有产，省级规划重点，企业申报	***	单个标准申报
16			高效贵重金属催化材料	国家规划重点，省内有产，多项材料尚没有相关标准	**	系列标准，与现有标准项目对比无重复后立项

续表 4-1

序号	材料分类	标准分类	预立项标准	标准来源	优先级	标准立项方式
17			稀有金属超细纳米晶	国家规划重点,省内有产(碳化钨等)	**	系列标准
18			稀有金属特粗晶粒	国家规划重点,省内有产(碳化钨等)	**	系列标准
19		测试方法标准	用于半导体技术的材料测试——用 ICP-MS 在水溶液中测定多种元素的方法分析硅晶圆表面	相关材料为国家和省级规划重点,有技术机构申报	*	单个标准
20			新型半导体材料	多种材料是国家规划重点,且省内有产	**	系列标准,与现有标准比对无重复后立项
21	电磁学材料	材料技术标准	高性能靶材 铬硅系列靶材	企业申报	*	系列标准
			钨钛系列靶材	企业申报	*	系列标准
			硅铝系列靶材	国家规划重点,省内有产	**	系列标准
			氧化锌锡系列靶材	省级规划重点,省内有产	**	系列标准
			铜铟镓硒系列靶材	国家规划重点,省内有产,省级规划重点	**	系列标准
			其他靶材	—	*	—
22			储能材料	部分产品是国家规划重点,省内有产	**	系列标准
23			新型电磁屏蔽材料	国家规划重点,企业申报	***	系列标准,与现有标准项目比对无重复后立项
24			高磁感取向硅钢	国家规划重点,省内有产	**	系列标准
25			大型钛基钛锰合金涂层阳极	国家规划重点,省内有产	**	系列标准
26			磁控管用铼钍钨丝	企业申报	*	系列标准
27			电子元器件端电极电镀材料	企业申报	*	系列标准

续表 4-1

序号	材料分类	标准分类	预立项标准	标准来源	优先级	标准立项方式
28	金属薄膜材料	材料技术标准	薄膜光伏材料	多个种类是国家规划重点，省内有产，已有行业标准"建筑用薄膜光伏中空玻璃一致性评定要求"	**	系列标准，与现有标准项目比对无重复后立项
29			高精度铝箔	省内规划重点	**	系列标准
30			电子铝箔	省内规划重点	**	系列标准
31			亲水金属箔	省内规划重点，亲水铝箔已有两项相关行业标准"铝及铝合金板、带、箔行业清洁生产水平评价技术要求 第5部分：亲水铝箔"和"亲水铝箔安全生产规范"，其他亲水金属箔还没有标准	**	系列标准
32			超薄电解铜箔	省内规划重点，有行业标准"铜箔、铝箔饰面人造板"，和电解铜箔不同	**	系列标准
33	金属粉体材料	材料技术标准	超细预合金粉	国家规划重点，省内有产，省内规划重点；有多项合金粉行业标准，但没有超细合金粉标准	**	系列标准
34			超细金属粉体	国家规划重点，省内有产，省内规划重点；只有一项行业标准"超硬磨料制品用预混合金属粉末"	**	系列标准
35			超细金属氧化物粉体	部分种类企业申报，省内规划重点	***	系列标准
36			3D打印金属粉体材料	省内规划重点，企业申报	***	系列标准
37	其他功能金属材料	材料技术标准	非晶纳米晶合金材料	省级规划重点，省内有产	**	系列标准
38			精密密封金属材料	国家规划重点，省内有产	**	系列标准
39			耐磨涂层与薄膜	部分种类是国家规划重点，省内有产，省内规划重点	**	系列标准

续表 4-1

序号	材料分类	标准分类	预立项标准	标准来源	优先级	标准立项方式
40	材料		微型拉拔模具	国家规划重点，省内有产	**	系列标准
41			高效吸附金属—有机多孔材料	国家规划重点，省内有产	**	系列标准
42			高温吸附金属多孔材料	国家规划重点，省内有产	**	系列标准
43			铁铬铝金属纤维多孔材料	国家规划重点，省内有产	**	系列标准
44	新型轻合金材料	材料技术标准	高性能铝合金	国家规划重点，省内有产，省级规划重点	**	系列标准
45			高性能钛铝合金	国家规划重点，省内有产	**	系列标准
46			高性能镁合金	国家规划重点，省内有产，省级规划重点	**	系列标准
47			高性能镁铝合金	省级规划重点，省内有产	**	系列标准
48			高强轻质钛合金	国家规划重点，省内有产，省级规划重点	**	系列标准
49			其他高性能轻合金材料	—	—	—
50		应用技术标准	铝镁硅（铜）合金汽车车身材料	国家规划重点，省内有产	**	单个标准
51			经济节能型铝—镁—硅裸绞线	企业申报	*	单个标准
52	高端金属结构材料	材料技术标准	汽车板用的细晶 TRIP 钢	国家规划重点，省内有产，省内规划重点	**	单个标准
53			建筑结构用大直径高强度钢绞线	企业申报	*	单个标准
54			颗粒或纤维增强金属材料	省级规划重点，省内有产	**	系列标准
55			高强高导铜合金材料	省级规划重点，省内有产	**	系列标准
56			其他高性能材料	—	—	—
新型无机非金属材料						
57	陶瓷材料	测试方法标准	纤维增强陶瓷材料室温下开孔张力强度的试验方法	ISO 14603：2012	*	单个标准
58			用于陶瓷材料制备的氮化硼粉末化学成分分析方法	ISO/DIS 17942	*	单个标准

续表 4-1

序号	材料分类	标准分类	预立项标准	标准来源	优先级	标准立项方式
59			用于陶瓷材料制备的氮化硅粉末化学成分分析方法	ISO/DIS 17947	*	单个标准
60			陶瓷粉堆密度的测试方法	ISO 23145：2012 系列	*	单个标准
61			多孔陶瓷材料的抗热震性测试方法	ISO 28703：2011	*	单个标准
62			多孔陶瓷材料的循环弯曲疲劳抗热震性测试方法	ISO 28704：2011	*	单个标准
63			微波陶瓷材料微波安全性试验方法	ASTM C1607—1	*	单个标准
64			高性能建筑陶瓷材料	省内规划重点	**	系列标准
65			超薄建筑陶瓷材料	省内规划重点，已有行业标准"轻质陶瓷砖"和"薄型陶瓷砖"	**	系列标准
66		材料技术标准	纤维和纳米颗粒增强陶瓷	省内规划重点	**	系列标准
67			抗菌陶瓷	省级规划重点	**	系列标准
68			自洁陶瓷	省级规划重点，已有一项测试行业标准"建筑陶瓷自清洁性能测试方法"	**	系列标准
69			高效分离陶瓷膜	省级规划重点	**	系列标准
70			功能陶瓷粉体	省级规划重点	**	系列标准
71			石油钻井泥浆泵缸套复合氧化锆陶瓷材料	企业申报	*	单个标准
72	玻璃材料	测试方法标准	防爆玻璃的分级与试验方法	DIN EN 356	*	单个标准，直接采用
73			防火建筑玻璃防火性能试验方法与等级分类	DIN EN 357	*	单个标准，直接采用
74			可再生玻璃材料试验方法	ASTM C1663—09（耐久性试验）；ASTM E688—2011；ASTM E708—2011（材料可再生性能试验）	*	系列标准，修改采用
75			建筑玻璃辐射性试验方法	DIN EN 12898	*	单个标准，修改采用

续表 4-1

序号	材料分类	标准分类	预立项标准	标准来源	优先级	标准立项方式
76		材料技术标准	平板玻璃抗冲击试验方法及分类	DIN EN 12758	*	单个标准，修改采用
77			高性能车用玻璃	省级规划重点	**	系列标准
78			低辐射玻璃	国家规划重点，省级规划重点，企业申报	***	系列标准
79			镀膜功能玻璃	部分材料为省级规划重点，多个材料已有企业申报	***	系列标准
80			电子显示用玻璃基板	国家规划重点，省级规划重点	**	系列标准
81			超薄玻璃	省级规划重点	**	系列标准
82			玻璃制品原料用再生玻璃	ASTM E688—94（2011）；ASTM E708—79（2011）	*	系列标准
83	水泥材料	通用基础标准	纤维增强聚合物水泥材料性能设计导则	ISO 14484：2013	*	单个标准，修改采用
84		测试方法标准	纤维增强聚合物水泥材料试验方法	ISO 10406：2008；ISO 8336：2009；DIN EN 1170	*	系列标准，修改采用或自行制定
85		材料技术标准	塑性水泥	ASTM C1328/C1328M—12	*	单个标准，修改采用
86			橡胶水泥	ASTM D816—06（2011）	*	单个标准，修改采用
87			聚合物增强水泥预制板	DIN EN 15564	*	单个标准，修改采用
88			干混膨胀玻化微珠保温隔热防火砂浆生产技术规范	企业申报	*	单个标准
89			ICF 保温节能建筑系统	ASTM C195—07（2013）；ASTM E2634—11	*	单个标准，修改采用
90			高性能抗氯盐水泥	企业申报	*	单个标准

续表 4-1

序号	材料分类	标准分类	预立项标准	标准来源	优先级	标准立项方式
91	无机纤维	材料技术标准	矿物纤维喷涂吸声隔热材料	ASTM C1014—08（2013）	*	单个标准，修改采用
92			水泥和混凝土增强用耐碱玻璃纤维	ASTM C1666/C1666M—08	*	单个标准，修改采用
93			石墨或碳纤维盘根	ASTM F2191—02（2008）	*	单个标准，修改采用
94			工业用气动耐高温绝热纤维	ASTM C1685—08	*	单个标准，修改采用
95			高性能耐高温纤维毡	ASTM C892—10	*	单个标准，修改采用
96	无机涂层	通用基础标准	搪瓷和陶瓷—金属体系术语	ASTM C286—09	*	单个标准，修改采用
97		测试方法标准	隔热水泥涂层导热性的试验方法	JIS R 1611：2010	*	单个标准，修改采用
98			隔热无机涂层线性膨胀系数的试验方法	DIN 51177；JIS H 8455：2010	*	单个标准，修改采用
99			搪瓷铝板	企业申报	*	单个标准
100			搪瓷不锈钢板	企业申报	*	单个标准
101		材料技术标准	隔热保温陶瓷涂料	省级规划重点	* *	系列标准
102			微晶玻璃涂层	国家重点（微晶玻璃）；省内规划重点（微晶玻璃）；省内有产	* *	系列标准
103	光学材料	测试方法标准	精细陶瓷薄膜在润湿状态下光谱传输性能试验方法	ISO 10678：2010	*	单个标准，直接采用
104			带透明基底的陶瓷薄膜光传输性能试验方法	ISO/DIS 17861；ISO 20508：2003	*	单个标准，直接采用
105			光纤微弯敏感性试验方法	IEC/TR 62221	*	单个标准，直接采用
106			氮化镓衬底片测试方法	企业申报	*	单个标准
107			氮化镓自支撑衬底片	企业申报	*	单个标准
108			氮化镓复合衬底片	企业申报	*	单个标准

续表 4-1

序号	材料分类	标准分类	预立项标准	标准来源	优先级	标准立项方式
109	电磁学材料	测试方法标准	离子导电精细陶瓷的导电性试验方法	ISO 11894：2013 系列	*	系列标准，直接或修改采用
110		材料技术标准	X射线防护玻璃板	IEC 61331—2	*	单个标准，修改采用
111			透明导电氧化物玻璃	国家规划重点	**	系列标准
112			电子浆料	企业申报，省内规划重点	***	单个标准
113			多层片式瓷介电容器用陶瓷介质材料	企业申报，国家标准"电容器用陶瓷介质材料"为1996年版，无其他陶瓷介质材料标准	*	单个标准
高性能有机高分子材料						
114	合成树脂	通用基础标准	聚醚酰亚胺类材料（PEIs）分类、术语和基础标准	ASTM D5205—10	*	单个标准，修改采用
115			液晶聚合物（LCP）分类、术语和基础标准	ASTM D5138—11，省级规划重点	*	单个标准，修改采用
116		材料技术标准	高性能含氟聚合物	ASTM D2116—07（2012）；ASTM D3307—10，国家规划重点	**	单个标准，修改采用
117			聚醚酮	ASTM D6262—12，国家规划重点，省级规划重点	**	单个标准，修改采用
118			聚苯硫醚（PPS）	ASTM D4067—11；ASTM D6358—11；国家规划重点	**	单个标准，修改采用
119			聚酰胺酰亚胺（PAI）材料	ASTM D7292—12	*	单个标准，修改采用
120			聚醚酰亚胺（PEI）材料	ASTM D7293—1	*	单个标准，修改采用
121			氯化乙烯—醋酸乙烯（EVA）共聚物	企业申报	*	单个标准
122			松香聚氧乙烯醚材料	企业申报	*	单个标准

续表 4-1

序号	材料分类	标准分类	预立项标准	标准来源	优先级	标准立项方式
123			聚乙烯醇缩丁醛树脂	企业申报	*	单个标准
124			氯化聚丙烯	企业申报	*	单个标准
125			交联聚乙烯（PEX）	企业申报	*	单个标准
126			高性能聚丙烯	省级规划重点	* *	单个标准
127			用于3D打印高分子复合材料	省级规划重点，企业申报多项	* * *	系列标准
128	合成纤维	测试方法标准	非织造过滤材料孔隙特征测试方法	企业申报	*	单个标准
129			非织造空气过滤布过滤性能试验方法	企业申报	*	单个标准
130		材料技术标准	超高分子量聚乙烯纤维	省级规划重点	* *	单个标准
131			高性能纺织纤维	多个种类为省级规划重点	* *	单个标准
132		应用技术标准	干式潜水衣	企业申报	*	单个标准
133			纤维素纤维及其混纺交织免烫梭织衬衫	企业申报	*	单个标准
134	工程塑料	测试方法标准	碳纤维增强树脂基复合材料试验方法	企业申报多个性能的测试方法	*	系列标准
135		材料技术标准	高性能碳纤维增强丙烯腈—丁二烯—苯乙烯（ABS）	企业申报	*	单个标准
136			智能电表外壳用聚碳酸酯	企业申报	*	单个标准
137			笔记本外壳用碳纤维增强聚酰胺	企业申报	*	单个标准
138		应用技术标准	交联和耐热聚乙烯管的塑料嵌件	企业申报	*	单个标准
139			用于交联聚乙烯管路的增强交联聚乙烯环冷膨胀嵌件	企业申报	*	单个标准
140	特种橡胶	材料技术标准	功能橡胶材料	为高性能改性橡胶材料留位置	*	系列标准
141			高性能橡胶材料	省级规划重点，国家重点规划中多个类目	* *	系列标准
142			特种专用橡胶	为专用橡胶材料留位置	*	系列标准

续表 4-1

序号	材料分类	标准分类	预立项标准	标准来源	优先级	标准立项方式
143	光学材料	测试方法标准	透明或半透明高分子材料中双折射和残余应变的光弹性试验方法	ASTM D4093—95（2010）	*	单个标准，修改采用
144			透明有机塑料折射率试验方法	ASTM D542—13	*	单个标准，修改采用
145			强化塑胶板散射因子试验方法	ASTM D1494—12	*	单个标准，修改采用
146			塑料薄板透明度试验方法	ASTM D1746—09	*	单个标准，修改采用
147			透明塑料的光投射系数试验方法	ASTM D1003—13	*	单个标准，修改采用
148		材料技术标准	塑料光纤材料	省级规划重点，已有多项转向器或连接器国家标准和行业标准，已有行业标准"通信用塑料光纤"	**	系列标准，对比已有标准无重复后立项
149			PET 光栅片材	企业申报	*	单个标准
150			LED 用反光高分子材料	企业申报	*	单个标准
151			LED 透镜用 UV 光固化树脂	企业申报	*	单个标准
152	电磁学材料	材料技术标准	永久抗静电丙烯腈—丁二烯—苯乙烯（ABS）塑料	企业申报	*	单个标准
153			复合导电塑料	企业申报	*	单个标准
154			导电耐高温塑料	企业申报	*	单个标准
155			ITO 导电基膜	企业申报	*	单个标准
156			电子基环氧树脂	省级规划重点	**	单个标准
157			电子基聚酰亚胺树脂	省级规划重点	**	单个标准
158		应用技术标准	高功率 LED 封装用白色基板	企业申报，主要强调绝缘和电磁屏蔽性能	*	单个标准
159			半导体封装用覆铜箔层压板	企业申报	*	单个标准
160			电动汽车用高可靠性覆铜箔层压板	企业申报	*	单个标准

续表 4-1

序号	材料分类	标准分类	预立项标准	标准来源	优先级	标准立项方式
161	热力学材料	材料技术标准	LED封装有机硅树脂	省级规划重点，主要强调耐高温和导热性能	**	单个标准
162			LED照明灯具用高导热高分子复合材料	企业申报，主要强调导热性能	*	单个标准
163			耐高温尼龙	企业申报	*	系列标准
164			辐射散热聚合物	企业申报	*	系列标准
165			散热型水溶电泳涂层	企业申报	*	系列标准
166			隔热用喷涂聚氨酯泡沫	ISO 8873：2006	*	单个标准，修改采用
167			外墙隔热和装饰用发泡聚苯乙烯	ASTM E2430/E2430M—13	*	单个标准，修改采用
168	薄膜材料	测试方法标准	塑料薄膜水蒸气透过率试验方法	ASTM D7407—07（2012）	*	单个标准，修改采用
169			塑料薄膜/片材氧气透过率试验方法	ASTM F2622—08（2013）；ASTM D3985—05（2010）	*	单个标准，修改采用
170			各向异性光学薄膜的雾度检测方法	企业申报	*	单个标准，修改采用
171		材料技术标准	压纹通孔真空复合薄膜	省级规划重点，企业申报	***	单个标准
172			陶瓷涂层锂离子电池隔膜	省级规划重点，企业申报	***	单个标准
173			透湿型塑料薄膜	企业申报	*	单个标准
174			紫外光固化压敏胶PE保护膜	企业申报	*	单个标准
175			轻离型聚酯薄膜	企业申报	*	单个标准
176			电子产品屏幕保护膜	企业申报	*	单个标准
177			聚乙烯醇缩丁醛(PVB)膜	企业申报	*	单个标准
178	涂覆材料	通用基础标准	水性玻璃涂料中有害物质限量	企业申报	*	单个标准
179			不流胶半固化规范	企业申报	*	单个标准
180		测试方法标准	热裂解气相色谱质谱法（PyGCMS）鉴定水性内外墙涂料成膜物质	企业申报	*	单个标准

续表 4-1

序号	材料分类	标准分类	预立项标准	标准来源	优先级	标准立项方式
181			聚氨酯类木器涂料耐黄变性质快速鉴定方法	企业申报	*	单个标准
182			使用近红外光谱法（NIR）快速检测涂料中的有害物质含量方法	企业申报	*	单个标准
183			环保低温固化型粉末涂料	省级规划重点，企业申报	***	系列标准
184			水性工业涂料	省级规划重点，企业申报	***	系列标准
185			隔热涂料	JIS A5547—2003	*	系列标准，部分参考采用
186		材料技术标准	光学涂料	参考 ISO 9211：2012；DIN 67510 系列标准	*	系列标准，参考采用
187			可剥离陶瓷辊棒保护涂料	企业申报	*	单个标准
188			辐射散热涂料	省级规划重点，多个产品类型已有企业申报	***	系列标准，对比现有标准项目无重复后立项
189			水性复膜胶	企业申报	*	单个标准
190			水性低温玻璃釉	企业申报	*	单个标准
191		通用基础标准	可回收高分子材料的回收和利用指南	DIN EN 15343	*	单个标准，修改采用
192	再生材料（省级规划重点）		会议、展览等用环保高分子材料的评估和选择	ASTM E2746—11	*	单个标准，修改采用
193			回收再生聚乙烯塑料	DIN EN 15344	*	单个标准，修改采用
194			回收再生聚丙烯塑料	DIN EN 15345	*	单个标准，修改采用
195		材料技术标准	回收再生聚氯乙烯塑料	DIN EN 15346	*	单个标准，修改采用
196			回收再生 PET 塑料	DIN EN 15348	*	单个标准，修改采用

续表 4-1

序号	材料分类	标准分类	预立项标准	标准来源	优先级	标准立项方式
197		应用技术标准	包含回收再生成分的聚氯乙烯（PVC）不耐压管材	ASTM F1760—01（2011）	*	单个标准，修改采用
198			回收再生聚乙烯模塑和挤出材料	ASTM D5203—07	*	单个标准，修改采用
199			再生聚氯乙烯排水管	ASTM F1732—12	*	单个标准，修改采用
200	可降解材料（省级规划重点）	材料技术标准	海洋环境中不漂浮可生物降解高分子材料	ASTM D7081—05	*	单个标准，修改采用
201			淀粉基全生物降解材料	企业申报	*	单个标准
202			生物降解地膜	企业申报	*	单个标准
203			生物降解印刷薄膜	企业申报	*	单个标准
204			可降解塑料标签	ASTM D6868—11；ASTM D6400—12	*	单个标准，修改采用
特种精细化工材料						
205	电子或电子信息产业用精细化工材料	测试方法标准	高纯试剂试验方法	JIS K8007；JIS K8001	*	单个标准，修改采用
206			导电胶体积电阻率试验方法	ASTM D2739—2010	*	单个标准，修改采用
207		材料技术标准	超净高纯试剂	省级规划重点；参考 SEMI—C1，MOS 试剂标准，SEMI—C7，电子纯 BV—Ⅲ试剂标准，德国依默克试剂标准，ACS 试剂标准	*	系列标准，修改采用
208			高分辨率感光材料	省级规划重点	**	系列标准
209			磁性墨水	省级规划重点，ISO 1004：2013	**	单个标准，修改采用
210			导电油墨	省级规划重点，IEC 61249	**	单个标准，修改采用
211			导电胶	省级规划重点	**	系列标准
212			水性镀铝膜转移复合胶	企业申报	*	单个标准

续表 4-1

序号	材料分类	标准分类	预立项标准	标准来源	优先级	标准立项方式
213	机动车领域用精细化工材料（省级规划重点）	通用基础标准	电子绝缘用硅油	ASTM D4652—05（2012）	*	单个标准，修改采用
214			LED 封装用化学品	省级规划重点	*	系列标准
215			机动车用冷却液 术语和分类	ASTM D4725—13	*	单个标准，修改采用
216			自动传动液等级评估与分类	企业申报	*	单个标准
217		材料技术标准	高性能合成制动液	企业申报	*	单个标准
218			高效玻璃防雾剂	JIS K2399—2001	*	单个标准，修改采用
219			机动车用挡风玻璃清洗剂	JIS K2398—2009	*	单个标准，修改采用
220			汽车美容精细化学品	企业申报	*	单个标准
221	建筑行业用精细化工材料	测试方法标准	高性能建筑用结构胶粘剂试验方法	ASTM D1144—99（2011）；ASTM C882/C882M—13；DIN 54457—2007；DIN 54461—2005；DIN 68141—2008；DIN EN 302—3—2013	*	系列标准，修改采用
222			高性能建筑业用结构胶粘剂	ASTM C881/C881M—10；ASTM C1059/C1059M—99（2008）；DIN EN 15275—2011	*	系列标准，修改采用
223			建筑用环保结构胶粘剂	ASTM D4690—12	*	单个标准，修改采用
224		材料技术标准	建筑用高性能粘合剂	JIS K6806—2003；DIN EN 301—2013；DIN EN 15425—2008	*	系列标准，部分修改采用，部分自行制定
225			新型高效混凝土添加剂	JIS A6204—2011；ASTM C882/C882M—13；DIN EN 934 系列标准	*	系列标准，部分修改采用，部分自行制定

续表 4-1

序号	材料分类	标准分类	预立项标准	标准来源	优先级	标准立项方式
226	高分子加工行工用精细化工材料	材料技术标准	高分子材料无卤阻燃改性剂	企业申报	*	系列标准
227			高分子晶型改性剂	企业申报	*	系列标准
228			不饱和酸酐改性橡胶高性能增韧剂	企业申报	*	系列标准
229			高分子材料微发泡剂	企业申报	*	系列标准
230			高分子材料加工润滑助剂	企业申报	*	系列标准
231			橡胶材料抗老化助剂	企业申报	*	系列标准
232	造纸产业用精细化工材料	材料技术标准	碳酸钙合成纸	企业申报	*	单个标准
233			新型造纸助剂	参考 DIN 55626 系列标准 2005 年以后新增的多项标准	*	系列标准，修改采用或自行制定
234	日化产业用精细化工材料	通用基础标准	环保表面活性剂 术语或通用要求	省级规划重点	* *	单个标准
235		测试方法标准	合成洗涤剂生物降解性能试验方法	JIS K3363	*	单个标准，修改采用
236		材料技术标准	环保表面活性剂	省级规划重点	* *	系列标准
237			硅氟表面改性剂	省级规划重点	* *	系列标准
238			其他新型表面活性剂	—	—	—
239	石化行业精细化工材料	测试方法标准	润滑油氧化稳定性试验方法	JIS K2514 系列标准（2013）	*	系列标准，修改采用
240			水性油墨性能试验方法	ASTM D6531—00（2010）；	*	单个标准，修改采用
241			润滑油及其添加剂化学分析方法	DIN 51363 系列标准；DIN 51399 系列标准	*	系列标准，修改采用
242		材料技术标准	新型高效石油和润滑油添加剂	JIS K2395—2009	*	系列标准，修改采用
243			新型高效润滑油	JIS K2220—2013；IEC 61221—2004	*	系列标准，修改采用
244			环保染料和油墨	省级规划重点，企业申报	* *	系列标准
245			光学染料和油墨	参考 ISO 9211：2012；DIN 67510 系列标准	*	系列标准，修改采用

续表 4-1

序号	材料分类	标准分类	预立项标准	标准来源	优先级	标准立项方式
246	金属加工行业用精细化工材料	材料技术标准	铸造用化学品助剂	部分材料企业申报	*	系列标准
247			其他金属加工助剂	—	—	—
248	环境精细化工材料	通用基础标准	抗菌消毒剂 术语	省级规划重点，ASTM E2756—10	***	单个标准，修改采用
249		测试方法标准	用琼脂片技术评定抗菌制剂的试验方法	ASTM E1882—10	*	单个标准，修改采用
250			聚合物或疏水材料中微生物灭杀成分的活性试验方法	ASTM E2180—07（2012）	*	单个标准，修改采用
251			涂层材料中生物灭杀成分释放率试验方法	ISO 10890：2010；ASTM D6903—07（2013）	*	单个标准，修改采用
252		材料技术标准	新型高效饮用水处理剂	省级规划重点；DIN EN 1197—2006；DIN EN 12678—2008 等	**	系列标准，修改采用
253			新型高效饮用游泳池水处理剂	DIN EN 15797—2010 等	*	系列标准，修改采用或自行制定
254			二氧化碳富吸材料	省级规划重点	**	系列标准
255			新型消毒抗菌剂	企业申报	*	系列标准
前沿新型材料						
256	纳米材料（省级规划重点）	通用基础标准	纳米材料的分类	ISO/TR 11360：2010	**	单个标准，直接采用
257			纳米材料的特性辨别指南	ISO/TS 12805：2011	**	单个标准，直接采用
258			含纳米材料产品自愿性标签指南	ISO/TS 13830：2013	**	单个标准，直接采用
259		安全技术标准	职业环境中释放产生的纳米粒子处理指南	ASTM E2535—07（2013）；ISO/TS 12025：2012；ISO/AWI TR 18637	**	单个标准，修改采用

续表 4-1

序号	材料分类	标准分类	预立项标准	标准来源	优先级	标准立项方式
260	纳米材料（省级规划重点）	测试方法标准	超细纳米颗粒和纳米结构气溶胶—吸入状态特征与危害性评估	ISO/TR 27628：2007	**	单个标准，直接采用
261			纳米材料的职业风险管理	ISO/TS 12901：2012；ISO/AWI TR 18637	**	单个标准，修改采用
262			纳米材料对细胞活力的影响试验方法	ISO/AWI 19007	**	单个标准，直接采用
263			纳米粒子的溶血性试验方法	ASTM E2524—08（2013）	**	单个标准，直接采用
264		材料技术标准	碳纳米管电气性能测试方法	IEC 62624	**	单个标准，直接采用
265			锂电池阴极纳米材料	IEC/TS 62607—4—1	**	单个标准，直接采用
266			其他纳米材料	—	—	
267	新能源材料（省级规划重点）	通用基础标准	光伏组件生态设计技术规范	企业申报	***	单个标准
268		测试方法标准	光伏组件用乙烯—醋酸乙烯共聚物（EVA）中醋酸乙烯（VA）含量测试方法	企业申报	***	单个标准
269			光伏组件封装材料测试方法	企业申报多个项目	**	系列标准
270			蜂窝夹心核心材料的静能量吸收性能试验方法	ASTM D7336/D7336M—12	**	单个标准，修改采用
271			太阳能模拟光源的光谱分布计算	ISO/DTR 18486	**	单个标准，修改采用
272		材料技术标准	动力电池级 镍钴锰酸锂	企业申报	***	单个标准
273			镍锰酸锂	企业申报	***	单个标准
274			镍钴酸锂	企业申报	***	单个标准
275			镍钴铝酸锂	企业申报	***	单个标准
276			锰酸锂	省级规划重点，省内有产，已有行业标准"镍钴锰酸锂"	***	单个标准

续表 4-1

序号	材料分类	标准分类	预立项标准	标准来源	优先级	标准立项方式
277			磷酸铁锂	省级规划重点，省内有产，已有行业标准"通信用磷酸铁锂电池组 第1部分：集成式电池组"	***	单个标准
278			燃料电池双极板	省级规划重点，省内有产	***	单个标准
279			高性能电解液	省级规划重点，省内有产	***	系列标准
280			薄膜太阳能电池	IEC 61646：2008	**	单个标准，修改采用
281			其他新型电池材料	—	—	—
282	智能材料	通用基础标准	形状记忆材料 术语	JIS H 7001：2009	*	单个标准，修改采用
283			镍钛形状记忆合金通用标准	ASTM F2005—2005（2010）	*	单个标准，修改采用
284			智能纤维 定义和分类	DIN CEN/TR 16298—2012	*	单个标准，修改采用
285		测试方法标准	形状记忆合金试验方法	JIS H 7106：2002；JIS H7104：2002；ASTM F2082—2006；JIS H 7103：2012；JIS H 7105：2012，刚发布两项试验方法行业标准，还未实施	*	系列标准，修改采用，对比已有标准项目无重复后立项
286			形状记忆合金	ASTM F2633—2007，ASTM F2063—2005，国家规划重点，已有行业标准"形状记忆合金丝"，刚发布还未实施	*	系列标准，修改采用，对比已有标准项目无重复后立项
287		材料技术标准	电磁声学传感器	ASTM E1774—1996（2007）	*	单个标准，修改采用
288			电水壶温敏磁控开关	企业申报	*	单个标准
289			磁敏传感器	企业申报	*	单个标准
290			辐射感应薄膜	DIN 15551	*	单个标准，修改采用

续表 4-1

序号	材料分类	标准分类	预立项标准	标准来源	优先级	标准立项方式
291	智能材料	应用技术标准	磁致伸缩传感器	国家规划重点，省内规划重点，省内有产	**	单个标准
292			智能玻璃	多类材料省级规划重点（自动调温、调湿等，温度预警、压力预警等）	**	系列标准
293			压敏电控装置	IEC 60730—2—6	*	单个标准，修改采用
294			温敏电控装置	IEC 60730—2—9	*	单个标准，修改采用
295			湿敏电控装置	IEC 60730—2—13	*	单个标准，修改采用
296			气流、水流和水位敏感电控装置	IEC 60730—2—15	*	单个标准，修改采用
297	超材料	通用基础标准	电磁超材料 术语	企业申报	*	单个标准
298			电磁超材料材料选择与性能设计导则	企业申报	*	单个标准
299		材料技术标准	电磁超材料及其制品	企业申报	*	单个标准
300	生物基材料	材料技术标准	生物基塑料	企业申报	*	单个标准
301			生物基能源材料	引领标准	*	系列标准
302	石墨烯基材料	材料技术标准	石墨烯基光学材料	引领标准	*	系列标准
303			石墨烯基电学材料	引领标准	*	系列标准
304			石墨烯基器件	引领标准	*	系列标准
305			石墨烯基水处理剂	引领标准	*	系列标准

第五章　广东省新材料产业标准体系实施环境分析与产业标准化路线图

一、标准体系规划实施环境分析

随着科技的迅猛发展，特别是经济全球化、一体化的加速，组织所处的环境更为开放和动荡。因此，环境分析成为一项日益重要的政策分析活动。环境发展趋势可分为两大类：一类表示环境威胁，另一类表示环境机会。环境威胁是指环境中不利的发展趋势所形成的挑战，如果不积极应对，它将导致组织竞争地位的削弱。环境机会则是对组织行为富有吸引力的领域，在这一领域中，该组织将拥有竞争优势。对组织环境进行分析的一种简明扼要的方法是 PSET 分析。其中，广东省新材料相关政策如表 5-1 所示。

表 5-1　广东省新材料相关政策一览表

序号	政策文件名	新材料相关政策要点
1	《关于贯彻落实国务院加快培育和发展战略性新兴产业决定的意见》	大力发展稀土功能材料、平板显示材料、半导体照明材料等新型功能材料，推广低能耗、轻污染、可循环的新型材料制造技术。提升碳纤维、芳纶、超高分子量聚乙烯纤维等高性能纤维及其复合材料发展水平。
2	国家《新材料产业标准化工作三年行动计划》	到2015年，完成200项重点标准制修订工作，立项并启动300项新材料标准研制，开展50项重点标准；覆盖《新材料产业"十二五"发展规划》提出的400个重点新材料产品，基本形成重点领域发展急需的、具有创新成果和国际水平的重要技术标准体系；新材料国际标准化工作取得实质性进展，提出20项新材料国际标准提案，推进若干国际标准的立项和制定，在稀土新材料、稀贵金属材料等领域实现重大突破。
3	广东省《2011年促进战略性新兴产业加快发展行动方案》	研究制定新材料产业发展指导目录；建立和完善促进发展的新材料、高端装备制造、太阳能光伏等五大重点产业的评估指标体系。
4	《广东省战略性新兴产业发展"十二五"规划》	确定了新材料、新能源汽车和半导体照明等领域作为广东重点培育和发展的战略性新兴产业；面向高端电子信息、新能源汽车、半导体照明等重点产业发展对新型材料的需求，重点发展先进金属等新型材料，加快培育和布局发展前沿新型材料。

续表 5-1

序号	政策文件名	新材料相关政策要点
5	广东省《新材料产业"十二五"发展规划》	到 2015 年，新材料产业总产值达到 2 万亿元，年均增长率超过 25%；重点新材料企业研发投入占销售收入比重达到 5%，建成一批新材料工程技术研发和公共服务平台；打造 10 个创新能力强、具有核心竞争力、新材料销售收入超 150 亿元的综合性龙头企业，培育 20 个新材料销售收入超过 50 亿元的专业性骨干企业，建成若干主业突出、产业配套齐全、年产值超过 300 亿元的新材料产业基地和产业集群；新材料产品综合保障能力提高到 70%，关键新材料保障能力达到 50%，实现碳纤维等先进储能材料、半导体材料、膜材料等关键品种产业化、规模化。
6	《广东省新材料产业发展专项规划》	成立专项课题组历时近半个月，赴广州、佛山、江门等 6 市现场进行调研与考察；通过规划引导，突出重点，合理布局，加快培育和发展新材料产业。
7	《广州综合性国家高技术产业基地发展规划》	新材料产业方面，依托广州新材料国家高技术产业基地建设，促进新材料产业建成现代新材料产业体系。到 2015 年，力争实现新材料产业总产值达 1800 亿元，出现销售收入达 150 亿元的标杆企业；到 2020 年力争实现产业总产值 3000 亿元，出现销售收入达 200 亿元的龙头企业。
8	《广州新材料产业国家高技术产业基地总体发展规划》	广州新材料产业总产值年均增长 20% 以上，2010 年达到 900 亿元，约占全市工业总产值的比重为 7.4%，工业增加值 200 亿元，约占全市 GDP 2.3%；届时，年销售收入超亿元的新材料企业将超过 140 家，其中，超 10 亿元的企业 23 家、超 100 亿元的企业 3 家。到 2015 年，新材料技术产品将形成 1800 亿元的产业规模。而其建设的总目标是建成产业结构高级化、产业发展聚集化、产业水平国际化的现代新材料产业体系。
9	《深圳新材料产业振兴发展政策》	重点发展支撑领域新材料、优势领域新材料、新兴领域新材料等；制定了到 2015 年"新材料产业规模达到 1500 亿元，努力成为世界知名、国内领先的新材料产业基地"的发展目标；明确了每年 5 亿元设立新材料产业发展专项资金，用于支持新材料产业发展。
10	《关于开展 2015 年广州市战略性新兴产业（生物、新材料、新能源与节能环保）示范工程专项的通知》	支持新材料、新能源和技能环保等产业重点领域的应用示范，促进产业规模发展及基础能力建设；通过财政补助或股权投资的方式对新材料等符合要求的企业进行支持。

续表 5-1

序号	政策文件名	新材料相关政策要点
11	河源《关于"三个50工程"扶持政策的实施意见》	加大对稀土深加工等产业企业扶持力度的主要优惠点有：新投产的企业，四年内由本级财政安排资金给予支持；投产企业向金融机构贷款的，经企业申请，按其所需支付贷款利息的20%给予一次性贴息扶持，每个项目的贴息扶持最高限额为50万元。

随着近年来广东建材、纺织服装等传统产业转型升级步伐加快，新材料对传统产业转型升级的支撑和促进作用日益增强，相关产业对新材料的需求也在逐年扩大。通过建立新材料产业园和基地，广东大力吸引新材料产业相关厂家落户，加强产学研结合，提高自主创新能力，促进新材料产业集群发展。目前，广东已经初步形成了广州新材料产业国家高技术产业基地、深圳国家半导体照明基地、佛山光伏产业基地等一批特色鲜明的新材料产业集聚区，并培育出一批处于国内领先地位的新材料龙头骨干企业，新材料产业发展势头良好，产业集群态势已初步形成。

其中，位于南海的广东省新材料产业基地政府共投资15亿元，用于基础设施、孵化器、公共平台等建设。该基地建成后将重点发展新能源材料、新型金属材料、新型显示材料、高性能复合材料、功能陶瓷材料、生物医用材料六大新材料。基地以"龙头企业+技术平台+特色园区"为发展模式，按照"高起点规划、高标准建设、高效能管理、高水平引资"的原则，着力于打造国内一流并具有国际竞争力的新材料产业集群。

据统计，2012年广东省新材料产业实现工业总产值1339.09亿元，同比增长6.1%，实现工业增加值299.16亿元，同比增长7.9%，实现销售产值1293.8亿元，同比增长4.1%，实现主营业务收入1289.7亿元，同比增长0.8%。目前，规模以上高新技术企业有600多家，行业从业人员约10万人，广州、深圳、佛山和东莞4市的新材料产业规模占全省60%以上。

以上的分析表明，广东的新材料行业不仅应用前景广阔，且产业规模初具，已经具备了强大的大型项目支撑能力。表5-2为广东省新材料项目应用概况及典型案例。

表5-2 重大项目支撑能力举例

序号	项目类别	应用概况及典型案例
1	先进金属材料	非晶和微晶材料、高比强的铝锂合金、金属基复合材料以及形状记忆合金等新型功能金属材料，已分别在航空航天、能源、机电等各个领域获得了应用。如中山金胜铝业研发了一种可显著提高铝合金耐热性能的金属化合物，它应用到打印机的定影辊基材之中，可将材料热稳定性提升一倍，加快了热传导速度，满足了高速激光打印的需要。

续表 5-2

序号	项目类别	应用概况及典型案例
2	新型无机非金属材料	包括先进陶瓷、特种玻璃及其他无机非金属材料。其中精细熔融石英陶瓷坩埚、陶瓷过滤膜和新型无毒蜂窝陶瓷脱硝催化剂等产品已经初具规模；低辐射（Low-E）镀膜玻璃、涂膜玻璃、真空节能玻璃广泛应用于建筑节能、平板显示和太阳能利用等领域；功能性超硬材料、高性能玻璃纤维和绿色新型耐火材料等产品在新型建筑产业应用前景广阔。如中山格兰特生产的低辐射镀膜玻璃已成为业内知名的金色 Low-E 玻璃，与高校产学研合作的自洁玻璃也达到了国际先进水平。
3	高性能有机高分子材料及复合材料	高分子聚合物与金属粉末或陶瓷颗粒组成的双组分或多组分的复合材料，在设备维护领域方面取得了突破性的进展，除用于连接、密封、堵漏、绝缘外，还广泛应用于机械设备耐磨损、耐腐蚀、耐冲击修复，也可用于修补设备上的各种缺陷。深圳市龙邦新材料有限公司是全球除美国杜邦以外，唯一实现芳纶复合材料工业化量产的企业，其产品已经为"神舟七号"载人航天工程所采用，并成为陆航直升机项目蜂窝结构件材料提供商，赢得国际主流厂商的认可。
4	特种精细化工材料	主要包括有机硅材料、有机氟材料、工程塑料、特种橡胶、高性能纤维、生物基新材料六小类产品；二次加工的新材料主要指在化学合成的新材料基础上，与其他辅助材料和助剂相配合，通过混配、复合等工艺所生产的材料，如氟涂料、硅涂料、有机硅胶粘剂、功能性膜材料等。例如，深圳材质科技股份有限公司专门从事锂离子电池隔膜及其他高分子功能膜产品设计开发，公司自主研发掌握了隔膜干法、湿法生产工艺，打破了国外技术封锁，填补了国内空白。公司已经成为动力锂电池产品的主要供应商，并且成为国际市场的有力竞争者，为美国 A123、韩国 LG 等国外多家知名企业批量供货。
5	新型稀土功能材料	稀土磁、光、电等功能材料在新能源汽车、风力发电、新型显示与照明、机器人、电子信息、航空航天、国防军工、节能环保及高端装备制造等战略性新兴产业中均发挥着不可或缺的核心基础材料的作用。广东是我国稀土功能材料应用第一大省。广东稀土研发实力也不容小觑，在稀土发光材料、稀土储氢材料等领域的研究成果处于国内领先水平。2012 年，我国首家稀土全产业链大型集团"广东省稀土产业集团"在广州成立，这意味着广东率先在我国稀土产业新版图中占据了一席之地。
6	前沿新型材料	主要包括纳米材料、超材料及智能材料等，其中超材料广泛应用于隐形材料的制备；智能材料能感知外部刺激，是未来打造智能生活的重要原材料；光电材料是指用于制造各种光电设备，主要包括红外材料、激光材料、光纤材料等。2012 年，全球第一条超材料生产线正式落户深圳。其主导者深圳光启高等理工研究院为广东和深圳首批引进的海外创新团队，拥有世界超材料领域最前沿的创新技术，成立不到 2 年已申请 1589 件底层技术专利及应用专利，在该领域核心知识产权上具有主导控制权。目前其产品主要包括超材料平板卫星天线、超材料小天线、超材料双工器等。

进入21世纪,以新材料为代表的战略性新兴产业正在成为引领经济发展的重要力量,各国高度重视新材料开发应用。标准作为新材料开发、产业化及推广应用的重要支撑,是规范新材料市场秩序、促进企业参与国际竞争、维护产业利益和经济安全的重要手段。建立完善的新材料产业标准体系,对于加快培育发展新材料产业、促进材料工业转型升级、支撑战略性新兴产业发展、保障国民经济重大工程建设和国防科技工业具有重要意义。

我国有色金属、石化、建材等原材料工业规模巨大,是国民经济的基础产业。据统计,截至2012年,我国原材料工业现行有效标准11814项,占工业和通信业现行有效标准的20%。近年来,各行业日益重视新材料标准化工作,新材料标准制修订步伐加快,仅2010年以来就发布了碳纤维、光学功能薄膜、功能陶瓷等100余项新材料标准,推动了原材料工业结构调整和转型升级。

广东历来重视标准的制修订工作,积极参与国家有关标准的研究和制定。近年来在新材料标准的制定上开展了一系列的研究工作,多个专业化的行业TC顺利组建,多项与新材料相关的地方标准成功问世。

2012年底,广东省稀土标准化技术委员会在江门正式成立,负责稀土技术领域的标准化归口工作。广东省稀土标准化技术委员会由23人组成,设主任委员1人,副主任委员2人。国内最大的稀土发光材料生产企业江门市科恒实业股份有限公司承担着该标准化技术委员会秘书处的工作。广东省稀土标准化技术委员会为广东稀土行业提供了有力的技术支撑,对增强企业参与国际国内标准化活动的话语权,把握技术发展的新动向,推动全省实施技术标准战略工作有重要的意义。

2013年11月,全国首个电磁超材料技术及制品标准化技术委员会在深圳成立。这是我国在全球率先启动电磁超材料标准化工作。该标准化技术委员会首届委员25人,涵盖了超材料技术从开发到应用,从原材料到成品,从设计到验证测试的全部领域。秘书处设在我国超材料技术领域龙头单位深圳光启高等理工研究院。目前,光启共申请国内外专利2428个,使我国超材料领域年度专利申请量保持在全球第一。电磁超材料技术及制品标准化技术委员会的成立,标志着我国超材料发展走入了规范有序的快车道,有利于我国在该领域产业链的形成和推广应用,对于抢占国际竞争的制高点,率先形成先发优势,具有重大的战略意义。

二、SWOT分析

SWOT分析法又称为道斯矩阵、态势分析法,被广泛应用于组织的战略规划中。SWOT分析涵盖了组织的优势(Strengths)、劣势(Weaknesses)、机会(Opportunities)和威胁(Threats)。它通过对组织内外部因素各方面内容进行综合和概括,进而分析组织的优劣势、面临的机会和挑战。SWOT分析可以有效地帮助组织或项目把资源聚集在优势和机会最多的地方,在组织或项目规划实施前期,预期和保障组织或项目目标的实现(见表5-3)。

（一）优势

（1）国家积极扶持新材料产业发展。1999年国家颁布《当前国家优先发展的高技术产业化重点领域指南》，对新材料进行扶持；2000年发布《国家计委关于组织实施新材料高技术产业化专项的公告》，明确了发展新材料对国民经济有重要支撑作用；"十五"规划将新材料列为最重要的发展领域之一。

（2）广东省政府把新材料产业列为高新技术产业发展的重点领域。"十五"期间开始，广东将新材料列为重点发展产业，并出台了一系列配套的产业政策给予重点支持。

（3）建立了较完善的新材料产业创新服务体系和产业链。早在2003年，广东省佛山市沧江工业园就被批准为国家火炬计划新材料基地。目前，广东已经初步形成了广州新材料产业国家高技术产业基地、深圳国家半导体照明基地、佛山光伏产业基地等一批新材料产业集聚区，产业集群态势已初步形成。

（4）广东省自主创新基础良好，新材料产业的研发潜力巨大。截至2010年，广东已有新材料领域的5个国家重点实验室、11个国家重点工程中心和30多个省级工程中心，例如，致力于场致发射平板显示材料、一维纳米材料的中山大学光电材料与技术国家重点实验室，以及华南理工大学材料科学与工程学院，拥有聚合物新型成型装备等多个国家工程（技术）研究中心。广东在一些重点、关键新材料的制备技术、工艺技术、新产品开发及节能、环保和资源综合利用等方面潜力巨大。

（5）广东作为改革开放的排头兵，一直保持着良好的对外合作关系。这有助于引进吸收国际先进的新材料标准化研究成果，为最大限度地进行集成创新奠定了良好的基础。

（二）劣势

（1）科研成果转化为生产力的水平低。例如我国稀土资源储量占世界总储量的80%，产量占世界总产量的70%，但其中2/3以资源或初级产品的方式出口国外，尚未形成真正的核心技术优势。

（2）新材料产品缺乏市场竞争力。例如我国钢铁产量已居世界前列，但达到世界主要钢铁强国质量水平的钢材不足20%，每年仍需进口1000多万吨优质钢材；此外，我国高性能通用高分子材料与国外差距也较大，目前大量进口，而工业领域主要用到的工程塑料更是难以满足需求。

（3）国防建设、国民经济建设和国计民生的关键新材料亟待开发，前瞻性新材料和具有自主知识产权的材料研发能力不足。近年来，超导材料、纳米材料、信息材料等基础研究领域有了新的研究成果，而这些成果多为发达国家所取得，这对我国的新材料标准化可能带来许多的专利壁垒。

（4）面临国际竞争日益激烈的严峻挑战。加入WTO后，为满足国民待遇原则、非歧视原则等，我国新材料组织难以继续获得税收优惠，一些资源垄断性材料产业生产的产品在缺乏政府政策优惠和财政补贴的情况下，将面临极为严峻的挑战。

表 5-3 SWOT 分析表

	优势(Strengths)	劣势(Weaknesses)
内部	S1. 国家积极扶持新材料产业发展 S2. 地方政府对新材料产业的支持力度空前 S3. 建立了较完善的新材料产业创新服务体系和产业链 S4. 广东省自主创新能力基础较好 S5. 拥有较为完善的检验检测技术 S6. 广东省对外合作关系密切,有助于引进吸收国际先进的新材料标准化研究成果 S7. 处于广东产业结构转型升级中,新材料产业进入黄金发展期	W1. 材料标准体系仍以传统材料标准为主,新材料产业标准体系尚未健立 W2. 关键标准前期研究、技术攻关相对不足,标准制定所需的工艺参数、材料性能等基础数据缺乏 W3. 对高端产品综合检验、检测能力不足 W4. 标准化人员配置不足,综合素质有待提升;新材料标准的制定多属于创新工作,难度相对较大 W5. 国际标准突破不多,难以满足新材料国际交流合作需求 W6. 标准实施效益不明显,标准宣传和贯彻的力度不够 W7. 新材料行业的标准化投入有待提升
机会(Opportunities) O1. 全球经济竞争格局正处于深度变革期,带来重大历史机遇 O2. 新材料应用领域日益广阔,市场需求空间大 O3. 广东经济发展进入了调整结构阶段,面临转型升级的机遇	SO 维持策略(发挥优势,抓住机遇) S1. O1 结合,积极落实政府对新材料产业标准化工作进行顶层规划和指导,实现新材料标准体系布局 S2. S3. S4. S5. O1. O4 结合,积极引导企业进行转型升级,推动当地企业产品的升级 S3. S4. O3 结合,大力推动科技服务业的发展水平,实现新材料研发到产业化的高效结合,提升科技成果转化率	WO 强化策略(利用机会,克服劣势) W1. O3 结合,对新材料标准路线进行科学规划,有的放矢,逐步建立完善的新材料标准体系 W3. O1 结合,通过新材料基地建设等措施,带动检验检测机构软硬件的升级;积极引进国外先进的检测设备和技术 W2. W3. W4. O2. O3. O4 结合,出台系列政策,引导人才、资金等资源向新材料标准化相关工作倾斜,壮大标准化工作队伍的实力

续表5-3

O4. 具备较强的经济实力和综合竞争力,为培育和发展新材料产业提供了基础设施、研发、人才等重要保障	S5. O4 结合,进一步推动新材料产业集群建设,并实现集群内检验检测设备、人才的配套升级	W6. O4 结合,加强新材料标准化人才的培养和引进,形成稳定、可持续发展的新材料标准化队伍
O5. 社会与企业的标准化意识和水平逐步提升	S3. O5 结合,继续推动企业和社会标准化意识的提升,通过创建"标准化良好行为企业"等活动来提升企业标准化水平	W5. W7. O5 结合,增加新材料标准化工作的投入,鼓励企业和标准化机构积极参与国际标准的研究和讨论,提升社会对标准的认知度
O6. 许多标准尚处于空白状态,是广东建立新材料标准话语权的重大机遇	S2. S7. O6 结合,进一步加大标准化工作的资源投入,积极抢占新材料国际标准的话语权	W5. W7. O6 结合,抓住历史机遇,加大新材料标准化工作投入,抢占新材料标准的国际话语权
威胁(Threats)	ST 防御策略（利用优势,化威胁为机遇）	WT 避险策略（减少劣势,规避威胁）
T1. 各地纷纷出台鼓励政策措施推动新材料产业发展,资金、技术、人才、标准、市场等资源配置竞争更加激烈	S4. S5. T1 结合,完善新材料产业激励政策,进一步巩固广东对新材料产业资金、技术与人才的吸引力	W1. W2. T1. T2 结合,提前对新材料标准体系建设进行规划布局,通过出台相应的配套政策来吸引高素质标准化人才等相关资源
T2. 新材料技术发展迅速,标准制修订的滞后影响产业发展	S1. T2 结合,对新材料标准的制修订工作程序进行调整,缩短新材料标准制修订的立项时间,加快标准制修订的时效性	W3. W5. W6. T3. T4. T5 结合,根据发展规划,结合广东实际,在新材料领域选定若干领域各个击破,从而为新材料的标准化奠定技术基础
T3. 核心技术太少,产业发展差距大,面临一定的专利壁垒	S4. T3 结合,通过科技专项等政策促进新材料核心技术的攻关,加大对国外新材料科技先进技术的引进、消化、再吸收	W5. T2. T3. T4 结合,引导企业和科研机构积极参与标准的国际化活动,加大对国际标准制定与参与的奖励
T4. 国内的检验检测设备、技术可能跟不上性能指标的发展	S2. T4 结合,引进国际先进的检验检测设备,积极参与国际化标准活动	W4. T1. T5 结合,加大新材料标准化人才培育方面的投入,建立一支综合实力强的标准化人才队伍
T5. 与标准相关的法令、规定不能实现配套,标准的执行效果有待进一步提升	S3. S4. S5. S7. T5 结合,完善相关法律法规,规范企业的生产行为,引导企业以标准治企	W6. T5 结合,增加对标准的适宜性与实施效益的考核,确保标准的制定与实际相吻合,并保证标准的有效实施

（三）发展机遇

（1）全球经济竞争格局正处于深度变革期，各国纷纷加大投入，布局新能源、新材料、节能环保等新兴技术产业。这为广东深度参与国际产业分工，缩短与发达国家发展战略性新兴产业的差距带来历史机遇。

（2）我国正处于经济社会战略转型期，加快形成新的经济增长点、促进产业结构升级和经济发展方式转变成为经济发展的头等任务，高新技术产业将带动新材料需求的增加。

（3）随着社会经济持续快速发展，特别是城市化、工业化进程的加快，新材料的应用领域将进一步拓宽，产业发展前景广阔。

（4）广东省已具备较强的经济实力和综合竞争力，为培育和发展战略性新兴产业提供了基础设施、研发创新、人才培育、产学研合作等必要保障。特别是珠江三角洲产业一体化格局加快形成，为促进战略性新兴产业发展营造了良好的环境，奠定了坚实的基础。

（5）省内支柱产业及高技术产业发展对新材料的需求不断扩大。特别是机械制造业、电子信息制造业、汽车工业、建筑业等支柱产业的快速发展对原材料在质量、性能等方面都提出了更高的要求。

（6）许多新材料标准尚处于空白状态，这是广东掌握新材料标准国际话语权的重大机遇。

（四）威胁因素

（1）应用领域宽广，涵盖了信息、能源、交通、医疗等各个领域，许多标准尚无先例，标准的制定工作具有一定的创新性，难度较高。

（2）新材料产业发展迅猛，标准的制修订具有一定的滞后性制约了产业的快速发展。

（3）新材料行业涉及自然科学和工程技术，多学科交叉渗透，知识和技术高度密集。投资密集是指研究开发和生产新材料产品要求有一定的投资强度。新材料行业标准的制定一次性投入大，要求高。

（4）新材料核心技术少，产业发展差距大，技术专利多被国外巨头垄断，可能遭遇一定的专利壁垒。

（5）国际标准日益完善，市场不断渗透并扩散，国内的检测标准、检测技术可能不能适应各类指标的更新。

（6）根据国家部署，各地纷纷出台鼓励战略性新兴产业发展的政策措施，以培育和发展战略性新兴产业为重点的新一轮地区之间资金、技术、人才、标准、市场等资源配置竞争更加激烈，给广东抢占发展先机带来新挑战。

分析表明，建立科学合理的新材料标准体系和规划路线图，将有效地推动广东省新材料产业的高速发展，推动新材料产业成为主导产业和支柱产业，并将广东建设成为全国新材料产业发展的重要策源地和集聚地。

通过以上的 SWOT 分析可以看到，及时对广东省新材料标准化工作进行系统规划，是广东省做大做强新材料产业，实现经济结构转型的应有之义。建立完善的新材料标准体系，引导企业不断参与地方标准、国家标准甚至是国际标准的讨论和制定，将极大地提升广东省新材料产业的标准化水平。具体来说，广东的新材料标准化工作应着重从以下几个方面着手展开：

1. 加强协调，完善工作机制

新材料行业是新兴产业，属于多学科交叉领域。新材料标准立项难，给标准制定的及时开展造成一定的困扰。因此，需进一步建立协调有力、运转顺畅的工作机制。各主管部门需进一步提高对新材料标准制修订及宣传贯彻工作的认识，做好协调服务工作，及时对本地区新材料标准制（修）定进行统筹规划。

与此同时，要鼓励新材料技术研发机构与相关科研院校，积极参与标准制定和宣传贯彻，充分发挥新新材料各个标准化技术委员会在标准体系建设中的重要作用，最终逐步形成政府引导、市场推动、社会参与、产学研相结合的良性格局。

2. 完善新材料标准体系

当前，新材料标准无论在数量上还是在质量上仍存在较大缺口，没有形成完整的标准体系，新材料标准路线图的制定，对于完善新材料标准体系十分必要，它将实现基础标准、方法标准、产品标准的有机结合。

由于新材料的应用极为广泛，涉及生物、环保、航空航天等诸多领域。长期以来，新材料标准分散在多部门和多系统，各行业标准体系之间既交叉重复，又有许多遗漏。针对这一问题，标准的研究制定机构有必要对整个新材料行业的标准体系进行全面的梳理研究，对新材料行业标准体系的现状进行摸底，在此基础上，结合广东省新材料产业发展的实际情况，逐步对标准体系进行完善。新材料标准路线图的制定，将有效解决当前新材料标准跨越领域大、零散未成体系的突出问题，将极大地促进广东新材料产业的良性发展。

3. 加强科学研究，提高标准制定水平

新材料行业属于新兴产业，许多产品及核心技术被国外组织垄断，新标准的制定尚没有相关的标准可以借鉴，属于创新型工作，难度较大。同时，由于新材料基础研究积累少，标准制定技术支撑薄弱。因此，应鼓励组织和科研单位把技术创新与相关的新材料标准基础研究结合起来，特别是与行业科研项目相结合，提高标准制定的科学性和适用性。

4. 夯实研究基础，提升标准的制修订能力

在新材料标准制定过程中，需要开展大量的标准前期研究工作。新材料标准的制定周期较长，资金要求更高，而目前新材料行业的标准科研经费紧缺，这直接影响了标准的前期研究。

作为一项公益性、技术性、基础性工作，政府部门应加大对新材料标准体系建设的投入，鼓励行业协会、组织和社会组织对制定标准的投入，形成标准制定经费的多元化投入机制。加快培养标准化人才，建立一支水平高、结构优的专家队伍，提高标准体系建设的科学性和适用性。

5. 加强标准的宣传贯彻工作，提升标准的实际效用

现阶段，广东新材料标准整体水平不高，与产业发展需求有一定脱节，特别是一些标准针对性、适用性不强，某些标准还存在缺失和滞后现象，这导致现行标准实施效果不理想，对规范生产与贸易行为没能发挥标准应有的作用。

标准的制定机构应加强标准的宣传贯彻工作，提高标准实施效益。通过标准宣传和培训，增强组织的标准化意识，引导新材料生产经营者按标准组织生产、加工、销售，提高行业的标准化水平。采取政府推动、标杆企业带动、行业自律联动等多种形式，扩大标准实施覆盖面，提高新材料组织贯彻标准的自觉性和社会对标准的认知度，探索建立标准宣传贯彻的有效途径。

6. 提升国际标准化活动能力

在经济全球化的大背景下，标准在国际贸易、市场准入等方面发挥着重要作用。进入21世纪，经济全球化和市场国际化趋势加快，市场竞争日益激烈，新材料出口企业频频遭遇各种技术性贸易壁垒，而这些贸易壁垒的核心，就是技术标准。

因此，应积极鼓励企业、相关科研机构积极参加ISO/TC年会等国际标准化活动，跟踪国内外标准化动态，承担更多的国际标准化技术组织工作。目前，化工行业，我国已经承担4个国际标准化技术组织秘书处工作，如ISO/TC61塑料技术委员会、ISO/TC59/SC8建筑结构标准化技术委员会建筑密封材料分会国际秘书处等。广东企业应进一步牢牢把握当前技术快速变革的历史机遇，争取更多的国际话语权。

三、广东省新材料产业联盟与政策推动

1. 设立广东省新材料相关的标准化技术委员会以及分技术委员会

新材料是各材料领域的前沿，产业覆盖范围较宽，几乎可以涉足所有的材料领域。在标准制修订的过程中，从专业领域考虑，需要分别设立标准技术委员会，独立开展工作。以广东省新材料相关的标准技术委员会为基础，结合各专业技术委员会的设立与合作，是解决新材料标准化难题的最佳方案（见表5-4）。

表5-4 拟成立标准化技术委员会与其他已建立新材料相关标准化技术委员会

序号	拟成立的标准化技术委员会名称	标准化任务	拟定成立时间	备注
1	新材料	高性能跨学科改性材料、初步形成产业或尚未形成产业的前沿新型材料的标准化。	2015	产业引导性材料的标准化工作，数量有限但不能被其他标准技术委员会覆盖

续表 5-4

序号	拟成立的标准化技术委员会名称	标准化任务	拟定成立时间	备注
2	功能有色金属	高性能铝合金、金属粉体材料、铝箔、亲水箔、电子铝箔、汽车轻量化高性能镁铝合金材料、轨道交通用大规格工业铝型材，钨基合金材料、高纯阴极铜、高性能铜合金、超薄电解铜箔等，高性能镁合金，高性能钛合金，记忆合金，生物相容镁合金材料，核级海绵锆，特种用途轻质金属基复合材料，ZTO（氧化锌锡）靶材、CIGS（铜铟镓硒）靶材、磁控溅射用靶材、电极材料、高纯金属有机源（MO源），高纯和低偏析材料、快速凝固金属与合金、固相连续复合层状金属材料、颗粒或纤维增强金属基复合材料等高性能特殊功能金属材料，以及铜电解工艺、高性能有色金属合金材料成分设计、触变挤压技术、半固态加工技术、电磁附加成形技术、激光快速成形技术、粉末注射成形技术等标准。	2015	对口 SAC/TC 243
3	纳米材料	纳米材料相关标准。	2015	SAC/TC 279 国家纳米技术委员会于 2005 年成立，该技术委员会的工作内容主要是纳米技术，不包括纳米产品
4	工业陶瓷与特种陶瓷	新能源陶瓷、节能环保陶瓷、新型陶瓷色料、高强高韧结构陶瓷材料、超薄建筑陶瓷材料、高性能陶瓷基复合材料、纤维和纳米颗粒增强材料、污水处理与过滤材料、自洁材料、抗菌材料、陶瓷膜、导电陶瓷材料、片式无源电子元件用陶瓷材料、电子敏感陶瓷材料、高压高功率电力电子元件用陶瓷材料、功能陶瓷粉体、器件及配套材料等材料及相关标准。	2015	对口 SAC/TC 194
5	生物芯片	生物芯片材料技术、检测方法、安全性及应用技术标准等。	2015	对口 SAC/TC421

续表 5-4

序号	拟成立的标准化技术委员会名称	标准化任务	拟定成立时间	备注
6	无机纤维	玻璃纤维、碳纤维及相关材料技术、检测方法、设备技术、安全性及应用技术标准等。	2015	对口 SAC/TC245
7	光电材料	感光材料、电磁材料等标准。	2016	广东省没有相关标准化技术委员会覆盖，国家有多个标准化技术委员会覆盖，但太分散。而这个领域的材料标准重要，但数量不多
8	环保产品	吸附净化材料、生物基材料、环保涂料和密封材料、降解材料、可再生资源材料及其材料技术等标准。	2016	对口 SAC/TC 275 环保产品
9	特种玻璃	电子工业用功能玻璃，Low-E（低辐射）节能玻璃，超薄玻璃，镀膜玻璃，高性能车用玻璃，超薄、超厚、超白等优质浮法玻璃及相关材料标准。	2016	对口 SAC/TC447
10	磁性元件与铁氧体材料	磁性元件、磁性元件与铁氧体材料技术、检测方法、安全性及应用技术标准等。	2016	对口 SAC/TC89
11	电磁超材料	电磁超材料相关标准。	2016	对口 SAC/TC545
12	石墨烯	石墨烯材料技术、检测方法、设备技术、安全性及应用技术标准等。	2016	对口 SAC/TC 2013 年开始筹建
13	合成树脂和橡胶	高性能薄膜材料、高性能聚丙烯、特种合成橡胶、热收缩材料、新型热塑性弹性体、高性能热熔胶、硅酮密封胶、塑代钢材料、钢塑复合材料、ABS（工程塑料）、PMMA（有机玻璃）、聚醚醚酮、液晶聚合物、聚碳酸酯、MDI 聚氨酯、聚丙烯酸类材料、电子级环氧树脂与电子用聚酰亚胺树脂、光学硅胶、电子和 LED 封装材料、高性能粘合剂、导电胶等材料相关标准。	—	2010 年已成立，秘书处：茂名市质量计量监督检测所
14	太阳光伏能源系统	太阳能光伏系统用材料相关标准。	—	2010 年已成立，秘书处：兴业太阳能公司

续表 5-4

序号	拟成立的标准化技术委员会名称	标准化任务	拟定成立时间	备注
15	LED 光源	OLED、LED 引线框架和封装材料、LED 用导热胶、硅单晶片及外延层、非晶硅材料、衬底材料、散热材料等相关标准。	—	2011 年已成立，秘书处：东莞质量监督检测中心
16	化学用品	化学试剂：超净高纯试剂、光刻胶配套试剂、蚀刻溶剂等材料相关标准；高效水处理剂、环境友好表面活性剂、以硅和氟为基础合成的表面改性剂相关标准；高效催化剂相关标准；化学工业和高分子材料加工助剂相关标准；汽车产业用精细化工材料、船舶产业用精细化工材料、航空航天产业用精细化工材料相关标准。	—	2011 年已成立，秘书处：广东省石油和化学工业协会
17	建筑材料	大尺寸玻璃基板，轻质、高强、隔热、保温的新型墙体材料，隔音和吸音材料，建筑物用自动调温和调湿材料，自动预警温度、压力等的智能材料和节能建筑材料等标准；建筑材料绿色制造关键技术标准，生产高性能隔热保温建筑材料技术标准。	—	2011 年已成立，秘书处：广东省建筑材料研究院、广东省建筑材料行业协会
18	纺织服装业	耐高温尼龙、高性能芳纶、涤纶、尼龙、超高分子量聚乙烯、环保医疗卫生纺织产品等材料相关标准。	—	2011 年已成立，秘书处：广州市纤维产品检测院
19	医疗仪器设备及器械	高性能口腔材料和器械设备用材料标准，高性能外科植入物和矫形器械用材料标准。	—	2011 年已成立，秘书处：广东省医疗器械质量监督检验所、广州市计量检测技术研究院
20	水泥及制品	水泥基磁性材料和电磁屏蔽水泥等材料相关标准。	—	2011 年已成立，秘书处：广州市建筑材料工业研究所有限公司、广东省水泥行业协会
21	太阳能	太阳能材料相关标准。	—	2012 年已成立，秘书处：顺德区质量技术监督标准与编码所

续表5-4

序号	拟成立的标准化技术委员会名称	标准化任务	拟定成立时间	备注
22	塑料与塑料制品	新型高性能或功能塑料及其合金相关标准。	—	2012年已成立,秘书处:佛山佛塑科技集团股份有限公司
23	新能源动力电池	新型电池材料,以及电池用隔膜、电解液、储氢、氢氧化亚镍、高纯石墨负极、锰酸锂、钛酸锂、磷酸铁锂等新能源材料、锂离子电池用电解液、燃料电池双极板材料、氢能及燃料电池、超级电容器等电池材料、电池隔膜材料、双轴拉伸聚乙烯薄膜、电池专用胶粘、电解液带等材料相关标准。	—	2012年已成立,秘书处:广东质量监督检测研究院
24	电力电子系统和设备	薄膜晶体管液晶显示器、金属氧化物TFT、电子墨水、载流子输运材料、电子浆料、驱动芯片等相关标准。	—	2012年已成立,秘书处:广东省珠海市质量计量监督检测所
25	稀土	照明、显示用稀土发光材料、稀土烧结、粘结永磁材料、混合动力汽车用储氢材料、稀土功能助剂、高性能稀土铝/镁合金材料、磁致冷材料、超磁致伸缩材料等稀土磁性材料、高性能固态储氢材料、纳米稀土抗菌材料、稀土精密抛光材料等稀土粉体材料相关标准。	—	2013年已成立,秘书处:江门市科恒实业股份有限公司
26	石材	新型石材产品相关标准。	—	2013年已成立,秘书处:广东省质量监督石材产品检验站
27	表面工程	耐磨涂层、耐腐蚀涂层、耐高温表面涂层等材料标准。	—	2013年已成立,秘书处:南海区标准化研究与促进中心、广东科富科技股份有限公司

2. 建立标准化示范点

新材料产业的特点决定了其标准示范的重要意义。标准化作为产业发展的重要导向，以标准示范的作用促进产业扩大，保证产业技术水平，推动产业发展，最终实现产业集群或产业联盟，使其成为新材料发展的重要基地。新材料产业的发展现状，也决定了建立标准化示范点的重要性。新材料产业发展需要政策的支持和推动。标准化示范点的建立，有助于定位政策落脚点，真正落实政策、发挥作用，使其成为产业发展的有力抓手（见表5-5）。

表5-5 拟建立的标准化示范点

序号	拟建立的标准化示范点	拟实施和推广的标准项目	预期成果或经验	拟建设时间
1	新能源电池材料	电池用隔膜、电解液、储氢、氢氧化亚镍、高纯石墨负极、锰酸锂、钛酸锂、磷酸铁锂等新能源材料，锂离子电池用电解液、燃料电池双极板材料、氢能及燃料电池、超级电容器等电池材料，电池隔膜材料、双轴拉伸聚乙烯薄膜、电池专用胶粘、电解液带等材料相关标准。	1. 提升锂离子电池和高性能铅酸电池的质量水平，提升行业门槛，规范产业发展； 2. 实现锂硫电池、液流电池等新型电池材料的产业化。	2016
2	高分子材料用改性助剂	各类高分子材料用改性助剂相关标准。	1. 提升产品质量水平； 2. 设立产业门槛； 3. 规范产业发展。	2016
3	乙酸仲丁酯	乙酸仲丁酯国家和地方标准。	1. 设立行业门槛； 2. 规范产业发展。	2016
4	可再生资源	可再生资源材料回收、材料技术等标准。	1. 提升可再生资源材料回收标准，和材料质量水平； 2. 设立产业门槛，规范产业发展。	2016
5	功能纺织材料	耐高温尼龙、高性能芳纶、涤纶、尼龙、超高分子量聚乙烯、环保医疗卫生纺织产品等材料相关标准。	1. 规范功能纺织材料市场； 2. 提升广东省功能纺织材料质量水平。	2017
6	环保涂料	环保涂料相关标准。	1. 提升产品质量水平； 2. 设立产业门槛； 3. 规范产业发展。	2017
7	功能陶瓷材料	功能陶瓷材料相关标准。	1. 提升产品质量水平； 2. 设立产业门槛； 3. 规范产业发展。	2017

续表 5-5

序号	拟建立的标准化示范点	拟实施和推广的标准项目	预期成果或经验	拟建设时间
8	高性能薄膜材料	1. 实施各类薄膜材料生产和产品标准； 2. 制定联盟标准。	提升各类功能薄膜材料标准化，提升行业门槛，规范产业市场。	2017
9	高效水处理剂	高效水处理剂相关标准。	1. 提升产品质量水平； 2. 设立产业门槛； 3. 规范产业发展。	2017
10	高性能水泥材料	水泥基磁性材料和电磁屏蔽水泥等材料相关标准。	1. 提升产品质量水平； 2. 设立产业门槛； 3. 规范产业发展。	2018
11	特种玻璃	电子工业用功能玻璃，Low-E（低辐射）节能玻璃，超薄玻璃，镀膜玻璃，高性能车用玻璃，超薄、超厚、超白等优质浮法玻璃及相关材料标准。	1. 提升产品质量水平； 2. 设立产业门槛； 3. 规范产业发展。	2018
12	高性能钢材	高强、耐蚀、耐候、耐磨合金钢，非晶纳米晶合金，石油天然气输送钢管，高性能轻量化汽车覆盖件钢，汽车用高强高韧钢，大型风力发电机组用钢材，短流程薄板坯连铸连轧产品，高性能特种钢等材料标准；熔融还原、洁净钢生产、连铸连轧、连铸连挤等高精度、高质量产品深加工等技术标准。	1. 提升功能钢材的质量，规范行业发展； 2. 提升钢材加工技术的标准化。	2018
13	功能有色金属	稀土和稀有功能材料标准。	1. 促进材料产业链的形成和材料产业化； 2. 规范行业发展。	2018
14	超高纯试剂	超高纯试剂相关技术和产品标准。	促进产业发展。	2018
15	形状记忆合金	形状记忆合金国家标准和地方标准的实践。	1. 促进形状记忆合金产业化； 2. 规范产业发展。	2018

3. 产业标准技术联盟建设

以标准化技术委员会为技术中心，联合相关企业、检测机构、社会机构、公共服务平台共建产业联盟，以较低的风险实现较大范围的资源调配，使企业优势互补、拓展发展空间，以集体的力量提高产业或行业竞争力，实现超常规发展。相对于传统产业，新材料产业对资金、政策导向、社会认可的需求度更强,新材料产业的发展对产业联盟建设的依赖度更高。

以新材料标准化技术委员会为中心,在开展标准化工作的同时,凝聚一批具有影响力的新材料相关机构,推进标准项目的推广和应用,帮助行业转型升级,推动联盟标准的制修订,共同推动广东省新材料产业的发展(见表 5-6)。

表 5-6 拟建立的标准联盟

序号	拟建立的标准联盟	联盟成员类型	预期成果	拟建设时间
1	新能源电池材料	基础材料及相关配套生产企业; 相关标准化技术委员会; 相关行业协会; 相关质量检验机构或部门; 高校和研究院所; 科技服务机构等。	1. 新材料及其制品产量增加; 2. 新材料及其制品技术水平稳定; 3. 新材料及其制品市场拓展; 4. 打造出行业品牌。	2017
2	高分子材料加工助剂			2017
3	乙酸仲丁酯			2017
4	人造石材			2017
5	功能纺织材料			2018
6	可再生资源			2018
7	形状记忆合金			2018
8	高性能钢材			2018
9	金属功能材料			2018
10	环保涂料			2018
11	功能陶瓷材料			2018
12	高性能薄膜材料			2018

四、广东省新材料产业标准化路线图

标准体系主要包括标准研究、标准化体系建设、科技服务平台建设、人才培养和政策措施,启动时间为 2015 年,预计在 2019 年年底前完成。前期主要工作是成立配套的标准化技术委员会,完成新材料相关标准项目的转化或制修订。后期集中建立标准示范点和标准联盟。在整个工作期间,逐渐建成和完善新材料标准化人才库和科技服务平台。每个分类的规划内容按照五个方面进行分解,分类推进标准化进程(见图 5-1)。

标准化专项内容	2015—2016	2017—2018	2019
标准研究	标准和产业技术研究 转化一批国际国外先进标准 制定一批国内外空白的先进标准		
标准化体系建设	成立1个TC 建立15个以上标准化示范点	成立5个TC	成立6个TC 建立11个以上标准联盟
科技服务平台建设	信息服务、科技成果转化服务、第三方科技中介服务、贸易技术措施服务平台		
人才培养	培养新材料标准化专家,建设新材料技术人才数据库		
政策措施	1.建立标准化推动机制,如建立新材料标准化专项资金,对具有高技术含量的、取得显著经济效益的标准化项目进行奖励; 2.建立标准化示范点特殊通道,将示范点企业纳入"重点企业直通车"的服务对象中,鼓励企业设立标准化示范点; 3.市场激励机制,如建立专项资金对企业或市场进行引导性补贴。		

(a)

标准化专项内容	2015—2016	2017—2018	2019	标准化专项类别
先进金属材料	特种金属功能材料和高端金属结构材料范围内的8种新材料类型			标准化对象
		稀土功能材料7项标准		标准化研究
		稀土金属材料11项标准		
		电磁学材料9项标准		
		金属薄膜材料5项标准		
		金属粉体材料4项标准		
	其他功能材料7项标准			
	新型轻合金材料8项标准			
		高端金属结构材料5项标准		
	建立功能有色金属、磁性元件和铁氧体两个标准化技术委员会,联合稀土标准化技术委员会开展标准化工作			标准化体系建设
	建立高性能钢材和金属功能材料的标准化示范点和标准联盟			
	建设以新材料科技成果转化技术平台为基础,企业和高校、研究机构为支撑的科技服务平台			标准化服务平台
	建立以高校、研究院所为核心,联合企业技术人员,共同推进标准化建设的专家团队			人才培养

(b)

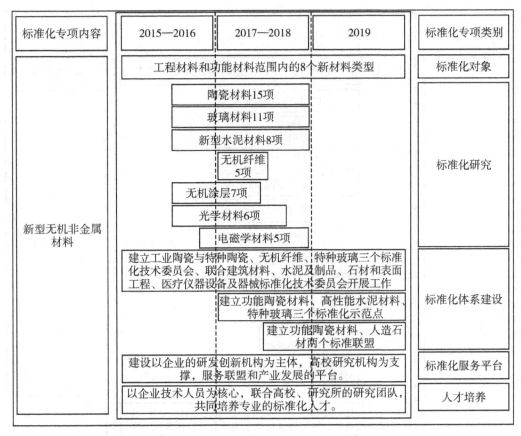

（c）

标准化专项内容	2015—2016	2017—2018	2019	标准化专项类别
高性能有机高分子材料		高端工程材料和功能高分子材料范围内的12个新材料类型		标准化对象
		合成树脂14项标准		标准化研究
		特种橡胶3项标准		
		合成纤维6项标准		
		工程塑料6项标准		
		光学材料9项标准		
		电磁学材料9项标准		
		热力学材料7项标准		
		薄膜材料10项标准		
		涂覆材料23项材料		
		再生材料9项标准		
	可降解材料5项标准			
	联合合成树脂与橡胶、塑料与塑料制品、纺织服装业、医疗仪器设备及器械等标准化技术委员会开展标准化工作			标准化体系建设
	建立可再生资源材料、功能纺织材料、环保涂料、高性能薄膜材料四个标准化示范点			
	建立可再生资源材料、功能纺织材料、环保涂料、高性能薄膜材料四个标准联盟			
	建设以相关企业与高校、研究院所共同支撑，加强政策引导、推动的标准化服务平台			标准化服务平台
	建立15人以上不同专业的专家团队			人才培养

（d）

标准化专项内容	2015—2016	2017—2018	2019	标准化专项类别
特种精细化工材料	10个产业领域的特种精细化工新材料类型			标准化对象
	电子与电子信息产业用精细化工材料10项标准			标准化研究
	机动车用精细化工材料6项标准			
	建筑行业用精细化工材料5项标准			
	高分子加工用精细化工材料6项标准			
		造纸产业用精细化工材料2项标准		
		日化产业用精细化工材料5项标准		
		石化行业用精细化工材料7项标准		
		金属加工行业用精细化工材料2项标准		
		环境精细化工材料8项标准		
	联合化学用品、电力电子系统和设备等标准化技术委员会开展标准化工作			标准化体系建设
	建立高分子材料加工助剂、乙酸仲丁酯、高效水处理剂、超高纯试剂四个标准化示范点			
	高分子材料加工助剂、乙酸仲丁酯标准联盟			
	以相关企业为发展主体，联合高校和研究院所，标准化和发展新型研究成果			标准化服务平台
	建立10人以上不同专业的专家团队			人才培养

(e)

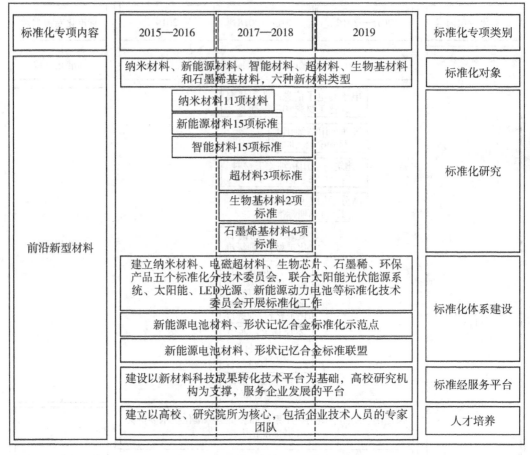

(f)

图 5-1 广东省新材料产业标准化路线图

附录1 ISO 标准列表

序号	材料分类	标准类型	标准名称
1. 先进金属标准			
1	新型黑金属及复合材料	通用基础标准	ISO 7989-1-2006, Steel wire and wire products — Non-ferrous metallic coatings on steel wire — Part 1: General principles
2			ISO 3134-1:1985, Light metals and their alloys — Terms and definitions — Part 1: Materials
3		测试方法标准	ISO 437-1982, Steel and cast iron — Determination of total carbon content — Combustion gravimetric method
4			ISO 439-2010, Steel and iron — Determination of total silicon content — Gravimetric method
5			ISO 629-1982, Steel and cast iron — Determination of manganese content — Spectrophotometric method
6			ISO 671-1982, Steel and cast iron — Determination of sulphur content — Combustion titrimetric method
7			ISO 1461:2009, Hot dip galvanized coatings on fabricated iron and steel articles — Specifications and test methods
8			ISO 3651-1-1998, Determination of resistance to intergranular corrosion of stainless steels — Part 1: Austenitic and ferritic-austenitic (duplex) stainless steels — Corrosion test in nitric acid medium by measurement of loss in mass (Huey test) 9:31 2014/2/25
9			ISO 3651-2-1998, Determination of resistance to intergranular corrosion of stainless steels — Part 2: Ferritic, austenitic and ferritic-austenitic (duplex) stainless steels — Corrosion test in media containing sulfuric acid
10			ISO 3690-2001, Welding and allied processes — Determination of hydrogen content in arc weld metal
11			ISO 4687-1:1992, Iron ores — Determination of phosphorus content — Part 1: Molybdenum blue spectrophotometric method

续表

序号	材料分类	标准类型	标准名称
12			ISO 4829-1-1986, Steel and cast iron — Determination of total silicon content — Reduced molybdosilicate spectrophotometric method — Part 1: Silicon contents between 0.05% and 1.0%
13			ISO 4829-2-1988, Steel and iron — Determination of total silicon content — Reduced molybdosilicate spectrophotometric method — Part 2: Silicon contents between 0.01% and 0.05%
14			ISO 4934-2003, Steel and iron — Determination of sulfur content — Gravimetric method
15			ISO 4935-1989, Steel and iron — Determination of sulfur content — Infrared absorption method after combustion in an induction furnace
16			ISO 4937-1986, Steel and iron — Determination of chromium content — Potentiometric or visual titration method
17			ISO 4938-1988, Steel and iron — Determination of nickel content — Gravimetric or titrimetric method
18			ISO 4939-1984, Steel and cast iron — Determination of nickel content — Dimethylglyoxime spectrophotometric method
19			ISO 4940-1985, Steel and cast iron — Determination of nickel content — Flame atomic absorption spectrometric method
20			ISO 4941-1994, Steel and iron — Determination of molybdenum content — Thiocyanate spectrophotometric method
21			ISO 4942-1988, Steel and iron — Determination of vanadium content — N-BPHA spectrophotometric method
22			ISO 4943-1985, Steel and cast iron — Determination of copper content — Flame atomic absorption spectrometric method
23			ISO 4946-1984, Steel and cast iron — Determination of copper content — 2, 2′-Diquinolyl spectrophotometric method
24			ISO 4947-1986, Steel and cast iron — Determination of vanadium content — Potentiometric titration method
25			ISO 4993-2009, Steel and iron castings — Radiographic inspection
26			ISO 8249-2000, Welding — Determination of Ferrite Number (FN) in austenitic and duplex ferritic-austenitic Cr-Ni stainless steel weld metals

续表

序号	材料分类	标准类型	标准名称
27			ISO 8502-2: 2005, Preparation of steel substrates before application of paints and related products — Tests for the assessment of surface cleanliness — Part 2: Laboratory determination of chloride on cleaned surface
28			ISO 8502-3: 1992, Preparation of steel substrates before application of paints and related products — Tests for the assessment of surface cleanliness — Part 3: Assessment of dust on steel surfaces prepared for painting (pressure-sensitive tape method)
29			ISO 8502-4: 1993, Preparation of steel substrates before application of paints and related products — Tests for the assess
30			ISO 8502-5: 1998, Preparation of steel substrates before application of paints and related products — Tests for the assessment of surface cleanliness — Part 5: Measurement of chloride on steel surfaces prepared for painting (ion detection tube method)
31			ISO 8502-6: 2006, Preparation of steel substrates before application of paints and related products — Tests for the assessment of surface cleanliness — Part 6: Extraction of soluble contaminants for analysis — The Bresle method
32			ISO 8502-9: 1998, Preparation of steel substrates before application of paints and related products — Tests for the assessment of surface cleanliness — Part 9: Field method for the conductometric determination of water-soluble salts
33			ISO 8502-11: 2006, Preparation of steel substrates before application of paints and related products — Tests for the assessment of surface cleanliness — Part 11: Field method for the turbidimetric determination of water-soluble sulfate
34			ISO 8502-12-2003, Preparation of steel substrates before application of paints and related products — Tests for the assessment of surface cleanliness — Part 12: Field method for the titrimetric determination of water-soluble ferrous ions
35			ISO 8829-1: 2009, Aerospace — Test methods for polytetrafluoroethylene (PTFE) inner-tube hose assemblies — Part 1: Metallic (stainless steel) braid

续表

序号	材料分类	标准类型	标准名称
36			ISO 8829-2：2006, Aerospace — Test methods for polytetrafluoroethylene (PTFE) inner-tube hose assemblies — Part 2：Non-metallic braid
37			ISO 9516-1：2003, Iron ores — Determination of various elements by X-ray fluorescence spectrometry — Part 1：Comprehensive procedure
38			ISO 9556-2001, Steel and iron — Determination of total carbon content — Infrared absorption method after combustion in an induction furnace
39			ISO 9647-1989, Steel and iron — Determination of vanadium content — Flame atomic absorption spectrometric method
40			ISO 9682-1：2009, Iron ores — Determination of manganese content — Part 1：Flame atomic absorption spectrometric method
41			ISO 9682-2：2006, Iron ores — Determination of manganese content — Part 2：Periodate spectrophotometric method
42			ISO 9685：1991, Iron ores — Determination of nickel and/or chromium contents — Flame atomic absorption spectrometric method
43			ISO/TR 9769-1991, Steel and iron — Review of available methods of analysis
44			ISO 10138-1991, Steel and iron — Determination of chromium content — Flame atomic absorption spectrometric method
45			ISO 10280-1995, Steel and iron — Determination of titanium content — Diantipyrylmethane spectrometric method
46			ISO 10308：2006, Metallic coatings — Review of porosity tests
47			ISO 10700-1995, Steel and iron — Determination of manganese content — Flame atomic absorption spectrometric method
48			ISO 10701：1994, Steel and iron - Determination of sulfur content — Methylene blue spectrophotometric method
49			ISO 10702-1993, Steel and iron — Determination of nitrogen content — Titrimetric method after distillation
50			ISO 10714-2002, Steel and iron — Determination of phosphorus content — Phosphovanadomolybdate spectrophotometric method

续表

序号	材料分类	标准类型	标准名称
51			ISO 10720-1997, Steel and iron — Determination of nitrogen content — Thermal conductimetric method after fusion in a current of inert gas
52			ISO 10893-1: 2011, Non-destructive testing of steel tubes — Part 1: Automated electromagnetic testing of seamless and welded (except submerged arc-welded) steel tubes for the verification of hydraulic leaktightness
53			ISO 10893-2: 2011, Non-destructive testing of steel tubes — Part 2: Automated eddy current testing of seamless and welded (except submerged arc-welded) steel tubes for the detection of imperfections
54			ISO 10893-3: 2011, Non-destructive testing of steel tubes — Part 3: Automated full peripheral flux leakage testing of seamless and welded (except submerged arc-welded) ferromagnetic steel tubes for the detection of longitudinal and/or transverse imperfections
55			ISO 10893-4: 2011, Non-destructive testing of steel tubes — Part 4: Liquid penetrant inspection of seamless and welded steel tubes for the detection of surface imperfections
56			ISO 10893-5-2011, Non-destructive testing of steel tubes — Part 5: Magnetic particle inspection of seamless and welded ferromagnetic steel tubes for the detection of surface imperfections
57			ISO 10893-6: 2011, Non-destructive testing of steel tubes — Part 6: Radiographic testing of the weld seam of welded steel tubes for the detection of imperfections
58			ISO 10893-7: 2011, Non-destructive testing of steel tubes — Part 7: Digital radiographic testing of the weld seam of welded steel tubes for the detection of imperfections
59			ISO 10893-8: 2011, Non-destructive testing of steel tubes — Part 8: Automated ultrasonic testing of seamless and welded steel tubes for the detection of laminar imperfections
60			ISO 10893-9: 2011, Non-destructive testing of steel tubes — Part 9: Automated ultrasonic testing for the detection of laminar imperfections in strip/plate used for the manufacture of welded steel tubes

续表

序号	材料分类	标准类型	标准名称
61			ISO 10893-10-2011, Non-destructive testing of steel tubes — Part 10: Automated full peripheral ultrasonic testing of seamless and welded (except submerged arc-welded) steel tubes for the detection of longitudinal and/or transverse imperfections
62			ISO 10893-11:2011, Non-destructive testing of steel tubes — Part 11: Automated ultrasonic testing of the weld seam of welded steel tubes for the detection of longitudinal and/or transverse imperfections
63			ISO 10893-12:2011, Non-destructive testing of steel tubes — Part 12: Automated full peripheral ultrasonic thickness testing of seamless and welded (except submerged arc-welded) steel tubes
64			ISO 11533:2009, Iron ores — Determination of cobalt — Flame atomic absorption spectrometric method
65			ISO 11535:2006, Iron ores — Determination of various elements — Inductively coupled plasma atomic emission spectrometric method
66			ISO 11652-1997, Steel and iron — Determination of cobalt content — Flame atomic absorption spectrometric method
67			ISO 11653:1997, Steel — Determination of high cobalt content — Potentiometric titration method after separation by ion exchange
68			ISO 11971-2008, Steel and iron castings — Visual examination of surface quality
69			ISO 13311:1997, Iron ores — Determination of lead content — Flame atomic absorption spectrometric method
70			ISO 13520-2002, Determination of ferrite content in austenitic stainless steel castings
71			ISO 13898-1-1997, Steel and iron — Determination of nickel, copper and cobalt contents — Inductively coupled plasma atomic emission spectrometric method — Part 1: General requirements and sample dissolution
72			ISO 13898-2-1997, Steel and iron — Determination of nickel, copper and cobalt contents — Inductively coupled plasma atomic emission spectrometric method — Part 2: Determination of nickel content
73			ISO 13898-3-1997, Steel and iron — Determination of nickel, copper and cobalt contents — Inductively coupled plasma atomic emission spectrometric method — Part 3: Determination of copper content

续表

序号	材料分类	标准类型	标准名称
74			ISO 13898-4-1997, Steel and iron — Determination of nickel, copper and cobalt contents — Inductively coupled plasma atomic emission spectrometric method — Part 4: Determination of cobalt content
75			ISO/TS 13899-3: 2005, Steel — Determination of Mo, Nb and W contents in alloyed steel — Inductively coupled plasma atomic emission spectrometric method — Part 3: Determination of W content
76			ISO 13902-1997, Steel and iron — Determination of high sulfur content — Infrared absorption method after combustion in an induction furnace
77			ISO 14284-2002, Steel and iron — Sampling and preparation of samples for the determination of chemical composition
78			ISO 15350-2010, Steel and iron — Determination of total carbon and sulfur content — Infrared absorption method after combustion in an induction furnace (routine method)
79			ISO 15351-2010, Steel and iron — Determination of nitrogen content — Thermal conductimetric method after fusion in a current of inert gas (Routine method)
80			ISO 15353-2001, Steel and iron — Determination of tin content — Flame atomic absorption spectrometric method (extraction as Sn-SCN)
81			ISO 15634: 2005, Iron ores — Determination of chromium content — Flame atomic absorption spectrometric method
82			ISO 16918-1-2009, Steel and iron — Determination of nine elements by the inductively coupled plasma mass spectrometric method — Part 1: Determination of tin, antimony, cerium, lead and bismuth
83			ISO 17053-2005, Steel and iron — Determination of oxygen — Infrared method after fusion under inert gas
84			ISO/TR 17055: 2002, Steel — Determination of silicon content — Inductively coupled plasma atomic emission spectrometric method
85			ISO 17058-2004, Steel and iron — Determination of arsenic content — Spectrophotometric method
86			ISO 18632: 2010, Alloyed steel — Determination of manganese — Potentiometric and visual titration method

续表

序号	材料分类	标准类型	标准名称
87			ISO 22778-2006, Metallic coatings — Physical vapour-deposited coatings of cadmium on iron and steel — Specification and test methods
88			ISO 28764-2011, Vitreous and porcelain enamels — Production of specimens for testing enamels on sheet steel, sheet aluminium and cast iron
89			ISO 3353-1：2002, Aerospace — Lead and runout threads — Part 1：Rolled external threads
90			ISO 3353-2：2002, Aerospace — Lead and runout threads — Part 2：Internal threads
91			ISO 3506-1：2009, Mechanical properties of corrosion-resistant stainless steel fasteners — Part 1：Bolts, screws and studs
92			ISO 3506-2：2009, Mechanical properties of corrosion-resistant stainless steel fasteners — Part 2：Nuts
93			ISO 3506-3：2009, Mechanical properties of corrosion-resistant stainless steel fasteners — Part 3：Set screws and similar fasteners not under tensile stress
94			ISO 3506-4：2009, Mechanical properties of corrosion-resistant stainless steel fasteners — Part 4：Tapping screws
95			ISO 3575：2011, Continuous hot-dip zinc-coated carbon steel sheet of commercial and drawing qualities
96			ISO 4990：2003, Steel castings — General technical delivery requirements
97			ISO 4999：2011, Continuous hot-dip terne (lead alloy) coated cold-reduced carbon steel sheet of commercial, drawing and structural qualities
98			ISO 5000：2011, Continuous hot-dip aluminium-silicon-coated cold-reduced carbon steel sheet of commercial and drawing qualities
99			ISO 5001：2012, Cold-reduced carbon steel sheet for vitreous enamelling
100			ISO 5002：2013, Hot-rolled and cold-reduced electrolytic zinc-coated carbon steel sheet of commercial and drawing qualities
101			ISO 5778：1998, Ships and marine technology — Small weathertight steel hatches

续表

序号	材料分类	标准类型	标准名称
102			ISO 5950：2012, Electrolytic tin-coated cold-reduced carbon steel sheet of commercial and drawing qualities
103			ISO 6042：1998, Ships and marine technology — Weathertight single-leaf steel doors
104			ISO 6305-2-2007, Railway components — Technical delivery requirements — Part 2: Non-alloy carbon steel baseplates
105			ISO 6305-3-1983, Railway components — Technical delivery requirements — Part 3: Steel sleepers
106			ISO 6305-4-1985, Railway components — Technical delivery requirements — Part 4: Untreated steel nuts and bolts and high-strength nuts and bolts for fish-plates and fastenings
107			ISO 6410-1：1993, Technical drawings — Screw threads and threaded parts — Part 1: General conventions
108			ISO 7046-2：2011, Countersunk flat head screws (common head style) with type H or type Z cross recess — Product grade A — Part 2: Steel screws of property class 8.8, stainless steel screws and non-ferrous metal screws
109			ISO 7257：1983, Aircraft — Hydraulic tubing joints and fittings — Rotary flexure test
110			ISO 8501-1：2007, Preparation of steel substrates before application of paints and related products — Visual assessment of surface cleanliness — Part 1: Rust grades and preparation grades of uncoated steel substrates and of steel substrates after overall removal of previous coatings
111			ISO 9182-4：2013, Tools for pressing — Guide pillars — Part 4: Type C, pillars with taper lead and bush
112			ISO 9444-1：2009, Continuously hot-rolled stainless steel — Tolerances on dimensions and form — Part 1: Narrow strip and cut lengths
113			ISO 9444-2：2009, Continuously hot-rolled stainless steel — Tolerances on dimensions and form — Part 2: Wide strip and sheet/plate
114			ISO 9445-1：2009, Continuously cold-rolled stainless steel — Tolerances on dimensions and form — Part 1: Narrow strip and cut lengths

续表

序号	材料分类	标准类型	标准名称
115			ISO 9445-2：2009，Continuously cold-rolled stainless steel — Tolerances on dimensions and form — Part 2：Wide strip and plate/sheet
116			ISO 9587-2007，Metallic and other inorganic coatings — Pretreatment of iron or steel to reduce the risk of hydrogen embrittlement
117			ISO 9588-1999，Metallic and other inorganic coatings — Post-coating treatments of iron or steel to reduce the risk of hydrogen embrittlement
118			ISO 11692-1994，Ferritic-pearlitic engineering steels for precipitation hardening from hot-working temperatures
119			ISO 11950：1995，Cold-reduced electrolytic chromium/chromium oxide-coated steel
120			ISO 11951：1995，Cold-reduced blackplate in coil form for the production of tinplate or electrolytic chromium/chromium oxide-coated steel
121			ISO 12686：1999，Metallic and other inorganic coatings — Automated controlled shot-peening of metallic articles prior to nickel, autocatalytic nickel or chromium plating, or as a final finish
122			ISO 13755：2012，Ships and marine technology — Ship's mooring and towing fittings — Steel rollers
123			ISO 13795：2012，Ships and marine technology — Ship's mooring and towing fittings — Welded steel bollards for sea-going vessels
124			ISO 13798：2012，Ships and marine technology — Ship's mooring and towing fittings — Recessed bitts (Steel plate type)
125			ISO 13976：2005，Hot-rolled steel sheet in coils of structural quality and heavy thickness
126			ISO 14373：2006，Resistance welding — Procedure for spot welding of uncoated and coated low carbon steels
127			ISO 15156-2-2009，Petroleum and natural gas industries — Materials for use in H2S-containing environments in oil and gas production — Part 2：Cracking-resistant carbon and low-alloy steels, and the use of cast irons

续表

序号	材料分类	标准类型	标准名称
128			ISO 15787-2001, Technical product documentation — Heat-treated ferrous parts — Presentation and indications
129			ISO 15835：2009 系列标准, Steels for the reinforcement of concrete — Reinforcement couplers for mechanical splices of bars
130			ISO/TR15922：2011, Metallic and other inorganic coatings — Evaluation of properties of dark-stain phenomenon of chromated coiled or sheet product
131			ISO 16143-3：2005, Stainless steels for general purposes — Part 3：Wire
132			ISO 16120-3：2011, Non-alloy steel wire rod for conversion to wire — Part 3：Specific requirements for rimmed and rimmed substitute, low-carbon steel wire rod
133			ISO 16432：2006, Resistance welding — Procedure for projection welding of uncoated and coated low carbon steels using embossed projection（s）
134			ISO 16433：2006, Resistance welding — Procedure for seam welding of uncoated and coated low carbon steels
135			ISO/TR 17671-2-2002, Welding — Recommendations for welding of metallic materials — Part 2：Arc welding of ferritic steels
136			ISO 18172-1：2007, Gas cylinders — Refillable welded stainless steel cylinders — Part 1：Test pressure 6 MPa and below
137			ISO 18172-2：2007, Gas cylinders — Refillable welded stainless steel cylinders — Part 2：Test pressure greater than 6 MPa
138			ISO18286：2008, Hot-rolled stainless steel plates — Tolerances on dimensions and shape
139			ISO 21968：2005, Non-magnetic metallic coatings on metallic and non-metallic basis materials — Measurement of coating thickness — Phase-sensitive eddy-current method
140			ISO 24314：2006, Structural steels — Structural steels for building with improved seismic resistance — Technical delivery conditions

续表

序号	材料分类	标准类型	标准名称
141	新型有色金属及复合材料	通用基础标准	ISO 197-1:1983, Copper and copper alloys — Terms and definitions — Part 1: Materials
142			ISO 197-2:1983, Copper and copper alloys — Terms and definitions — Part 2: Unwrought products (Refinery shapes)
143		测试方法标准	ISO 310:1992, Manganese ores and concentrates — Determination of hygroscopic moisture content in analytical samples — Gravimetric method
144			ISO 548:1981, Manganese ores — Determination of barium oxide content — Barium sulphate gravimetric method
145			ISO 796:1973, Aluminium alloys — Determination of copper — Electrolytic method
146			ISO 1169:2006, Zinc alloys — Determination of aluminium content — Titrimetric method
147			ISO 1553:1976, Unalloyed copper containing not less than 99.90% of copper — Determination of copper content — Electrolytic method
148			ISO 1554:1976, Wrought and cast copper alloys — Determination of copper content — Electrolytic method
149			ISO 1976:1975, Zinc alloys — Determination of copper content — Electrolytic method
150			ISO 2085:2010, Anodizing of aluminium and its alloys — Check for continuity of thin anodic oxidation coatings — Copper sulfate test
151			ISO 2106:2011, Anodizing of aluminium and its alloys — Determination of mass per unit area (surface density) of anodic oxidation coatings — Gravimetric method
152			ISO 2143:2010, Anodizing of aluminium and its alloys — Estimation of loss of absorptive power of anodic oxidation coatings after sealing — Dye-spot test with prior acid treatment
153			ISO 2624:1990, Copper and copper alloys — Estimation of average grain size
154			ISO 3750:2006, Zinc alloys — Determination of magnesium content — Flame atomic absorption spectrometric method

续表

序号	材料分类	标准类型	标准名称
155			ISO 3815-1：2005, Zinc and zinc alloys — Part 1：Analysis of solid samples by optical emission spectrometry
156			ISO 3815-2：2005, Zinc and zinc alloys — Part 2：Analysis by inductively coupled plasma optical emission spectrometry
157			ISO 4173：1980, Ferromolybdenum — Determination of molybdenum content — Gravimetric method
158			ISO 4740：1985, Copper and copper alloys — Determination of zinc content — Flame atomic absorption spectrometric method
159			ISO 6101-4：1997, Rubber — Determination of metal content by atomic absorption spectrometry — Part 4：Determination of manganese content
160			ISO 6271-1：2004, Clear liquids — Estimation of colour by the platinum-cobalt scale — Part 1：Visual method
161			ISO 6271-2：2004, Clear liquids — Estimation of colour by the platinum-cobalt scale — Part 2：Spectrophotometric method
162			ISO 7530-1：1990, Nickel alloys — Flame atomic absorption spectrometric analysis — Part 1：General requirements and sample dissolution
163			ISO 9606-5：2000, Approval testing of welders — Fusion welding — Part 5：Titanium and titanium alloys, zirconium and zirconium alloys
164			ISO 9681：1990, Manganese ores and concentrates — Determination of iron content — Flame atomic absorption spectrometric method
165			ISO 9915：1992, Aluminium alloy castings — Radiography testing
166			ISO 10251：2006, Copper, lead, zinc and nickel concentrates — Determination of mass loss of bulk material on drying
167			ISO 10278：1995, Steel — Determination of manganese content — Inductively coupled plasma atomic emission spectrometric method
168			ISO 10378：2005, Copper, lead and zinc sulfide concentrates — Determination of gold and silver — Fire assay gravimetric and flame atomic absorption spectrometric method
169			ISO 10675-1-2008, Non-destructive testing of welds — Acceptance levels for radiographic testing — Part 1：Steel, nickel, titanium and their alloys

续表

序号	材料分类	标准类型	标准名称
170			ISO 11047：1998, Soil quality — Determination of cadmium, chromium, cobalt, copper, lead, manganese, nickel and zinc — Flame and electrothermal atomic absorption spectrometric methods
171			ISO 11400：1992, Nickel, ferronickel and nickel alloys — Determination of phosphorus content — Phosphovanadomolybdate molecular absorption spectrometric method
172			ISO 11433：1993, Nickel alloys — Determination of titanium content — Diantipyrylmethane molecular absorption spectrometric method
173			ISO 11437-2：1994, Nickel alloys — Determination of trace-element content by electrothermal atomic absorption spectrometric method — Part 2：Determination of lead content
174			ISO 11707：2011, Magnesium and its alloys — Determination of lead and cadmium
175			ISO 11790：2010, Copper, lead, zinc and nickel concentrates — Guidelines for the inspection of mechanical sampling systems
176			ISO 11794：2010, Copper, lead, zinc and nickel concentrates — Sampling of slurries
177			ISO 12742：2007, Copper, lead, and zinc sulfide concentrates — Determination of transportable moisture limits — Flow-table method
178			ISO 12743：2006, Copper, lead, zinc and nickel concentrates — Sampling procedures for determination of metal and moisture content
179			ISO 12744：2006, Copper, lead, zinc and nickel concentrates — Experimental methods for checking the precision of sampling
180			ISO 12830：2011, Paper, board and pulps — Determination of acid-soluble magnesium, calcium, manganese, iron, copper, sodium and potassium
181			ISO 13292：2006, Copper, lead, zinc and nickel concentrates — Experimental methods for checking the bias of sampling
182			ISO 13543：1996, Copper, lead and zinc sulfide concentrates — Determination of mass of contained metal in a lot
183			ISO/TR 15855：2001, Copper, lead and zinc sulfide concentrates — Step-by-step procedure for the testing of static scales

续表

序号	材料分类	标准类型	标准名称
184			ISO 16962: 2005, Surface chemical analysis — Analysis of zinc and/or aluminium-based metallic coatings by glow-discharge optical-emission spectrometry
185			ISO 17331: 2004, Surface chemical analysis — Chemical methods for the collection of elements from the surface of silicon-wafer working reference materials and their determination by total-reflection X-ray fluorescence (TXRF) spectroscopy
186			ISO 17925: 2004, Zinc and/or aluminium based coatings on steel — Determination of coating mass per unit area and chemical composition — Gravimetry, inductively coupled plasma atomic emission spectrometry and flame atomic absorption spectrometry
187			ISO 19959: 2005, Visual examination of the surface condition of investment castings — Steel, nickel alloys and cobalt alloys
188			ISO 20081: 2005, Zinc and zinc alloys — Method of sampling-Specifications
189			ISO 22725: 2007, Nickel alloys — Determination of tantalum — Inductively coupled plasma atomic emission spectrometric method
190			ISO 22778-2006, Metallic coatings — Physical vapour-deposited coatings of cadmium on iron and steel — Specification and test methods
191			ISO 22779: 2006, Metallic coatings — Physical vapour-deposited coatings of aluminium — Specification and test methods
192			ISO 22960: 2008, Titanium and titanium alloys — Determination of iron — Molecular absorption spectrometry using 1, 10-phenanthroline
193			ISO 22961: 2008, Titanium and titanium alloys — Determination of iron — Atomic absorption spectrometry
194			ISO 22962: 2008, Titanium and titanium alloys — Determination of iron — Inductively coupled plasma atomic emission spectrometry
195			ISO 22963: 2008, Titanium and titanium alloys — Determination of oxygen — Infrared method after fusion under inert gas
196		材料技术标准	ISO 301: 2006, Zinc alloy ingots intended for castings
197			ISO 1118: 1978, Aluminium and aluminium alloys — Determination of titanium — Spectrophotometric chromotropic acid method

续表

序号	材料分类	标准类型	标准名称
198			ISO 1456：2009, Metallic and other inorganic coatings — Electro-deposited coatings of nickel, nickel plus chromium, copper plus nickel and of copper plus nickel plus chromium
199			ISO 1553：1976, Unalloyed copper containing not less than 99.90% of copper — Determination of copper content — Electrolytic method
200			ISO 1554：1976, Wrought and cast copper alloys — Determination of copper content — Electrolytic method
201			ISO 1456：2009, Metallic and other inorganic coatings — Electro-deposited coatings of nickel, nickel plus chromium, copper plus nickel and of copper plus nickel plus chromium
202			ISO 2063：2005, Thermal spraying — Metallic and other inorganic coatings — Zinc, aluminium and their alloys
203			ISO 2081：2008, Metallic and other inorganic coatings — Electro-plated coatings of zinc with supplementary treatments on iron or steel
204			ISO 2082：2008, Metallic and other inorganic coatings — Electro-plated coatings of cadmium with supplementary treatments on iron or steel
205			ISO 2377：1972, Magnesium alloy sand castings — Reference test bar
206			ISO 3613：2010, Metallic and other inorganic coatings — Chromate conversion coatings on zinc, cadmium, aluminium-zinc alloys and zinc-aluminium alloys — Test methods
207			ISO 4382-1：1991, Plain bearings — Copper alloys — Part 1: Cast copper alloys for solid and multilayer thick-walled plain bearings
208			ISO 4382-2：1991, Plain bearings — Copper alloys — Part 2: Wrought copper alloys for solid plain bearings
209			ISO 4521：2008, Metallic and other inorganic coatings — Electro-deposited silver and silver alloy coatings for engineering purposes — Specification and test methods
210			ISO 4525：2003, Metallic coatings — Electroplated coatings of nickel plus chromium on plastics materials
211			ISO 4998：2011, Continuous hot-dip zinc-coated carbon steel sheet of structural quality

续表

序号	材料分类	标准类型	标准名称
212			ISO 5000：2011, Continuous hot-dip aluminium-silicon-coated cold-reduced carbon steel sheet of commercial and drawing qualities
213			ISO 5817：2003, Welding — Fusion-welded joints in steel, nickel, titanium and their alloys (beam welding excluded) — Quality levels for imperfections
214			ISO 6158：2011, Metallic and other inorganic coatings — Electro-deposited coatings of chromium for engineering purposes
215			ISO 6361-1：2011, Wrought aluminium and aluminium alloys — Sheets, strips and plates — Part 1：Technical conditions for inspection and delivery
216			ISO 6361-2：2011, Wrought aluminium and aluminium alloys — Sheets, strips and plates — Part 2：Mechanical properties
217			ISO 6361-3：2011, Wrought aluminium and aluminium alloys — Sheets, strips and plates — Part 3：Strips：Tolerances on shape and dimensions
218			ISO 6361-4：2011, Wrought aluminium and aluminium alloys — Sheets, strips and plates — Part 4：Sheets and plates：Tolerances on shape and dimensions
219			ISO 6363-3：2012, Wrought aluminium and aluminium alloys — Cold-drawn rods/bars, tubes and wires — Part 3：Drawn round bars and wires — Tolerances on form and dimensions (symmetric plus and minus tolerances on diameter)
220			ISO 6363-5：2012, Wrought aluminium and aluminium alloys — Cold-drawn rods/bars, tubes and wires — Part 5：Drawn square and hexagonal bars and wires — Tolerances on form and dimensions
221			ISO 6537-1982, Pneumatic fluid power systems — Cylinder barrels — Requirements for non-ferrous metallic tubes
222			ISO 6847：2013, Welding consumables — Deposition of a weld metal pad for chemical analysis
223			ISO 7271：2011, Aluminium and aluminium alloys — Foil and thin strip — Dimensional tolerances
224			ISO 7530-1：1990, Nickel alloys — Flame atomic absorption spectrometric analysis — Part 1：General requirements and sample dissolution

续表

序号	材料分类	标准类型	标准名称
225			ISO 7530-2：1990, Nickel alloys — Flame atomic absorption spectrometric analysis — Part 2：Determination of cobalt content
226			ISO 7530-3：1990, Nickel alloys — Flame atomic absorption spectrometric analysis — Part 3：Determination of chromium content
227			ISO 7530-4：1990, Nickel alloys — Flame atomic absorption spectrometric analysis — Part 4：Determination of copper content
228			ISO 7530-6：1990, Nickel alloys — Flame atomic absorption spectrometric analysis — Part 6：Determination of manganese content
229			ISO 7530-7：1992, Nickel alloys — Flame atomic absorption spectrometric analysis — Part 7：Determination of aluminium content
230			ISO 7530-8：1992, Nickel alloys — Flame atomic absorption spectrometric analysis — Part 8：Determination of silicon content
231			ISO 7722：1985, Aluminium alloy castings produced by gravity, sand, or chill casting, or by related processes — General conditions for inspection and delivery
232			ISO 7989-1-2006, Steel wire and wire products — Non-ferrous metallic coatings on steel wire — Part 1：General principles
233			ISO 7989-2-2007, Steel wire and wire products — Non-ferrous metallic coatings on steel wire — Part 2：Zinc or zinc-alloy coating
234			ISO 8287：2011, Magnesium and magnesium alloys — Unalloyed magnesium — Chemical composition
235			ISO 8839-1986, Mechanical properties of fasteners — Bolts, screws, studs and nuts made of non-ferrous metals
236			ISO 9152：1998, Aerospace — Bolts, with MJ threads, in titanium alloys, strength class 1100 MPa — Procurement specification
237			ISO 9216：2002, Aerospace — Nuts, hexagonal, slotted (castellated), for pulleys, in alloy steel and cadmium plated or in corrosion-resistant steel and passivated — Dimensions and masses
238			ISO 9217：2002, Aerospace — Washers, chamfered, with counterbore, for pulleys, in alloy steel and cadmium plated or in corrosion-resistant steel and passivated — Dimensions and masses
239			ISO 9218：2002, Aerospace — Washers, flat, for pulleys, in alloy steel and cadmium plated or in corrosion-resistant steel and passivated — Dimensions and masses

续表

序号	材料分类	标准类型	标准名称
240			ISO 9219: 2002, Aerospace — Bolts, thin hexagonal head, for pulleys, close tolerance shank, short thread, in alloy steel and cadmium plated or in titanium alloy and MoS2 lubricated or in corrosion-resistant steel and passivated — Dimensions and masses
241			ISO 9364: 2011, Continuous hot-dip 55% aluminium/zinc alloy-coated steel sheet of commercial, drawing and structural qualities
242			ISO 9388: 1992, Nickel alloys — Determination of phosphorus content — Molybdenum blue molecular absorption spectrometric method
243			ISO 9606-3: 1999, Approval testing of welders — Fusion welding — Part 3: Copper and copper alloys
244			ISO 9916: 1991, Aluminium alloy and magnesium alloy castings — Liquid penetrant inspection
245			ISO 10042: 2005, Welding — Arc-welded joints in aluminium and its alloys — Quality levels for imperfections
246			ISO 10049: 1992, Aluminium alloy castings — Visual method for assessing the porosity
247			ISO 11435: 2011, Nickel alloys — Determination of molybdenum content — Inductively coupled plasma/atomic emission spectrometric method
248			ISO 12745: 2008, Copper, lead and zinc ores and concentrates — Precision and bias of mass measurement techniques
249			ISO 13092: 2012, Titanium and titanium alloys — Titanium sponge
250			ISO 13521: 1999, Austenitic manganese steel castings
251			ISO 13770: 1997, Aluminium alloy gas cylinders — Operational requirements for avoidance of neck and shoulder cracks
252			ISO 13832: 2013, Aerospace — Wire, aluminium alloy and copper-clad aluminium conductors — General performance requirements
253			ISO 14657: 2005, Zinc-coated steel for the reinforcement of concrete
254			ISO 14713-1999, Zinc coatings — Guidelines and recommendations for the protection against corrosion of iron and steel in structures
255			ISO 14713-1-2009, Zinc coatings — Guidelines and recommendations for the protection against corrosion of iron and steel in structures

续表

序号	材料分类	标准类型	标准名称
256			ISO 14713-2-2009, Zinc coatings — Guidelines and recommendations for the protection against corrosion of iron and steel in structures
257			ISO 14713-3-2009, Zinc coatings — Guidelines and recommendations for the protection against corrosion of iron and steel in structures
258			ISO 14788：2011, Continuous hot-dip zinc-5% aluminium alloy coated steel sheet
259			ISO 15201：2006, Zinc and zinc alloys — Castings — Specifications
260			ISO 15614-1：2004, Specification and qualification of welding procedures for metallic materials — Welding procedure test — Part 1：Arc and gas welding of steels and arc welding of nickel and nickel alloys
261			ISO 15614-5：2004, Specification and qualification of welding procedures for metallic materials — Welding procedure test — Part 5：Arc welding of titanium, zirconium and their alloys
262			ISO 15726：2009, Metallic and other inorganic coatings — Electrodeposited zinc alloys with nickel, cobalt or iron
263			ISO 16220：2005, Magnesium and magnesium alloys — Magnesium alloy ingots and castings
264			ISO 17334：2008, Metallic and other inorganic coatings — Autocatalytic nickel over autocatalytic copper for electromagnetic shielding
265			ISO 18595：2007, Resistance welding — Spot welding of aluminium and aluminium alloys — Weldability, welding and testing
266			ISO 24034：2010, Welding consumables — Solid wire electrodes, solid wires and rods for fusion welding of titanium and titanium alloys-Classification
267			ISO 24373：2008, Welding consumables — Solid wires and rods for fusion welding of copper and copper alloys — Classification
268			ISO 26202：2007, Magnesium and magnesium alloys — Magnesium alloys for cast anodes
269			ISO 26945：2011, Metallic and other inorganic coatings — Electrodeposited coatings of tin-cobalt alloy
270			ISO 28401：2010, Light metals and their alloys — Titanium and titanium alloys — Classification and terminology

续表

序号	材料分类	标准类型	标准名称
271	稀有金属及复合材料	测试方法标准	ISO 4883：1978, Hardmetals — Determination of contents of metallic elements by X-ray fluorescence — Solution method
272			ISO 11174：1996, Workplace air — Determination of particulate cadmium and cadmium compounds — Flame and electrothermal atomic absorption spectrometric method
273			ISO 11210：1995, Determination of platinum in platinum jewellery alloys — Gravimetric method after precipitation of diammonium hexachloroplatinate
274			ISO 11427：1993, Determination of silver in silver jewellery alloys — Volumetric (potentiometric) method using potassium bromide
275			ISO 11489：1995, Determination of platinum in platinum jewellery alloys — Gravimetric determination by reduction with mercury (I) chloride
276			ISO 11490：1995, Determination of palladium in palladium jewellery alloys — Gravimetric determination with dimethylglyoxime
277			ISO 11494：2008, Jewellery — Determination of platinum in platinum jewellery alloys — Inductively coupled plasma (ICP) solution-spectrometric method using yttrium as internal standard element
278			ISO 11495：2008, Jewellery — Determination of palladium in palladium jewellery alloys — Inductively coupled plasma (ICP) solution-spectrometric method using yttrium as internal standard element
279			ISO 11873：2005, Hardmetals — Determination of sulfur and carbon contents in cobalt metal powders — Infrared detection method
280			ISO 11876：2010, Hardmetals — Determination of calcium, copper, iron, potassium, magnesium, manganese, sodium, nickel and zinc in cobalt metal powders — Flame atomic absorption spectrometric method
281			ISO 11877：2008, Hardmetals — Determination of silicon in cobalt metal powders — Photometric method
282			ISO 16794：2003, Nuclear energy — Determination of carbon compounds and fluorides in uranium hexafluoride infrared spectrometry

续表

序号	材料分类	标准类型	标准名称
283	功能金属材料	通用基础标准	ISO Guide 35：2006，Reference materials — General and statistical principles for certification
284			ISO 636：2004，Welding consumables — Rods，wires and deposits for tungsten inert gas welding of non-alloy and fine-grain steels-Classification
285			ISO 3134-1：1985，Light metals and their alloys — Terms and definitions — Part 1：Materials
286			ISO 16468：2005，Investment castings (steel，nickel alloys and cobalt alloys) — General technical requirements
287			ISO 21988：2006，Abrasion-resistant cast irons — Classification
288		测试方法标准	ISO 1352：2011，Metallic materials — Torque-controlled fatigue testing
289			ISO 3907：2009，Hardmetals — Determination of total carbon — Gravimetric method
290			ISO 3908：2009，Hardmetals — Determination of insoluble (free) carbon — Gravimetric method
291			ISO 9891：1994，Determination of carbon content in uranium dioxide powder and sintered pellets — High-frequency induction furnace combustion — Titrimetric/coulometric/infrared absorption methods
292			ISO 10113：2006，Metallic materials — Sheet and strip — Determination of plastic strain ratio
293			ISO 10271：2011，Dentistry — Corrosion test methods for metallic materials
294			ISO 10309：1994，Metallic coatings — Porosity tests — Ferroxyl test
295			ISO/TR 16060：2003，Destructive tests on welds in metallic materials — Etchants for macroscopic and microscopic examination
296			ISO 16794：2003，Nuclear energy — Determination of carbon compounds and fluorides in uranium hexafluoride infrared spectrometry
297			ISO 17352：2008，Hardmetals — Determination of silicon in cobalt metal powders using graphite-furnace atomic absorption

续表

序号	材料分类	标准类型	标准名称
298			ISO/TR 17641-3：2005, Destructive tests on welds in metallic materials — Hot cracking tests for weldments — Arc welding processes — Part 3：Externally loaded tests
299			ISO 18278-1：2004, Resistance welding — Weldability — Part 1：Assessment of weldability for resistance spot, seam and projection welding of metallic materials
300			ISO 20160：2006, Implants for surgery — Metallic materials — Classification of microstructures for alpha + beta titanium alloy bars
301			ISO 26482：2010, Hardmetals — Determination of lead and cadmium content
302		材料技术标准	ISO 1966：1973, Crimped joints for aircraft electrical cables
303			ISO 4386-1：2012, Plain bearings — Metallic multilayer plain bearings — Part 1：Non-destructive ultrasonic testing of bond of thickness greater than or equal to 0.5 mm
304			ISO 4386-2：2012, Plain bearings — Metallic multilayer plain bearings — Part 2：Destructive testing of bond for bearing metal layer thicknesses greater than or equal to 2 mm
305			ISO 4498：2010, Sintered metal materials, excluding hardmetals — Determination of apparent hardness and microhardness
306			ISO 5832-1：2007, Implants for surgery — Metallic materials — Part 1：Wrought stainless steel
307			ISO 5832-3：1996, Implants for surgery — Metallic materials — Part 3：Wrought titanium 6-aluminium 4-vanadium alloy
308			ISO 5832-4：1996, Implants for surgery — Metallic materials — Part 4：Cobalt-chromium-molybdenum casting alloy
309			ISO 5832-5：2005, Implants for surgery — Metallic materials — Part 5：Wrought cobalt-chromium-tungsten-nickel alloy
310			ISO 5832-6：1997, Implants for surgery — Metallic materials — Part 6：Wrought cobalt-nickel-chromium-molybdenum alloy
311			ISO 5832-7：1994, Implants for surgery — Metallic materials — Part 7：Forgeable and cold-formed cobalt-chromium-nickel-molybdenum-iron alloy

续表

序号	材料分类	标准类型	标准名称
312			ISO 5832-8：1997, Implants for surgery — Metallic materials — Part 8：Wrought cobalt-nickel-chromium-molybdenum- tungsten-iron alloy
313			ISO 5832-9：2007, Implants for surgery — Metallic materials — Part 9：Wrought high nitrogen stainless steel
314			ISO 5832-11：1994, Implants for surgery — Metallic materials — Part 11：Wrought titanium 6-aluminium 7-niobium alloy
315			ISO 5832-12：2007, Implants for surgery — Metallic materials — Part 12：Wrought cobalt-chromium-molybdenum alloy
316			ISO 5832-14：2007, Implants for surgery — Metallic materials — Part 14：Wrought titanium 15-molybdenum 5-zirconium 3-aluminium alloy
317			ISO 6158：2011, Metallic and other inorganic coatings — Electro-deposited coatings of chromium for engineering purposes
318			ISO 6847：2013, Welding consumables — Deposition of a weld metal pad for chemical analysis
319			ISO 9453：2006, Soft solder alloys — Chemical compositions and forms
320			ISO 9717：2010, Metallic and other inorganic coatings — Phosphate conversion coating of metals
321			ISO 10354：1992, Adhesives — Characterization of durability of structural-adhesive-bonded assemblies — Wedge rupture test
322			ISO 11130：2010, Corrosion of metals and alloys — Alternate immersion test in salt solution
323			ISO 13174：2012, Cathodic protection of harbour installations
324			ISO 13270：2013, Steel fibres for concrete — Definitions and specifications
325			ISO 13782：1996, Implants for surgery — Metallic materials — Unalloyed tantalum for surgical implant applications
326			ISO 14921：2010, Thermal spraying — Procedures for the application of thermally sprayed coatings for engineering components
327			ISO/TR 15608：2013, Welding — Guidelines for a metallic materials grouping system

续表

序号	材料分类	标准类型	标准名称
328			ISO 15614-6：2006, Specification and qualification of welding procedures for metallic materials — Welding procedure test — Part 6：Arc and gas welding of copper and its alloys
329			ISO/TR 20172：2009, Welding — Grouping systems for materials — European materials
330			ISO/TR 20173：2009, Welding — Grouping systems for materials — American materials
331			ISO 26945：2011, Metallic and other inorganic coatings — Electro-deposited coatings of tin-cobalt alloy
2. 新型无机非金属材料			
332	新型陶瓷材料	通用基础标准	ISO/WD 17889, Sustainability for ceramic tiling systems
333			ISO/CD 16575, Test methods and specifications for Cementitious Backer Units (CBUs)
334			ISO/CD 14448, Low modulus adhesives for exterior tile finishing
335		测试方法标准	ISO 14544：2013, Fine ceramics (advanced ceramics, advanced technical ceramics) — Mechanical properties of ceramic composites at high temperature — Determination of compression properties
336			ISO 14574：2013, Fine ceramics (advanced ceramics, advanced technical ceramics) — Mechanical properties of ceramic composites at high temperature — Determination of tensile properties
337			ISO 14603：2012, Fine ceramics (advanced ceramics, advanced technical ceramics) — Test method for open-hole tension of continuous fibre-reinforced ceramic matrix composites at room temperature
338			ISO 14628：2012, Fine ceramics (advanced ceramics, advanced technical ceramics) — Test method for rolling contact fatigue of silicon nitride ceramics at room temperature by balls-on-flat method
339			ISO 17092：2005, Fine ceramics (advanced ceramics, advanced technical ceramics) — Determination of corrosion resistance of monolithic ceramics in acid and alkaline solutions
340			ISO 17095：2013, Fine ceramics (advanced ceramics, advanced technical ceramics) — Test method for interfacial bond strength of ceramic materials at elevated temperatures

续表

序号	材料分类	标准类型	标准名称
341			ISO/DIS 17139, Fine ceramics (advanced ceramics, advanced technical ceramics) — Ceramic composites — Thermophysical properties — Determination of thermal expansion
342			ISO/DIS 17140, Fine ceramics (advanced ceramics, advanced technical ceramics) — Mechanical properties of ceramic composites at room temperature — Determination of fatigue properties at constant amplitude
343			ISO/DIS 17142, Fine ceramics (advanced ceramics, advanced technical ceramics) — Mechanical properties of ceramic composites at high temperature in air at atmospheric pressure — Determination of fatigue properties at constant amplitude
344			ISO/DIS 17161, Fine ceramics (advanced ceramics, advanced technical ceramics) — Ceramic composites — Determination of the degree of misalignment in uniaxial mechanical tests
345			ISO/WD 17841, Fine ceramics (advanced ceramics, advanced technical ceramics) — Test method for thermal fatigue of fine ceramics substrate
346			ISO 17562: 2001, Fine ceramics (advanced ceramics, advanced technical ceramics) — Test method for linear thermal expansion of monolithic ceramics by push-rod technique
347			ISO/DIS 17942, Fine ceramics (advanced ceramics, advanced technical ceramics) — Methods for chemical analysis of boron nitride powders
348			ISO/DIS 17947, Fine ceramics (advanced ceramics, advanced technical ceramics) — Methods for chemical analysis of fine silicon nitride powders
349			ISO/WD 18550, Fine Ceramics (Advanced ceramics, advanced technical ceramics) — Testing method for macroheterogeneity in microstructure
350			ISO 18755: 2005, Fine ceramics (advanced ceramics, advanced technical ceramics) — Determination of thermal diffusivity of monolithic ceramics by laser flash method
351			ISO 20509: 2003, Fine ceramics (advanced ceramics, advanced technical ceramics) — Determination of oxidation resistance of non-oxide monolithic ceramics

续表

序号	材料分类	标准类型	标准名称
352			ISO 23145：2012 系列标准，Fine ceramics (advanced ceramics, advanced technical ceramics) — Determination of bulk density of ceramic powders
353			ISO 23146：2012, Fine ceramics (advanced ceramics, advanced technical ceramics) — Test methods for fracture toughness of monolithic ceramics — Single-edge V-notch beam (SEVNB) method
354			ISO 24235：2007, Fine ceramics (advanced ceramics, advanced technical ceramics) — Determination of particle size distribution of ceramic powders by laser diffraction method
355			ISO 24369：2005, Fine ceramics (advanced ceramics, advanced technical ceramics) — Determination of content of coarse particles in ceramic powders by wet sieving method
356			ISO 24370：2005, Fine ceramics (advanced ceramics, advanced technical ceramics) — Test method for fracture toughness of monolithic ceramics at room temperature by chevron-notched beam (CNB) method
357			ISO 26423：2009, Fine ceramics (advanced ceramics, advanced technical ceramics) — Determination of coating thickness by crater-grinding method
358			ISO 26424：2008, Fine ceramics (advanced ceramics, advanced technical ceramics) — Determination of the abrasion resistance of coatings by a micro-scale abrasion test
359			ISO 26443：2008, Fine ceramics (advanced ceramics, advanced technical ceramics) — Rockwell indentation test for evaluation of adhesion of ceramic coatings
360			ISO 27447：2009, Fine ceramics (advanced ceramics, advanced technical ceramics) — Test method for antibacterial activity of semiconducting photocatalytic materials
361			ISO 27448：2009, Fine ceramics (advanced ceramics, advanced technical ceramics) — Test method for self-cleaning performance of semiconducting photocatalytic materials — Measurement of water contact angle

续表

序号	材料分类	标准类型	标准名称
362			ISO 28703：2011，Fine ceramics（advanced ceramics, advanced technical ceramics）— Test method for thermal-shock resistance of porous ceramics
363			ISO 28704：2011，Fine ceramics（advanced ceramics, advanced technical ceramics）— Test method for cyclic bending fatigue of porous ceramics at room temperature
364		材料技术标准	ISO 26602：2009，Fine ceramics（advanced ceramics, advanced technical ceramics）— Silicon nitride materials for rolling bearing balls
365		应用技术标准	ISO 10676：2010，Fine ceramics（advanced ceramics, advanced technical ceramics）— Test method for water purification performance of semiconducting photocatalytic materials by measurement of forming ability of active oxygen
366		通用基础标准	ISO 14484：2013，Performance guidelines for design of concrete structures using fibre-reinforced polymer（FRP）materials
367		测试方法标准	ISO 15673：2005，Guidelines for the simplified design of structural reinforced concrete for buildings
368			ISO 28842：2013，Guidelines for simplified design of reinforced concrete bridges
369	新型水泥材料		ISO 10406：2008 系列标准，Fibre-reinforced polymer（FRP）reinforcement of concrete — Test methods 系列标准
370		应用技术标准	ISO 8336：2009，Fibre-cement flat sheets — Product specification and test methods
371			ISO 10426-1：2009，Petroleum and natural gas industries — Cements and materials for well cementing
372			ISO 10904：2011，Fibre-cement corrugated sheets and fittings for roofing and cladding
373			ISO 22306：2007，Fibre-reinforced cement pipe, joints and fittings for gravity systems
374	新型玻璃材料	材料技术标准	ISO 9050：2003，Glass in building — Determination of light transmittance, solar direct transmittance, total solar energy transmittance, ultraviolet transmittance and related glazing factors
375			ISO 16293-1：2008，Glass in building — Basic soda lime silicate glass products

续表

序号	材料分类	标准类型	标准名称
376			ISO/CD 18178, Glass in building — Laminated solar PV glass
377			ISO 25537：2008, Glass in building — Silvered, flat-glass mirror
378	无机涂层材料	测试方法标准	Vitreous and porcelain enamels 系列测试方法标准
379			ISO 14604：2012, Fine ceramics (advanced ceramics, advanced technical ceramics) — Methods of test for ceramic coatings — Determination of fracture strain
380	耐火材料	测试方法标准	ISO 13765：2004 系列标准, Refractory mortars 系列标准
381			ISO 14719：2011, Chemical analysis of refractory material glass and glazes — Determination of Fe^{2+} and Fe^{3+} by the spectral photometric method with 1, 10-phenanthroline
382			ISO 21068-2009 系列标准, Chemical analysis of silicon-carbide-containing raw materials and refractory products
383			ISO 21078：2008 系列标准, Determination of boron (III) oxide in refractory products 系列标准
384			ISO 21079：2008 系列标准, Chemical analysis of refractories containing alumina, zirconia and silica — Refractories containing 5 percent to 45 percent of ZrO_2 (alternative to the X-ray fluorescence method) 系列标准
385			ISO 21587：2007 系列标准, Chemical analysis of aluminosilicate refractory products (alternative to the X-ray fluorescence method) 系列标准
386		材料技术标准	ISO 20292：2009, Materials for the production of primary aluminium — Dense refractory bricks — Determination of cryolite resistance
387	超硬材料	通用基础标准	ISO 513：2012, Classification and application of hard cutting materials for metal removal with defined cutting edges — Designation of the main groups and groups of application
388			ISO 6987：2012, Indexable hard material inserts with rounded corners, with partly cylindrical fixing hole — Dimensions
389		材料技术标准	ISO 9285：1997, Abrasive grains and crude — Chemical analysis of fused aluminium oxide
390			ISO 9286：1997, Abrasive grains and crude — Chemical analysis of silicon carbide

续表

序号	材料分类	标准类型	标准名称
391			ISO 15917:2012, Solid ball-nosed end mills with cylindrical shanks, made of carbide and ceramic materials
392			ISO 16462:2004, Cubic boron nitride inserts, tipped or solid — Dimensions, types
393			ISO 22917:2004, Superabrasives — Limit deviations and run-out tolerances for grinding wheels with diamond or cubic boron nitride
394		材料技术标准	ISO 22037:2007, Solid end mills with corner radii and cylindrical shanks made of hard cutting materials — Dimensions
395			ISO 10678:2010, Fine ceramics (advanced ceramics, advanced technical ceramics) — Determination of photocatalytic activity of surfaces in an aqueous medium by degradation of methylene blue
396			ISO 13125:2013, Fine ceramics (advanced ceramics, advanced technical ceramics) — Test method for antifungal activity of semi-conducting photocatalytic materials
397			ISO/DIS 17094, Fine ceramics (advanced ceramics, advanced technical ceramics) — Test method for antibacterial activity of semi-conducting photocatalytic materials under indoor lighting environment
398			ISO/NP 17721, Quantitative Determination of Antibacterial Activity of Ceramic Surfaces — Test Methods for Photocatalytic and Non-Photocatalytic Ceramic Tile Surface
399	光学材料	测试方法标准	ISO/DIS 17861, Fine ceramics (advanced ceramics, advanced technical ceramics) — Measurement method of spectral transmittance of fine ceramics thin films under humid condition
400			ISO/DIS 18061, Fine Ceramics (Advanced Ceramics, Advanced Technical Ceramics) — Determination of antiviral activity of semi-conducting photocatalytic materials — Test method using bacteriophage Q-beta
401			ISO/DIS 18560 系列标准, Fine ceramics (advanced ceramics, advanced technical ceramics) — Test method for air-purification performance of semiconducting photocatalytic materials by test chamber method under indoor lighting environment
402			ISO 20508:2003, Fine ceramics (advanced ceramics, advanced technical ceramics) — Determination of light transmittance of ceramic films with transparent substrate

续表

序号	材料分类	标准类型	标准名称
403		材料技术标准	ISO/NP 22197 系列标准，Fine ceramics (advanced ceramics, advanced technical ceramics) — Test method for air-purification performance of semiconducting photocatalytic materials 系列标准
404			ISO 6328：2000，Photography — Photographic materials — Determination of ISO resolving power
405			ISO 7187：1995，Photography — Materials for direct-positive colour-print cameras — Determination of ISO speed
406			ISO 10677：2011，Fine ceramics (advanced ceramics, advanced technical ceramics) — Ultraviolet light source for testing semiconducting photocatalytic materials
407			ISO 11382：2010，Optics and photonics — Optical materials and components — Characterization of optical materials used in the infrared spectral range from 0.78 μm to 25 μm
408			ISO/WD 18543，Glass in building — Electrochromic glazings — Accelerated aging test
409			ISO 18920：2011，Imaging materials — Reflection prints — Storage practices
410			Fine ceramics (advanced ceramics, advanced technical ceramics) — Light source for testing semiconducting photocatalytic materials used under indoor lighting environment
411	电学材料	测试方法标准	ISO 11894：2013 系列标准，Fine ceramics (advanced ceramics, advanced technical ceramics) — Test method for conductivity measurement of ion-conductive fine ceramics 系列标准
412		材料技术标准	ISO 20492：2008 系列标准，Glass in buildings - Insulating glass 系列标准
413	生物医药材料	通用基础标准	ISO 10451：2010，Dentistry — Contents of technical file for dental implant systems
414		测试方式标准	ISO 9693-1：2012，Dentistry — Compatibility testing — Part 1：Metal-ceramic systems
415		材料技术标准	ISO 3107：2011，Dentistry — Zinc oxide/eugenol cements and zinc oxide/non-eugenol cements
416			ISO 5833：2002，Implants for surgery — Acrylic resin cements

续表

序号	材料分类	标准类型	标准名称
417	生物医药材料		ISO 6474：2010系列标准，Implants for surgery — Ceramic materials 系列标准
418			ISO 6872：2008，Dentistry — Ceramic materials
419			ISO 6872：2008，Dentistry — Ceramic materials
420			ISO 9917-1：2007，Dentistry — Water-based cements
421			ISO 13356：2008，Implants for surgery — Ceramic materials based on yttria-stabilized tetragonal zirconia（Y-TZP）
422			SO 13779-1：2008，Implants for surgery — Hydroxyapatite
423			ISO 16402：2008，Implants for surgery — Acrylic resin cement — Flexural fatigue testing of acrylic resin cements used in orthopaedics
424		应用技术标准	ISO 12891-4：2000，Retrieval and analysis of surgical implants — Part 4：Analysis of retrieved ceramic surgical implants
3. 高性能有机高分子材料			
425	新型通用高分子材料	材料技术标准	ISO 4894-2系列标准，Plastics — Styrene/acrylonitrile（SAN）moulding and extrusion materials 系列标准
426			ISO 6402-2002系列标准，Plastics — Acrylonitrile-styrene-acrylate（ASA），acrylonitrile-（ethylene-propylene-diene）-styrene（AEPDS）and acrylonitrile-（chlorinated polyethylene）-styrene（ACS）moulding and extrusion materials 系列标准
427			ISO 10366-1：2002系列标准，Plastics-Methyl methacrylate-acrylonitrile-butadiene-styrene（MABS）moulding and extrusion materials
428			ISO 12086：2006系列标准，Plastics — Fluoropolymer dispersions and moulding and extrusion materials
429			ISO 14527：1999系列标准，Plastics — Urea-formaldehyde and urea/melamine-formaldehyde powder moulding compounds（UF- and UF/MF-PMCs）
430			ISO 14528：1999系列标准，Plastics — Melamine-formaldehyde powder moulding compounds（MF-PMCs）
431			ISO 14529：1999系列标准，Plastics — Melamine/phenolic powder moulding compounds（MP-PMCs）
432			ISO 14910-1：2013，Plastics — Thermoplastic polyester/ester and polyether/ester elastomers for moulding and extrusion

续表

序号	材料分类	标准类型	标准名称
433			ISO 15015：2011，Plastics — Extruded sheets of impact-modified acrylonitrile-styrene copolymers（ABS，AEPDS and ASA）— Requirements and test methods
434			ISO 15103：2007 系列标准，Plastics — Poly（phenylene ether）（PPE）moulding and extrusion materials
435			ISO/DIS 19066-1，Plastics-Methyl methacrylate-acrylonitrile-butadiene-styrene（MABS）moulding and extrusion materials
436			ISO 25137：2009 系列标准，Plastics — Sulfone polymer moulding and extrusion materials
437			ISO 28078-2：2009，Plastics — Poly（phenylene sulfide）（PPS）moulding and extrusion materials
438			ISO 28941：2008 系列标准，Plastics — Poly（phenylene ether）（PPE）moulding and extrusion materials
439		应用技术标准	ISO 15014：2007，Plastics — Extruded sheets of poly（vinylidene fluoride）（PVDF）— Requirements and test methods
440			ISO 527-4：1997，Plastics — Determination of tensile properties — Part 4：Test conditions for isotropic and orthotropic fibre-reinforced plastic composites
441			ISO 527-5：2009，Plastics — Determination of tensile properties — Part 5：Test conditions for unidirectional fibre-reinforced plastic composites
442			ISO 1268：2001 系列标准，Fibre-reinforced plastics — Methods of producing test plates
443	结构材料	测试方法	ISO 12815：2013，Fibre-reinforced plastic composites — Determination of plain-pin bearing strength
444			ISO 12817：2013，Fibre-reinforced plastic composites — Determination of open-hole compression strength
445			ISO 13003：2003，Fibre-reinforced plastics — Determination of fatigue properties under cyclic loading conditions
446			ISO 14125：1998，Fibre-reinforced plastic composites — Determination of flexural properties
447			ISO 14126：1999，Fibre-reinforced plastic composites — Determination of compressive properties in the in-plane direction

续表

序号	材料分类	标准类型	标准名称
448			ISO 14129：1997，Fibre-reinforced plastic composites — Determination of the in-plane shear stress/shear strain response, including the in-plane shear modulus and strength, by the plus or minus 45 degree tension test method
449			ISO 14130：1997，Fibre-reinforced plastic composites — Determination of apparent interlaminar shear strength by short-beam method
450			ISO 15024：2001，Fibre-reinforced plastic composites — Determination of mode I interlaminar fracture toughness, GIC, for unidirectionally reinforced materials
451			ISO/DIS 15114，Fibre-reinforced plastic composites — Determination of the mode II fracture resistance for unidirectionally reinforced materials using the calibrated end-loaded split (C-ELS) test and an effective crack length approach
452			ISO 15310：1999，Fibre-reinforced plastic composites — Determination of the in-plane shear modulus by the plate twist method
453			ISO/DIS 15512，Plastics — Determination of water content
454			ISO/DIS 16616，Test methods for Natural Fiber-reinforced Plastic Composite (NFC) Deck Boards
455			ISO 18352：2009，Carbon-fibre-reinforced plastics — Determination of compression-after-impact properties at a specified impact-energy level
456	光学材料	测试方法标准	ISO 489：1999，Plastics — Determination of refractive index
457			ISO 7686：2005，Plastics pipes and fittings — Determination of opacity
458			ISO 13468：1996 系列标准，Plastics — Determination of the total luminous transmittance of transparent materials — Part 1：Single-beam instrument
459			ISO 14782：1999，Plastics — Determination of haze for transparent materials
460			ISO/FDIS 17221，Plastics — Determination of image clarity (degree of sharpness of reflected or transmitted image)
461			ISO 18916：2007，Imaging materials — Processed imaging materials — Photographic activity test for enclosure materials

续表

序号	材料分类	标准类型	标准名称
462			ISO 18902:2013, Imaging materials — Processed imaging materials — Albums, framing and storage materials
463	热力学材料	测试方法标准	ISO 22007:2008 系列标准（ISO/DIS 2, 4, 6）, Plastics — Determination of thermal conductivity and thermal diffusivity
464		材料技术标准	ISO 8873:2006 系列标准, Rigid cellular plastics — Spray-applied polyurethane foam for thermal insulation
465		通用基础标准	ISO 25762:2009, Plastics — Guidance on the assessment of the fire characteristics and fire performance of fibre-reinforced polymer composites
466	阻燃高分子材料		ISO 9239:2002 系列标准, Reaction to fire tests for floorings
467		试验方法标准	ISO/TR 15655:2003, Fire resistance — Tests for thermo-physical and mechanical properties of structural materials at elevated temperatures for fire engineering design
468	太阳能相关材料	测试方法标准	ISO/DTR 18486, Plastics — Calculation of the goodness of fit of the spectral distribution of a solar simulator to a reference solar spectral distribution
469			ISO 2556:1974, Plastics — Determination of the gas transmission rate of films and thin sheets under atmospheric pressure — Manometric method
470			ISO 8296:2003, Plastics — Film and sheeting — Determination of wetting tension
471		测试方法标准	ISO 15105:2007 系列标准, Plastics — Film and sheeting — Determination of gas-transmission rate
472	高分子膜材料		ISO 15106:2003 系列标准（1-4, ISO/NP 5-7）, Plastics — Film and sheeting — Determination of water vapour transmission rate
473			ISO 23559:2011, Plastics — Film and sheeting — Guidance on the testing of thermoplastic films
474			ISO 11963:2012, Plastics — Polycarbonate sheets — Types, dimensions and characteristics
475		材料技术标准	ISO 13636:2012, Plastics — Film and sheeting — Non-oriented poly (ethylene terephthalate) (PET) sheets
476			ISO 15987:2003, Plastics — Film and sheeting — Biaxially oriented polyamide (nylon) films

续表

序号	材料分类	标准类型	标准名称
477			ISO 15988：2003，Plastics — Film and sheeting — Biaxially oriented poly（ethylene terephthalate）（PET）films
478			ISO 15989：2004，Plastics — Film and sheeting — Measurement of water-contact angle of corona-treated films
479			ISO 17555：2003，Plastics — Film and sheeting — Biaxially oriented polypropylene（PP）films
480			ISO 17557：2003，Plastics — Film and sheeting — Cast polypropylene（PP）films
481		通用基础 标准	ISO 8096：2005, Rubber or plastics-coated fabrics for water-resistant clothing -Specification
482			ISO 1420：2001、ISO/NP 1420，Rubber or plastics-coated fabrics — Determination of resistance to penetration by water
483			ISO 2286：1998 系列标准，Rubber or plastics-coated fabrics — Determination of roll characteristics
484			ISO 22196：2011，Measurement of antibacterial activity on plastics and other non-porous surfaces
485			ISO 2411：2000，Rubber or plastics-coated fabrics — Determination of coating adhesion
486	高分子涂覆材料	测试方法标准	ISO 3303：2012 系列标准，Rubber or plastics-coated fabrics — Determination of bursting strength
487			ISO 4674-1：2003，Rubber or plastics-coated fabrics — Determination of tear resistance
488			ISO 4675：1990，Rubber or plastics-coated fabrics — Low-temperature bend test
489			ISO 5470-2：2003，Rubber or plastics-coated fabrics — Determination of abrasion resistance
490			ISO 5978：1990，Rubber or plastics-coated fabrics — Determination of blocking resistance
491			ISO 5979：1982，Rubber or plastics coated fabrics — Determination of flexibility — Flat loop method
492			ISO 6452：2007，Rubber or plastics-coated fabrics — Determination of fogging characteristics of trim materials in the interior of automobiles

续表

序号	材料分类	标准类型	标准名称
493			ISO 7617：1988 系列标准，Plastics-coated fabrics for upholstery
494			ISO 7854：1995，Rubber or plastics-coated fabrics — Determination of resistance to damage by flexing
495			ISO 15100：2000，Plastics — Reinforcement fibres — Chopped strands — Determination of bulk density
496			ISO 32100：2010，Rubber or plastics-coated fabrics — Physical and mechanical tests — Determination of flex resistance by the flexometer method
497	电镀高分子材料	应用技术标准	ISO 4525：2003，Metallic coatings — Electroplated coatings of nickel plus chromium on plastics materials
498			ISO 62：2008，Plastics — Determination of water absorption
499			ISO 15512：2008（DIS），Plastics — Determination of water content
500	吸附材料	测试方法标准	ISO 17191：2004，Urine-absorbing aids for incontinence — Measurement of airborne respirable polyacrylate superabsorbent materials — Determination of dust in collection cassettes by sodium atomic absorption spectrometry
501			ISO 10210：2012，Plastics — Methods for the preparation of samples for biodegradation testing of plastic materials
502			ISO 13975：2012，Plastics — Determination of the ultimate anaerobic biodegradation of plastic materials in controlled slurry digestion systems — Method by measurement of biogas production
503			ISO 14851：1999，Determination of the ultimate aerobic biodegradability of plastic materials in an aqueous medium — Method by measuring the oxygen demand in a closed respirometer
504	环境友好高分子材料	测试方法标准	ISO 14852：1999，Determination of the ultimate aerobic biodegradability of plastic materials in an aqueous medium — Method by analysis of evolved carbon dioxide
505			ISO 14853：2005，Plastics — Determination of the ultimate anaerobic biodegradation of plastic materials in an aqueous system — Method by measurement of biogas production
506			ISO 14855-1：2012，Determination of the ultimate aerobic biodegradability of plastic materials under controlled composting conditions — Method by analysis of evolved carbon dioxide — Part 1：General method

续表

序号	材料分类	标准类型	标准名称
507			ISO 14855-2：2007，Determination of the ultimate aerobic biodegradability of plastic materials under controlled composting conditions — Method by analysis of evolved carbon dioxide — Part 2：Gravimetric measurement of carbon dioxide evolved in a laboratory-scale test
508			ISO 15985：2004（FIDS），Plastics — Determination of the ultimate anaerobic biodegradation and disintegration under high-solids anaerobic-digestion conditions — Method by analysis of released biogas
509			ISO 16929：2013，Plastics — Determination of the degree of disintegration of plastic materials under defined composting conditions in a pilot-scale test
510			ISO 17088：2012，Specifications for compostable plastics
511			ISO 17556：2012，Plastics — Determination of the ultimate aerobic biodegradability of plastic materials in soil by measuring the oxygen demand in a respirometer or the amount of carbon dioxide evolved
512			ISO/CD 18830，Plastics — Test method for determining aerobic biodegradation of plastic materials sunk at the sea water/sandy sediment interface
513			ISO 20200：2004、ISO/DIS 20200，Plastics — Determination of the degree of disintegration of plastic materials under simulated composting conditions in a laboratory-scale test
514	生物医药高分子材料	测试方法标准	ISO 15814：1999，Implants for surgery — Copolymers and blends based on polylactide — In vitro degradation testing
515		材料技术标准	ISO 4049：2009，Dentistry — Polymer-based restorative materials
516			ISO 6876：2012，Dentistry — Root canal sealing materials
517			Positive control material
518			ISO 14233：2003，Dentistry — Polymer-based die materials
519		应用技术标准	ISO 6874：2005，Dentistry — Polymer-based pit and fissure sealants
520			ISO 7206：2011 系列标准，Implants for surgery — Partial and total hip joint prostheses
521			ISO 15309：2013，Implants for surgery — Differential scanning calorimetry of poly ether ether ketone（PEEK）polymers and compounds for use in implantable medical devices

续表

序号	材料分类	标准类型	标准名称
4. 特种精细化工材料			
522	涂料	通用基础标准	ISO 28199-1：2009，Paints and varnishes — Evaluation of properties of coating systems related to the application process
523		测试方法标准	ISO 1518：2011 系列标准，Paints and varnishes — Determination of scratch resistance
524			ISO 1519：2011，Paints and varnishes — Bend test (cylindrical mandrel)
525			ISO 1522：2006，Paints and varnishes — Pendulum damping test
526			ISO/WD 2178，Non-magnetic coatings on magnetic substrates — Measurement of coating thickness — Magnetic method
527			ISO 2812：2007 系列标准，Paints and varnishes — Determination of resistance to liquids
528			ISO 2815：2003，Paints and varnishes — Buchholz indentation test
529			ISO 6272 系列标准，Paints and varnishes Rapid-deformation (impact resistance) tests
530			ISO 9117-2010 系列标准，Paints and varnishes — Drying tests
531			ISO 12137：2011，Paints and varnishes — Determination of mar resistance
532			ISO 14188：2012，Metallic and other inorganic coatings — Test methods for measuring thermal cycle resistance and thermal shock resistance for thermal barrier coatings
533			ISO 14604：2012，Fine ceramics (advanced ceramics, advanced technical ceramics) — Methods of test for ceramic coatings — Determination of fracture strain
534			ISO 15091：2012，Paints and varnishes — Determination of electrical conductivity and resistance
535			ISO 15184：2012，Paints and varnishes — Determination of film hardness by pencil test
536			ISO 15711：2003，Paints and varnishes — Determination of resistance to cathodic disbonding of coatings exposed to sea water
537			ISO 15715：2003，Binders for paints and varnishes — Determination of turbidity

续表

序号	材料分类	标准类型	标准名称
538	涂料	材料技术标准	ISO 16862：2003，Paints and varnishes — Evaluation of sag resistance
539			ISO 16927，Paints and varnishes — Determination of the overcoatability and recoatability of a coating
540			ISO 2360：2003，Non-conductive coatings on non-magnetic electrically conductive basis materials — Measurement of coating thickness — Amplitude-sensitive eddy-current method
541			ISO 4628：2003 系列标准，Paints and varnishes — Evaluation of degradation of coatings — Designation of quantity and size of defects, and of intensity of uniform changes in appearance
542			ISO 6158：2011，Metallic and other inorganic coatings — Electrodeposited coatings of chromium for engineering purposes
543			ISO 7143：2007，Binders for paints and varnishes — Methods of test for characterizing water-based binders
544			ISO 9211：2012 系列标准，Optics and photonics — Optical coatings
545			ISO 9717：2010，Metallic and other inorganic coatings — Phosphate conversion coating of metals
546			ISO 10283：2007，Binders for paints and varnishes — Determination of monomeric diisocyanates in isocyanate resins
547			ISO/NP 14232 系列标准，Thermal spraying — Powders
548			ISO 16805：2003，Binders for paints and varnishes — Determination of glass transition temperature
549			ISO/NP 18468，Epoxy coating (heeavy duty) of ductile iron fittings and accessories — requirements and testing method
550			ISO 29601：2011 paints and varnishes — Corrosion protection by protective paint systems — Assessment of porosity in a dry film
551			ISO 9587：2007，Metallic and other inorganic coatings — Pretreatment of iron or steel to reduce the risk of hydrogen embrittlement
552			ISO/WD 10110 系列标准，Optics and photonics — Preparation of drawings for optical elements and systems
553			ISO 10890：2010，Paints and varnishes — Modelling of biocide release rate from antifouling paints by mass-balance calculation
554			ISO 14921：2010，Thermal spraying — Procedures for the application of thermally sprayed coatings for engineering components

续表

序号	材料分类	标准类型	标准名称
555	颜料	测试方法标准	ISO 787：2009 系列标准，General methods of test for pigments and extenders
556		材料技术标准	ISO 1248：2006，Iron oxide pigments — Specifications and methods of test
557	油墨	测试方法标准	ISO 22754：2008，Pulp and paper — Determination of the effective residual ink concentration (ERIC number) by infrared reflectance measurement
558			ISO/IEC 24711：2007，Method for the determination of ink cartridge yield for colour inkjet printers and multi-function devices that contain printer components
559			ISO 2836：2004，Graphic technology — Prints and printing inks — Assessment of resistance of prints to various agents
560		应用技术标准	ISO 2846：2007 系列标准，Graphic technology — Colour and transparency of printing ink sets for four-colour printing
561	电子信息用化学品	通用基础标准	ISO 1004：2013 系列标准，Information processing — Magnetic ink character recognition
562		测试方法标准	ISO 10505：2009，Photography — Root mean square granularity of photographic films — Method of measurement
563			ISO 18909：2006，Photography — Processed photographic colour films and paper prints — Methods for measuring image stability
564			ISO 18916：2007，Imaging materials — Processed imaging materials — Photographic activity test for enclosure materials
565			ISO 18924：2013，Imaging materials — Test method for Arrhenius-type predictions
566			ISO 18939：2013，Imaging materials — Digital hard copy for medical imaging — Methods of measuring
567		材料技术标准	ISO 18902：2013，Imaging materials — Processed imaging materials — Albums, framing and storage materials
568			ISO 18938：2008，Imaging materials — Optical discs — Care and handling for extended storage
569	各种添加剂	通用基础标准	ISO/CD 17296 系列标准，Additive manufacturing

续表

序号	材料分类	标准类型	标准名称
570	粘合剂	测试方法标准	ISO 25179：2010，Adhesives — Determination of the solubility of water-soluble or alkali-soluble pressure-sensitive adhesives
571			ISO 26842-2：2013，Adhesives — Test methods for the evaluation and selection of adhesives for indoor wood products
572		材料技术标准	ISO 17087：2006，Specifications for adhesives used for finger joints in non-structural lumber products
573			ISO 29862：2007，Self adhesive tapes — Determination of peel adhesion properties
574			ISO 29863：2007，Self adhesive tapes — Measurement of static shear adhesion
575	表面活性剂及合成洗涤剂	测试方法标准	ISO 2870：2009，Surface active agents — Detergents — Determination of anionic-active matter hydrolysable and non-hydrolysable under acid conditions
576			ISO 2871：2010 系列标准，Surface active agents — Detergents — Determination of cationic-active matter content
577			ISO 4317：2011，Surface-active agents and detergents — Determination of water content — Karl Fischer methods
578			ISO 8799：2009，Surface active agents — Sulfated ethoxylated alcohols and alkylphenols — Determination of content of unsulfated matter
579			ISO/DIS 16560，Surface active agents — Determination of polyethylene glycol content in nonionic ethoxylated surfactants — HPLC method
580			ISO/FDIS 17293 系列标准，Surface active agents — Determination of chloroacetic acid（chloroacetate）in surfactants
581			ISO/DIS 17280，Surface active agents — Determination of 1,4-dioxan residues in surfactants obtained from epoxyethane by gas chromatography
582	医药精细化工	材料技术标准	ISO/NP 13779 系列标准，Implants for surgery — Hydroxyapatite
583			ISO/WD 17327，Non-active surgical implants — Implant coating
584	造纸工业用精细化工	测试方法标准	ISO 16532-1：2008，Paper and board — Determination of grease resistance

续表

序号	材料分类	标准类型	标准名称
5. 前沿新型材料			
585	纳米材料	通用基础标准	ISO/TR 11360：2010，Nanotechnologies — Methodology for the classification and categorization of nanomaterials
586			ISO/TR 14786，Nanotechnologies — Considerations for the development of chemical nomenclature for selected nano-objects
587			IEC/NP TS 80004-2，Nanotechnologies — Vocabulary — Part 2：Nano-objects：Nanoparticle，nanofibre and nanoplate
588			ISO/TS 80004-3：2010，Nanotechnologies — Vocabulary — Part 3：Carbon nano-objects
589			ISO/TS 80004-4：2011，Nanotechnologies — Vocabulary — Part 4：Nanostructured materials
590			ISO/TS 80004-5：2011，Nanotechnologies — Vocabulary — Part 5：Nano/bio interface
591			ISO/TS 80004-6：2013，Nanotechnologies — Vocabulary — Part 6：Nano-object characterization
592			ISO/AWI TS 80004-9，Nanotechnologies — Vocabulary — Part 9：Nano-enabled electrotechnical products and systems
593			ISO/AWI TS 80004-10，Nanotechnologies — Vocabulary — Part 10：Nano-enabled photonic components and systems
594			ISO/TS 12805：2011，Nanotechnologies — Materials specifications — Guidance on specifying nano-objects
595			ISO/TS 13830：2013，Nanotechnologies — Guidance on voluntary labelling for consumer products containing manufactured nano-objects
596			ISO/TS 27687：2008，Nanotechnologies — Terminology and definitions for nano-objects — Nanoparticle，nanofibre and nanoplate
597		安全技术标准	ISO/TS 12025：2012，Nanomaterials — Quantification of nano-object release from powders by generation of aerosols
598			ISO/TS 12901-1：2012，Nanotechnologies — Occupational risk management applied to engineered nanomaterials — Part 1：Principles and approaches
599			ISO/AWI TR 18637，General framework for the development of occupational exposure limits for nano-objects and their aggregates and agglomerates

续表

序号	材料分类	标准类型	标准名称
600	纳米材料	测试方法标准	ISO/TR 11811：2012，Nanotechnologies — Guidance on methods for nano- and microtribology measurements
601			ISO/TS 16195：2013，Nanotechnologies — Guidance for developing representative test materials consisting of nano-objects in dry powder form
602			ISO/AWI TR 18196，Nanotechnologies — Measurement method matrix for nano-objects
603			ISO/AWI 19007，Modified MTS assay for measuring the effect of nanoparticles on cell viability
604			ISO/TR 27628：2007，Workplace atmospheres — Ultrafine, nanoparticle and nano-structured aerosols — Inhalation exposure characterization and assessment
605	热敏材料	材料技术标准	ISO 7240-8：2007，Fire detection and alarm systems — Part 8：Carbon monoxide fire detectors using an electro-chemical cell in combination with a heat sensor
606			ISO 7240-15：2004，Fire detection and alarm systems — Part 15：Point type fire detectors using scattered light, transmitted light or ionization sensors in combination with a heat sensor
607			ISO 7240-27：2009，Fire detection and alarm systems — Part 27：Point-type fire detectors using a scattered-light, transmitted-light or ionization smoke sensor, an electrochemical-cell carbon-monoxide sensor and a heat sens
608			ISO/TR 27957：2008，Road vehicles — Temperature measurement in anthropomorphic test devices — Definition of the temperature sensor locations
609	压敏材料	应用技术标准	ISO 13856 系列标准，Safety of machinery — Pressure-sensitive protective devices
610			ISO/DIS 15106-5，Plastics — Film and sheeting — Determination of water vapour transmission rate — Part 5：Presssure sensor method
611	光敏材料	应用技术标准	ISO 15106-2：2003，Plastics — Film and sheeting — Determination of water vapour transmission rate — Part 2：Infrared detection sensor method
612			ISO 16844-3：2004，Road vehicles — Tachograph systems — Part 3：Motion sensor interface

续表

序号	材料分类	标准类型	标准名称
613			ISO/FDIS 17289, Water quality — Determination of dissolved oxygen — Optical sensor method
614			ISO/TS 19130: 2010, Geographic information-Imagery sensor models for geopositioning
615			ISO/TS 19130-2: 2014, Geographic information — Imagery sensor models for geopositioning — Part 2: SAR, InSAR, lidar and sonar
616			ISO/DTS 19159-1, Geographic information — Calibration and validation of remote sensing imagery sensors and data — Part 1: Optical sensors
617			ISO/AWI 19159-2, Geographic information — Calibration and validation of remote sensing imagery sensors — Part 2: Lidar
618	气敏材料	应用技术标准	ISO 15106-4: 2008, Plastics — Film and sheeting — Determination of water vapour transmission rate — Part 4: Gas-chromatographic detection sensor method
619		通用基础标准	ISO 12716: 2001, Non-destructive testing — Acoustic emission inspection — Vocabulary
620		测试方法标准	ISO 5347-15: 1993, Methods for the calibration of vibration and shock pick-ups — Part 15: Testing of acoustic sensitivity
621	声敏材料		ISO 10817-1: 1998, Rotating shaft vibration measuring systems — Part 1: Relative and absolute sensing of radial vibration
622		应用技术标准	ISO 12713: 1998, Non-destructive testing — Acoustic emission inspection — Primary calibration of transducers
623			ISO 12714: 1999, Non-destructive testing — Acoustic emission inspection — Secondary calibration of acoustic emission sensors
624			ISO/NP 18081, Non-destructive testing — Leak detection and location using surface-mounted acoustic emission sensors
625	湿敏材料	应用技术标准	ISO 15106-1: 2003, Plastics — Film and sheeting — Determination of water vapour transmission rate — Part 1: Humidity detection sensor method
626	电磁波感应材料	应用技术标准	ISO/ASTM 51539: 2013, Guide for use of radiation-sensitive indicators

续表

序号	材料分类	标准类型	标准名称
627	其他智能材料	应用技术标准	ISO/DTR 17522，Health informatics — Provisions for Health Applications on Mobile/Smart Devices
628			ISO 22896：2006，Road vehicles — Deployment and sensor bus for occupant safety systems
629			ISO 28902-1：2012，Air quality — Environmental meteorology — Part 1：Ground-based remote sensing of visual range by lidar
630			ISO/WD 28902-2，Air quality — Environmental meteorology — Part 2：Ground-based remote sensing by Doppler wind lidar
631			ISO/IEC CD 29167 系列标准，Information technology — Automatic identification and data capture techniques
632	光电材料	安全技术标准	ISO/DIS 15004-2，Ophthalmic instruments — Fundamental requirements and test methods — Part 2：Light hazard protection
633			ISO/AWI TR 20824，Ophthalmic instruments — Background for light hazard specification in ophthalmic instrument standards
634		测试方法标准	ISO 2827：1988，Photography — Electronic flash equipment — Determination of light output and performance
635			ISO 11315-1：1997，Photography — Projection in indoor rooms — Part 1：Screen illumination test for still projectors
636			ISO 11315-2：1997，Photography — Projection in indoor rooms — Part 2：Screen luminance test for still and video projection
637			ISO 12608：1996，Cinematography — Room and surround conditions for evaluating television display from telecine reproduction
638		材料技术标准	ISO 2910：2007，Cinematography — Screen luminance and chrominance for the projection of motion pictures
639			ISO/DIS 6742-1，Cycles — Lighting and retro-reflective devices — Part 1：Lighting and light signalling devices
640			ISO 9236 系列标准，Photography — Sensitometry of screen/film systems for medical radiography
641			ISO 9241 系列标准，Ergonomic requirements for office work with visual display terminals（VDTs）
642			ISO/TR 9241-309：2008，Ergonomics of human-system interaction — Part 309：Organic light-emitting diode（OLED）displays

续表

序号	材料分类	标准类型	标准名称
643			ISO 14648-1：2001，Micrographics — Quality control of COM recorders that generate images using a single internal display system — Part 1：Characteristics of the software test target
644			ISO 14648-2：2001，Micrographics — Quality control of COM recorders that generate images using a single internal display system — Part 2：Method of use
645			ISO/IEC TR 15938-8：2002/Amd 3：2007，Technologies for digital photo management using MPEG-7 visual tools
646			ISO/NP 17321-4，Graphic technology and photography — Colour characterisation of digital still cameras（DSCs）— Part 4：LED（Light Emitting Diode）colour target
647			ISO/IEC 17417：2011，Information technology — Telecommunications and information exchange between systems — Short Distance Visible Light Communication（SDVLC）
648			ISO/IEC 23000-3：2007，Information technology — Multimedia application format（MPEG-A）— Part 3：MPEG photo player application format
649			ISO/IEC 24755：2007，Information technology — Screen icons and symbols for personal mobile communication devices
650			ISO 26431-1：2008，Digital cinema（D-cinema）quality — Part 1：Screen luminance level, chromaticity and uniformity
651		应用技术标准	ISO/TR 9819：1991，Road vehicles — Comparison tables of regulations on photometric requirements of light signalling devices
652			ISO/IEC CD 11693 系列标准，Identification cards — Optical memory cards
653			ISO/IEC DIS 11694 系列标准，Identification cards — Optical memory cards — Linear recording method
654			ISO/IEC DIS 11695 系列标准，Identification cards — Optical memory cards — Holographic recording method
655			ISO/NP 12234 系列标准，Electronic still picture imaging — Removable memory
656			ISO/IEC DIS 16480，Information technology — Automatic identification and data capture techniques — Reading and display of ORM by mobile devices
657			ISO/TS 17915：2013，Optics and photonics — Measurement method of semiconductor lasers for sensing

续表

序号	材料分类	标准类型	标准名称
658	新能源材料	通用基础标准	ISO/CD 1213 系列标准，Solid mineral fuels — Vocabulary
659			ISO 7876 系列标准，Fuel injection equipment — Vocabulary
660			ISO/CD 8216 系列标准，Petroleum products — Fuels (class F) classification
661			ISO 16793：2005，Nuclear fuel technology — Guide for ceramographic preparation of UO_2 sintered pellets for microstructure examination
662			IS O/DTS 18683，Guidelines for systems and installations for supply of LNG as fuel to ships
663		安全技术标准	ISO 11311：2011，Nuclear criticality safety — Critical values for homogeneous plutonium-uranium oxide fuel mixtures outside of reactors
664			ISO/NP 12807，Nuclear fuel technology — Safe transport of radioactive materials — Leakage testing on packages
665			ISO 14943：2004，Nuclear fuel technology — Administrative criteria related to nuclear criticality safety
666			ISO 23273：2013，Fuel cell road vehicles — Safety specifications — Protection against hydrogen hazards for vehicles fuelled with compressed hydrogen
667			ISO 27468：2011，Nuclear criticality safety — Evaluation of systems containing PWR UOX fuels — Bounding burnup credit approach
668		设备技术标准	ISO 2929 系列标准，Rubber hoses and hose assemblies for bulk fuel delivery by truck — Specification
669			ISO 5772：1998，Rubber and Plastic Hoses and Hose Assemblies for measured fuel dispensing systems
670			ISO 6184 系列标准，Explosion protection systems
671			ISO 7840：2013，Small craft — Fire-resistant fuel hosesMore
672			ISO 8469：2013，Small craft — Non-fire-resistant fuel hosesMore
673			ISO 10979：1994，Identification of fuel assemblies for nuclear power reactors
674			ISO 13591：1997，Small craft — Portable fuel systems for outboard motors

续表

序号	材料分类	标准类型	标准名称
675			ISO/CD 13948 系列标准, Diesel engines — Fuel injection pumps and fuel injector low-pressure connections
676			ISO 13985: 2006, Liquid hydrogen — Land vehicle fuel tanks
677			ISO/TS 15869: 2009, Gaseous hydrogen and hydrogen blends — Land vehicle fuel tanks
678			ISO 16110 系列标准, Hydrogen generators using fuel processing technologies
679			ISO/FDIS 16380, Road Vehicles — Blended Fuels Refuelling Connector
680			ISO 21847 系列标准, Nuclear fuel technology — Alpha spectrometry
681		测试方法标准	ISO 334: 2013, Solid mineral fuels — Determination of total sulfur — Eschka method
682			ISO 587: 1997, Solid mineral fuels — Determination of chlorine using Eschka mixture
683			ISO 609: 1996, Solid mineral fuels — Determination of carbon and hydrogen — High temperature combustion method
684			ISO 622: 1981, Solid mineral fuels — Determination of phorphorus content — Reduced molybdophosphate photometric method
685			ISO 625: 1996, Solid mineral fuels — Determination of carbon and hydrogen — Liebig method
686			ISO 687: 2010, Solid mineral fuels — Coke — Determination of moisture in the general analysis test sample
687			ISO 925: 1997, Solid mineral fuels — Determination of carbonate carbon content — Gravimetric method
688			ISO 1171: 2010, Solid mineral fuels — Determination of ash
689			ISO 1928: 2009, Solid mineral fuels — Determination of gross calorific value by the bomb calorimetric method and calculation of net calorific value
690			ISO 1952: 2008, Solid mineral fuels — Determination of extractable metals in dilute hydrochloric acid
691			ISO 3012: 1999, Petroleum products — Determination of thiol (mercaptan) sulfur in light and middle distillate fuels — Potentiometric method

续表

序号	材料分类	标准类型	标准名称
692			ISO 3013：1997，Petroleum products — Determination of the freezing point of aviation fuels
693			ISO 3648：1994，Aviation fuels — Estimation of net specific energy
694			ISO 3734：1997，Petroleum products — Determination of water and sediment in residual fuel oils — Centrifuge method
695			ISO 3735：1999，Crude petroleum and fuel oils — Determination of sediment — Extraction method
696			ISO 4264：2007，Petroleum products — Calculation of cetane index of middle-distillate fuels by the four-variable equation
697			ISO/FDIS 5163，Petroleum products — Determination of knock characteristics of motor and aviation fuels — Motor method
698			ISO 5164：2005，Petroleum products — Determination of knock characteristics of motor fuels — Research method
699			ISO 5165：1998，Petroleum products — Determination of the ignition quality of diesel fuels — Cetane engine method
700			ISO 6246：1995，Petroleum products — Gum content of light and middle distillate fuels — Jet evaporation method
701			ISO 6249：1999，Petroleum products — Determination of thermal oxidation stability of gas turbine fuels — JFTOT method
702			ISO 6250：1997，Petroleum products — Determination of the water reaction of aviation fuels
703			ISO 6297：1997，Petroleum products — Aviation and distillate fuels — Determination of electrical conductivity
704			ISO/DIS 6460 系列标准，Motorcycles — Measurement method for gaseous exhaust emissions and fuel consumption
705			ISO 7097 系列标准，Nuclear fuel technology — Determination of uranium in solutions, uranium hexafluoride and solids
706			ISO 7476：2003，Nuclear fuel technology — Determination of uranium in uranyl nitrate solutions of nuclear grade quality — Gravimetric method
707			ISO 8217：2012，Petroleum products — Fuels (class F) — Specifications of marine fuels

续表

序号	材料分类	标准类型	标准名称
708			ISO 8298：2000，Nuclear fuel technology — Determination of milligram amounts of plutonium in nitric acid solutions — Potentiometric titration with potassium dichromate after oxidation by Ce（IV）and reduction by Fe（II）
709			ISO 8299：2005，Nuclear fuel technology — Determination of the isotopic and elemental uranium and plutonium concentrations of nuclear materials in nitric acid solutions by thermal-ionization mass spectrometry
710			ISO 8300：2013，Nuclear fuel technology — Determination of plutonium content in plutonium dioxide of nuclear grade quality — Gravimetric method
711			ISO 8310：2012，Refrigerated hydrocarbon and non-petroleum based liquefied gaseous fuels — General requirements for automatic tank thermometers on board marine carriers and floating storage
712			ISO 8425：2013，Nuclear fuel technology — Determination of plutonium in pure plutonium nitrate solutions — Gravimetric method
713			ISO 8691：1994，Petroleum products — Low levels of vanadium in liquid fuels — Determination by flameless atomic absorption spectrometry after ashing
714			ISO 9159：1988，Road vehicles — Nozzle spouts for leaded gasoline and diesel fuel
715			ISO 9463：2009，Nuclear energy — Nuclear fuel technology — Determination of plutonium in nitric acid solutions by spectrophotometry
716			ISO 10307 系列标准，Petroleum products — Total sediment in residual fuel oils
717			ISO 10478：1994，Petroleum products — Determination of aluminium and silicon in fuel oils
718			ISO 10645：1992，Nuclear energy — Light water reactors — Calculation of the decay heat power in nuclear fuels
719			ISO 10712：1995，Water quality — Pseudomonas putida growth inhibition test（Pseudomonas cell multiplication inhibition test）
720			ISO 10981：2004，Nuclear fuel technology — Determination of uranium in reprocessing-plant dissolver solution — Liquid chromatography method

续表

序号	材料分类	标准类型	标准名称
721			ISO 11483:2005, Nuclear fuel technology — Preparation of plutonium sources and determination of 238Pu/239Pu isotope ratio by alpha spectrometry
722			ISO 11452-3:2001, Road vehicles — Component test methods for electrical disturbances from narrowband radiated electromagnetic energy — Part 3: Transverse electromagnetic mode (TEM) cell
723			ISO 11561:1999, Ageing of thermal insulation materials — Determination of the long-term change in thermal resistance of closed-cell plastics (accelerated laboratory test methods)
724			ISO 11722:2013, Solid mineral fuels — Hard coal — Determination of moisture in the general analysis test sample by drying in nitrogen
725			ISO 11723:2004, Solid mineral fuels — Determination of arsenic and selenium — Eschka's mixture and hydride generation method
726			ISO 11724:2004, Solid mineral fuels — Determination of total fluorine in coal, coke and fly ash
727			ISO 11726:2004, Solid mineral fuels — Guidelines for the validation of alternative methods of analysis
728			ISO/TR 11954:2008, Fuel cell road vehicles — Maximum speed measurement
729			ISO 12156 系列标准, Diesel fuel — Assessment of lubricity using the high-frequency reciprocating rig (HFRR)
730			ISO 12205:1995, Petroleum products — Determination of the oxidation stability of middle-distillate fuels
731			ISO 12405 系列标准, Electrically propelled road vehicles — Test specification for lithium-ion traction battery packs and systems
732			ISO 12795:2004, Nuclear fuel technology — Uranium dioxide powder and pellets — Determination of uranium and oxygen/uranium ratio by gravimetric method with impurity correction
733			ISO 12800:2003, Nuclear fuel technology — Guide to the measurement of the specific surface area of uranium oxide powders by the BET method
734			ISO 12819:2009, Methods of evaluation of the battery life of a battery-powered watch

续表

序号	材料分类	标准类型	标准名称
735			ISO 13465：2009，Nuclear energy — Nuclear fuel technology — Determination of neptunium in nitric acid solutions by spectrophotometry
736			ISO 13759：1996，Petroleum products — Determination of alkyl nitrate in diesel fuels — Spectrometric method
737			ISO 14180：1998，Solid mineral fuels — Guidance on the sampling of coal seams
738			ISO 15167：1999，Petroleum products — Determination of particulate content of middle distillate fuels — Laboratory filtration method
739			ISO 15237：2003，Solid mineral fuels — Determination of total mercury content of coal
740			ISO 15238：2003，Solid mineral fuels — Determination of total cadmium content of coal
741			ISO 15239：2005，Solid mineral fuels — Evaluation of the measurement performance of on-line analysers
742			ISO 15387：2005，Space systems — Single-junction solar cells — Measurements and calibration procedures
743			ISO 15911：2000，Petroleum products — Estimation of net specific energy of aviation turbine fuels using hydrogen content data
744			ISO 16384：2012，Refrigerated hydrocarbon and non-petroleum based liquefied gaseous fuels — Dimethylether (DME) — Measurement and calculation on board ships
745			ISO 16424：2012，Nuclear energy — Evaluation of homogeneity of Gd distribution within gadolinium fuel blends and determination of Gd_2O_3 content in gadolinium fuel pellets by measurements of uranium and gadolinium elements
746			ISO 16795：2004，Nuclear energy — Determination of Gd_2O_3 content of gadolinium fuel pellets by X-ray fluorescence spectrometry
747			ISO 16796：2004，Nuclear energy — Determination of Gd_2O_3 content in gadolinium fuel blends and gadolinium fuel pellets by atomic emission spectrometry using an inductively coupled plasma source (ICP-AES)
748			ISO/FDIS 16861，Petroleum products — Fuels (class F) — Specifications of Dimethylether (DME)

续表

序号	材料分类	标准类型	标准名称
749			ISO 16966：2013，Nuclear energy — Nuclear fuel technology — Theoretical activation calculation method to evaluate the radioactivity of activated waste generated at nuclear reactors
750			ISO/FDIS 17196，Dimethyl ether（DME）for fuels — Determination of impurities — Gas chromatographic method
751			ISO/FDIS 17197，Dimethyl ether（DME）for fuels — Determination of water content — Karl Fischer titration method
752			ISO/FDIS 17198，Dimethyl ether（DME）for fuels — Determination of total sulfur, ultraviolet fluorescence method
753			ISO/FDIS 17786，Dimethyl ether（DME）for fuels — Determination of evaporation residues — Mass analysis method
754			ISO/CD 17827 系列标准，Solid Biofuels — Determination of particle size distribution for uncompressed fuels
755			ISO/CD 18300，Electrically propelled road vehicles — Specifications for lithium-ion cell and battery coupled with other types of battery and capacitor
756			ISO/DTS 18806，Solid mineral fuels — Determination of Chlorine content
757			ISO/NP 19090，Tissue-engineered medical products — Bioactive ceramics — Cell migration ability test for porous body
758			ISO 19579：2006，Solid mineral fuels — Determination of sulfur by IR spectrometry
759			ISO 20846：2011，Petroleum products — Determination of sulfur content of automotive fuels — Ultraviolet fluorescence method
760			ISO 20847：2004，Petroleum products — Determination of sulfur content of automotive fuels — Energy-dispersive X-ray fluorescence spectrometry
761			ISO 20884：2011，Petroleum products — Determination of sulfur content of automotive fuels — Wavelength-dispersive X-ray fluorescence spectrometry
762			ISO 21238：2007，Nuclear energy — Nuclear fuel technology — Scaling factor method to determine the radioactivity of low- and intermediate-level radioactive waste packages generated at nuclear power plants

续表

序号	材料分类	标准类型	标准名称
763			ISO 21483：2013，Determination of solubility in nitric acid of plutonium in unirradiated mixed oxide fuel pellets (U, Pu) O_2
764			ISO 21484：2008，Nuclear fuel technology — Determination of the O/M ratio in MOX pellets — Gravimetric method
765			ISO 22854 系列标准，Liquid petroleum products — Determination of hydrocarbon types and oxygenates in automotive-motor gasoline and in ethanol (E85) automotive fuel — Multidimensional gas chromatography method
766			ISO 23038：2006，Space systems — Space solar cells — Electron and proton irradiation test methods
767			ISO 23274 系列标准，Hybrid-electric road vehicles — Exhaust emissions and fuel consumption measurements
768			ISO 23828：2013，Fuel cell road vehicles — Energy consumption measurement — Vehicles fuelled with compressed hydrogen
769			ISO 26062：2010，Nuclear technology — Nuclear fuels — Procedures for the measurement of elemental impurities in uranium and plutonium-based materials by inductively coupled plasma mass spectrometry
770			ISO 29541：2010，Solid mineral fuels — Determination of total carbon, hydrogen and nitrogen content — Instrumental method
771			ISO 29945：2009，Refrigerated non-petroleum-based liquefied gaseous fuels — Dimethylether (DME) — Method of manual sampling onshore terminals
772		材料技术标准	ISO 1044：1993，Industrial trucks — Lead-acid traction batteries for electric trucks — Preferred voltages
773			ISO 4261：2013，Petroleum products — Fuels (class F) — Specifications of gas turbine fuels for industrial and marine applications
774			ISO/CD 8217，Petroleum products — Fuels (class F) — Specifications of marine fuels
775			ISO 9162：2013，Petroleum products — Fuels (class F) — Liquefied petroleum gases — Specifications
776			ISO 10276：2010，Nuclear energy — Fuel technology — Trunnions for packages used to transport radioactive material

续表

序号	材料分类	标准类型	标准名称
777			ISO 12183：2005，Nuclear fuel technology — Controlled-potential coulometric assay of plutonium
778			ISO/DIS 12749-3，Nuclear energy, nuclear technologie and radiological protection — Vocabulary — Part 3：Nuclear fuel cycle
779			ISO 13064 系列标准，Battery-electric mopeds and motorcycles — Performance
780			ISO 13463：1999，Nuclear-grade plutonium dioxide powder for fabrication of light water reactor MOX fuel — Guidelines to help in the definition of a product specification
781			ISO/TS 13605：2012，Solid mineral fuels — Major and minor elements in hard coal ash and coke ash — Wavelength dispersive X-ray fluorescence spectrometric method
782			ISO 14687-1：1999，Hydrogen fuel — Product specification — Part 1：All applications except proton exchange membrane (PEM) fuel cell for road vehicles
783			ISO 14687-2：2012，Hydrogen fuel — Product specification — Part 2：Proton exchange membrane (PEM) fuel cell applications for road vehicles
784			ISO 14687-3：2014，Hydrogen fuel — Product specification — Part 3：Proton exchange membrane (PEM) fuel cell applications for stationary appliances
785			ISO/FDIS 15366 系列标准，Nuclear fuel technology — Chemical separation and purification of uranium and plutonium in nitric acid solutions for isotopic and isotopic dilution analysis by solvent extraction chromatography
786			ISO/TR 15403 系列标准，Natural gas - Natural gas for use as a compressed fuel for vehicles
787			ISO/IEC PAS 16898：2012，Electrically propelled road vehicles — Dimensions and designation of secondary lithium-ion cells
788			ISO/FDIS 17225 系列标准，Solid biofuels — Fuel specifications and classes
789			ISO/CD 17546，Space systems — Lithium ion battery for space vehicles — Design and verification requirements

续表

序号	材料分类	标准类型	标准名称
790			ISO/CD 17588, Solid biofuels — Fuel quality assurance
791			ISO 18132 系列标准, Refrigerated hydrocarbon and non-petroleum based liquefied gaseous fuels — General requirements for automatic tank gauges
792			ISO/CD 18243, Electrically propelled mopeds and motorcycles — Specifications and safety requirements for lithium-ion traction battery systems
793			ISO/CD 18300, Electrically propelled road vehicles — Specifications for lithium-ion cell and battery coupled with other types of battery and capacitor
794			ISO/CD 19013 系列标准, Rubber hoses and tubing for fuel circuits for internal combustion engines — Specification
795		应用技术标准	ISO 6855 系列标准, Mopeds — Measurement method for gaseous exhaust emissions and fuel consumption
796			ISO/CD 7240-8, Fire detection and alarm systems — Part 8: Carbon monoxide fire detectors using an electro-chemical cell in combination with a heat sensor
797			ISO 7176-25: 2013, Wheelchairs — Part 25: Batteries and chargers for powered wheelchairs
798			ISO 10088: 2013, Small craft — Permanently installed fuel systems
799			ISO/FDIS 12614 系列标准, Road vehicles — Liquefied natural gas (LNG) fuel system components
800			SO/FDIS 12619 系列标准, Road vehicles — Compressed gaseous hydrogen (CGH2) and hydrogen/natural gas blend fuel system components
801			ISO/WD 15500 系列标准, Road vehicles — Compressed natural gas (CNG) fuel system components
802			ISO 15501 系列标准, Road vehicles — Compressed natural gas (CNG) fuel systems
803			ISO 23274 系列标准, Hybrid-electric road vehicles — Exhaust emissions and fuel consumption measurements

附录2 IEC 标准列表

序号	材料分类	标准类型	标准名称
1. 先进金属材料			
1	黑金属及合金材料	测试方法标准	IEC 60311, Electric irons for household or similar use — Methods for measuring performance
2			IEC/TR 62581, Electrical steel — Methods of measurement of the magnetostriction characteristics by means of single sheet and Epstein test specimens
3		材料技术标准	IEC 60329, Strip-wound cut cores of grain oriented silicon-iron alloy, used for electronic and telecommunication equipment
4			IEC 60335-2-3, Household and similar electrical appliances — Safety — Part 2-3: Particular requirements for electric irons
5			IEC 60335-2-44, Household and similar electrical appliances — Safety — Part 2-44: Particular requirements for ironers
6			IEC 60404-1-1, Magnetic materials — Part 1-1: Classification — Surface insulations of electrical steel sheet, strip and laminations
7			IEC 60404-2, Magnetic materials — Part 2: Methods of measurement of the magnetic properties of electrical steel strip and sheet by means of an Epstein frame
8			IEC 60404-3, Magnetic materials — Part 3: Methods of measurement of the magnetic properties of electrical steel strip and sheet by means of a single sheet tester
9			IEC 60404-4, Amendment 2 — Magnetic materials — Part 4: Methods of measurement of d. c. magnetic properties of magnetically soft materials
10			IEC 60404-8-3, Magnetic materials — Part 8-3: Specifications for individual materials — Cold-rolled electrical non-alloyed and alloyed steel sheet and strip delivered in the semi-processed state

续表

序号	材料分类	标准类型	标准名称
11			IEC 60404-8-4, Magnetic materials — Part 8-4: Specifications for individual materials — Cold-rolled non-oriented electrical steel strip and sheet delivered in the fully-processed state
12			IEC 60404-8-5, Magnetic materials — Part 8: Specifications for individual materials — Section Five: Specification for steel sheet and strip with specified mechanical properties and magnetic permeability
13			IEC 60404-8-6, Magnetic materials — Part 8-6: Specifications for individual materials — Soft magnetic metallic materials
14			IEC 60404-8-7, Magnetic materials — Part 8-7: Specifications for individual materials — Cold-rolled grain-oriented electrical steel strip and sheet delivered in the fully-processed state
15			IEC 60404-8-8, Magnetic materials — Part 8: Specifications for individual materials — Section 8: Specification for thin magnetic steel strip for use at medium frequencies
16			IEC 60404-9, Magnetic materials — Part 9: Methods of determination of the geometrical characteristics of magnetic steel sheet and strip
17			IEC 60404-8-10, Magnetic materials — Part 8-10: Specifications for individual materials — Magnetic materials (iron and steel) for use in relays
18			IEC 60404-13, Magnetic materials — Part 13: Methods of measurement of density, resistivity and stacking factor of electrical steel sheet and strip
19			IEC 60888, Zinc-coated steel wires for stranded conductors
20			IEC 60981, Extra heavy-duty electrical rigid steel conduits
21			IEC 61232, Aluminium-clad steel wires for electrical purposes
22			IEC 61394, Overhead lines — Requirements for greases for aluminium, aluminium alloy and steel bare conductors
23			IEC 61950, Cable management systems — Specifications for conduit fittings and accessories for cable installations for extra heavy duty electrical steel conduit

续表

序号	材料分类	标准类型	标准名称
24	有色金属及合金材料	测试方法标准	IEC 61189-11, Test methods for electrical materials, printed boards and other interconnection structures and assemblies — Part 11: Measurement of melting temperature or melting temperature ranges of solder alloys
25	有色金属及合金材料	测试方法标准	IEC 62739-1, Test method for erosion of wave soldering equipment using molten lead-free solder alloy — Part 1: Erosion test method for metal materials without surface processing
26	有色金属及合金材料	材料技术标准	IEC 60104, Aluminium-magnesium-silicon alloy wire for overhead line conductors
27	有色金属及合金材料	材料技术标准	IEC 60114, Recommendation for heat-treated aluminium alloy bus-bar material of the aluminium-magnesium-silicon type
28	有色金属及合金材料	材料技术标准	IEC 61190-1-3, Attachment materials for electronic assembly — Part 1-3: Requirements for electronic grade solder alloys and fluxed and non-fluxed solid solders for electronic soldering applications
29	有色金属及合金材料	材料技术标准	IEC 61394, Overhead lines — Requirements for greases for aluminium, aluminium alloy and steel bare conductors
30	有色金属及合金材料	材料技术标准	IEC 61755-3-5, Fibre optic connector optical interfaces — Part 3-5: Optical interface — 2.5 mm and 1.25 mm diameter cylindrical PC composite ferrule using Cu-Ni-alloy as fibre surrounding material, single mode fibre
31	有色金属及合金材料	材料技术标准	IEC 61755-3-6, Fibre optic connector optical interfaces — Part 3-6: Optical interface — 2.5 mm and 1.25 mm diameter cylindrical 8 degrees angled-PC composite ferrule using Cu-Ni-alloy as fibre surrounding material, single mode fibre
32	有色金属及合金材料	材料技术标准	IEC 61755-3-7, Fibre optic interconnecting devices and passive components — Fibre optic connector optical interfaces — Part 3-7: Optical interface, 2.5 mm and 1.25 mm diameter cylindrical PC composite ferrule using titanium as fibre surrounding material, single mode fibre
33	有色金属及合金材料	材料技术标准	IEC 61755-3-8, Fibre optic interconnecting devices and passive components — Fibre optic connector optical interfaces — Part 3-8: Optical interface, 2.5 mm and 1.25 mm diameter cylindrical 8 degrees angled-APC composite ferrule using titanium as fibre surrounding material, single mode fibre
34	有色金属及合金材料	材料技术标准	IEC 62004, Thermal-resistant aluminium alloy wire for overhead line conductor

续表

序号	材料分类	标准类型	标准名称
35	稀有金属及合金材料	材料技术标准	IEC 60973, Test procedures for germanium gamma-ray detectors
36			IEC 61275, Radiation protection instrumentation — Measurement of discrete radionuclides in the environment — In situ photon spectrometry system using a germanium detector
37			IEC 61435, Nuclear instrumentation — High-purity germanium crystals for radiation detectors — Measurement methods of basic characteristics
38			IEC 61452, Nuclear instrumentation — Measurement of gamma-ray emission rates of radionuclides — Calibration and use of germanium spectrometers
39			IEC 61788-3, Superconductivity — Part 3: Critical current measurement — DC critical current of Ag⁻ and/or Ag alloy-sheathed Bi-2212 and Bi-2223 oxide superconductors
40			IEC 61788-18, Superconductivity — Part 18: Mechanical properties measurement — Room temperature tensile test of Ag⁻ and/or Ag alloy-sheathed Bi-2223 and Bi-2212 composite superconductors
41			IEC 62483, Environmental acceptance requirements for tin whisker susceptibility of tin and tin alloy surface finishes on semiconductor devices
42	稀土金属及合金材料	测试方法标准	IEC/TR 62518, Rare earth sintered magnets — Stability of the magnetic properties at elevated temperatures
43	功能金属材料	材料技术标准	IEC 61249-5-1-1995, Materials for interconnection structures — Part 5: Sectional specification set for conductive foils and films with and without coatings — Section 1: Copper foils for the manufacture of copper-clad
44			IEC 61249-8-7-1996, Materials for interconnection structures — Part 8: Sectional specification set for non-conductive films and coatings — Section 7: Marking legend inks
45			IEC 61249-8-8-1997, Materials for interconnection structures — Part 8: Sectional specification set for non-conductive films and coatings — Section 8: Temporary polymer coatings

续表

序号	材料分类	标准类型	标准名称
2. 新型无机非金属材料			
46	新型陶瓷材料	测试方法标准	IEC 60168, Tests on indoor and outdoor post insulators of ceramic material or glass for systems with nominal voltages greater than 1000 V
47			IEC 60507, Artificial pollution tests on high-voltage ceramic and glass insulators to be used on a. c. systems
48		材料技术标准	IEC 60642（系列标准）, Piezoelectric ceramic resonators and resonator units for frequency control and selection
49			IEC 60672（系列标准）, Ceramic and glass insulating materials
50			IEC 61253-1（系列标准）, Piezoelectric ceramic resonators — A specification in the IEC quality assessment system for electronic components（IECQ）
51			IEC 61261-1, Piezoelectric ceramic filters for use in electronic equipment — A specification in the IEC quality assessment system for electronic components（IECQ）
52			IEC 61837-2, Surface mounted piezoelectric devices for frequency control and selection — Standard outlines and terminal lead connections — Part 2: Ceramic enclosures
53			IEC/TS 61994-4-2, Piezoelectric, dielectric and electrostatic devices and associated materials for frequency control, selection and detection — Glossary — Part 4-2: Piezoelectric and dielectric materials - Piezoelectric ceramics
54			IEC/TS 62371, Characteristics of hollow pressurised and unpressurised ceramic and glass insulators for use in electrical equipment with rated voltages greater than 1000 V
55	新型玻璃材料	材料技术标准	IEC 60317-0-5, Specifications for particular types of winding wires
56			IEC 61212-1, Insulating materials — Industrial rigid round laminated tubes and rods based on thermosetting resins for electrical purposes — Part 1: Definitions, designations and general requirements
57			IEC 61249-2-5（系列标准）, Materials for printed boards and other interconnecting structures
58			IEC 61331-2, Protective devices against diagnostic medical X-radiation — Part 2: Protective glass plates

续表

序号	材料分类	标准类型	标准名称
59	新型无机纤维	材料技术标准	IEC 60394（系列标准），Varnished fabrics for electrical purposes
60			IEC 60554（系列标准），Specification for cellulosic papers for electrical purposes
61			IEC 60667-1（系列标准），Specification for vulcanized fibre for electrical purposes
62			IEC 61067-1（系列标准），Specification for glass and glass polyester fibre woven tapes
63			IEC 61068-1（系列标准），Specification for polyester fibre woven tapes
64	抗震材料	测试方法标准	IEC 60068-3-3，Environmental testing — Part 3：Guidance. Seismic test methods for equipment
65			IEC 60255-21-3，Electrical relays — Part 21：Vibration, shock, bump and seismic tests on measuring relays and protection equipment — Section 3：Seismic tests
66			IEC 61587-2，Mechanical structures for electronic equipment — Tests for IEC 60917 and 60297 — Part 2：Seismic tests for cabinets and racks
67			IEC 61587-5，Mechanical structures for electronic equipment — Tests for IEC 60917 and IEC 60297 — Part 5：Seismic tests for chassis, subracks and plug-in units
68		材料技术标准	IEC/TS 61463，Bushings — Seismic qualification
69			IEC 62271-207，High-voltage switchgear and controlgear — Part 207：Seismic qualification for gas-insulated switchgear assemblies for rated voltages above 52 kV
70			IEC/TS 62271-210，High-voltage switchgear and controlgear — Part 210：Seismic qualification for metal enclosed and solid-insulation enclosed switchgear and controlgear assemblies for rated voltages above 1 kV and up to and including 52 kV
71			IEC/TR 62271-300，High-voltage switchgear and controlgear — Part 300：Seismic qualification of alternating current circuit-breakers
72		应用技术标准	IEC 60297-3-105（系列标准），Mechanical structures for electronic equipment — Dimensions of mechanical structures of the 482.6 mm (19 in) series — Part 3-105：Dimensions and design aspects for 1U high chassis

续表

序号	材料分类	标准类型	标准名称
73	电学材料	通用基础标准	IEC 60050-111（系列标准），International Electrotechnical Vocabulary
74			IEC 60073，Basic and safety principles for man-machine interface，marking and identification — Coding principles for indicators and actuators
75			IEC/TR 61200-704（系列标准），Electrical installation guide
76			IEC 80000-14，Quantities and units — Part 14：Telebiometrics related to human physiology
77		安全技术标准	IEC 60204-SER（系列标准），Safety of machinery — Electrical equipment of machines — ALL PARTS
78			IEC/TR 60513，Fundamental aspects of safety standards for medical electrical equipment
79			IEC 60519（系列标准），Safety in electroheating installations
80			IEC 60745（系列标准），Hand-held motor-operated electric tools — Safety
81			IEC 60950（系列标准），Information technology equipment — Safety
82			IEC 62115，Electric toys — Safety
83			IEC 62485-2，Safety requirements for secondary batteries and battery installations
84		测试方法标准	IEC 60068（系列标准），Environmental testing
85			IEC 60331（系列标准），Tests for electric cables under fire conditions — Circuit integrity
86			IEC 60332（系列标准），Tests on electric and optical fibre cables under fire conditions
87			IEC 60512（系列标准），Connectors for electronic equipment — Tests and measurements
88			IEC 60695（系列标准），Fire hazard testing
89			IEC 61034-1（系列标准），Measurement of smoke density of cables burning under defined conditions
90			IEC/TS 62073，Guidance on the measurement of wettability of insulator surfaces

续表

序号	材料分类	标准类型	标准名称
91		材料技术标准	IEC 60055-1, Paper-insulated metal-sheathed cables for rated voltages up to 18/30 kV (with copper or aluminium conductors and excluding gas-pressure and oil-filled cables)
92			IEC 60191(系列标准), Mechanical standardization of semiconductor devices
93			IEC 60216(系列标准), Electrical insulating materials — Thermal endurance properties
94			IEC 60305, Insulators for overhead lines with a nominal voltage above 1000 V — Ceramic or glass insulator units for a. c. systems — Characteristics of insulator units of the cap and pin type
95			IEC 60368-2-2, Piezoelectric filters — Part 2: Guide to the use of piezoelectric filters — Section 2: Piezoelectric ceramic filters
96			IEC 60371-3-7(系列标准), Insulating materials based on mica
97			IEC 60383-1(系列标准), Insulators for overhead lines with a nominal voltage above 1000 V
98			IEC 60384-8(系列标准), Fixed capacitors for use in electronic equipment
99			IEC 60404-14(系列标准), Magnetic materials
100			IEC 60433, Insulators for overhead lines with a nominal voltage above 1000 V — Ceramic insulators for a. c. systems — Characteristics of insulator units of the long rod type
101			IEC 60584-1(系列标准), Thermocouples
102			IEC 60684-3-165(系列标准), Flexible insulating sleeving
103			IEC 60747(系列标准), Discrete semiconductor devices and integrated circuits
104			IEC 60819(系列标准), Non-cellulosic papers for electrical purposes
105			IEC 60836, Specifications for unused silicone insulating liquids for electrotechnical purposes
106			IEC 61000(系列标准), TC/SC CIS/H Electromagnetic compatibility (EMC)
107			IEC 61086-1(系列标准), Coatings for loaded printed wire boards (conformal coatings)

续表

序号	材料分类	标准类型	标准名称
108			IEC 61229，Rigid protective covers for live working on a. c. installations
109			IEC 61249（系列标准），Materials for printed boards and other interconnecting structures
110			IEC 61621，Dry, solid insulating materials — Resistance test to high-voltage, low-current arc discharges
111			IEC 61747（系列标准），Liquid crystal display devices
112			IEC 62276，Single crystal wafers for surface acoustic wave（SAW）device applications — Specifications and measuring methods
113			IEC/TS 62282（系列标准），Fuel cell technologies
114			IEC 62541-4，OPC unified architecture
115		应用技术标准	IEC 60092-353，Electrical installations in ships
116			IEC 60364（系列标准），Low-voltage electrical installations
117			IEC 60730（系列标准）Automatic electrical controls
118			IEC 62219，Overhead electrical conductors — Formed wire, concentric lay, stranded conductors
119		通用基础标准	IEC/TR 61282-3，Fibre optic communication system design guides
120			IEC/TR 61930，Fibre optic graphical symbology
121			IEC 62005-1，Reliability of fibre optic interconnecting devices and passive components
122			IEC/TR 62721，Reliability of devices used in fibre optic systems — General and guidance
123	光学材料	安全技术标准	IEC 62305-1（系列标准），Protection against lightning
124			IEC/TR 62471-2（系列标准），Photobiological safety of lamps and lamp systems
125		测试方法标准	IEC 60811-100（系列标准），Electric and optical fibre cables — Test methods for non-metallic materials
126			IEC 61280-1-1（系列标准），Fibre optic communication subsystem basic test procedures
127			IEC 61290-1-1（系列标准），Optical amplifiers — Test methods
128			IEC 61744，Calibration of fibre optic chromatic dispersion test sets

续表

序号	材料分类	标准类型	标准名称
129			IEC 61745, End-face image analysis procedure for the calibration of optical fibre geometry test sets
130			IEC/TR 62221, Optical fibres — Measurement methods — Micro-bending sensitivity
131			IEC/TR 62284, Effective area measurements of single-mode optical fibres — Guidance
132			IEC/TR 62324, Single-mode optical fibres — Raman gain efficiency measurement using continuous wave method — Guidance
133			IEC/TR 62349, Guidance for polarization crosstalk measurement of optical fibre
134			IEC/TR 62469, Guidance for residual stress measurement of optical fibre
135			IEC 60793-1-21, Optical fibres
136			IEC 60794-1-1（系列标准）, Optical fibre cables
137			IEC 60869-1（系列标准）, Fibre optic interconnecting devices and passive components — Fibre optic passive power control devices
138			IEC 60874-14-1（系列标准）, Connectors for optical fibres and cables
139			IEC 61274-1-1（系列标准）, Fibre optic interconnecting devices and passive components — Adaptors for fibre optic connectors
140			IEC 61281-1, Fibre optic communication subsystems
141		材料技术标准	IEC 61290-6-1（系列标准）, Optical fibre amplifiers — Basic specification
142			IEC 61291-1（系列标准）, Optical amplifiers
143			IEC 61754-2（系列标准）, Fibre optic connector interfaces
144			IEC 61757-1（系列标准）, Fibre optic sensors
145			IEC 62007-1, Semiconductor optoelectronic devices for fibre optic system applications
146			IEC/TS 62033, Attenuation uniformity in optical fibres
147			IEC/TR 62048, Optical fibres — Reliability — Power law theory
148			IEC 62386-101（系列标准）, Digital addressable lighting interface

续表

序号	材料分类	标准类型	标准名称
149			IEC 62561-1（系列标准），Lightning protection system components（LPSC）
150			IEC/TS 62661-2-1（系列标准），Optical backplanes — Product specification
151			IEC/PAS 62717，LED modules for general lighting — Performance requirements
152			IEC/PAS 62722-1（系列标准），Luminaire performance
153			IEC 61300-2-51（系列标准），Fibre optic interconnecting devices and passive components — Basic test and measurement procedures
154			IEC 61314-1（系列标准），Fibre optic interconnecting devices and passive components — Fibre optic fan-outs
155			IEC 61315，Calibration of fibre-optic power meters
156			IEC 61746-1（系列标准），Calibration of optical time-domain reflectometers
157			IEC 61753-1（系列标准）Fibre optic interconnecting devices and passive components performance standard
158		应用技术标准	IEC/TR 62000，Guidance for combining different single-mode fibres types
159			IEC 62074-1，Fibre optic interconnecting devices and passive components — Fibre optic WDM devices
160			IEC 62077，Fibre optic interconnecting devices and passive components — Fibre optic circulators — Generic specification
161			IEC 62099，Fibre optic wavelength switches — Generic specification
162			IEC 62134-1（系列标准），Fibre optic interconnecting devices and passive components — Fibre optic closures
163			IEC 62148-1（系列标准），Fibre optic active components and devices — Package and interface standards
164			IEC/TR 62572-2，Fibre optic active components and devices — Reliability standards
165			IEC 62664-1-1（系列标准），Fibre optic interconnecting devices and passive components — Fibre optic connector product specifications
166			IEC/TR 62785，Guidance on the environmentally conscious design of fibre optics related products and subsystems

续表

序号	材料分类	标准类型	标准名称
167	太阳能产业用材料	通用基础标准	IEC/TS 61836, Solar photovoltaic energy systems — Terms, definitions and symbols
168		安全技术标准	IEC 61730 (系列标准), Photovoltaic (PV) module safety qualification
169			IEC 62109-1 (系列标准), Safety of power converters for use in photovoltaic power systems
170		测试方法标准	IEC 61345, UV test for photovoltaic (PV) modules
171			IEC 61683, Photovoltaic systems — Power conditioners — Procedure for measuring efficiency
172			IEC 61701, Salt mist corrosion testing of photovoltaic (PV) modules
173			IEC 61702, Rating of direct coupled photovoltaic (PV) pumping systems
174			IEC 61724, Photovoltaic system performance monitoring — Guidelines for measurement, data exchange and analysis
175			IEC 61829, Crystalline silicon photovoltaic (PV) array — On-site measurement of I-V characteristics
176			IEC 61853-1, Photovoltaic (PV) module performance testing and energy rating
177			IEC 62116, Test procedure of islanding prevention measures for utility-interconnected photovoltaic inverters
178			IEC 62716, Photovoltaic (PV) modules — Ammonia corrosion testing
179		材料技术标准	IEC 60904 (系列标准), Photovoltaic devices
180			IEC 61249-5-1 (系列标准), Materials for interconnection structures
181			IEC 61727, Photovoltaic (PV) systems — Characteristics of the utility interface
182			IEC 62116, Utility-interconnected photovoltaic inverters
183			IEC/TS 62600-100 (系列标准), Marine energy — Wave, tidal and other water current converter
184			IEC/TS 62727, Photovoltaic systems — Specification for solar trackers

续表

序号	材料分类	标准类型	标准名称
185		应用技术标准	IEC 61215, Crystalline silicon terrestrial photovoltaic (PV) modules — Design qualification and type approval
186			IEC 61646, Thin-film terrestrial photovoltaic (PV) modules — Design qualification and type approval
187			IEC 62093, Balance-of-system components for photovoltaic systems — Design qualification natural environments
188			IEC 62108, Concentrator photovoltaic (CPV) modules and assemblies — Design qualification and type approval
189			IEC/PAS 62111, Specifications for the use of renewable energies in rural decentralised electrification
190			IEC 62124, Photovoltaic (PV) stand alone systems — Design verification
191			IEC 62253, Photovoltaic pumping systems — Design qualification and performance measurements
192			IEC 62446, Grid connected photovoltaic systems — Minimum requirements for system documentation, commissioning tests and inspection
193			IEC 62509, Battery charge controllers for photovoltaic systems — Performance and functioning
194			IEC/TS 62548, Photovoltaic (PV) arrays — Design requirements
3. 高性能有机高分子材料及复合材料			
195	电学材料	通用基础标准	IEC 60455-3-5 (2006-03), Resin based reactive compounds used for electrical insulation — Part 3: Specifications for individual materials — Sheet 5: Unsaturated polyester based impregnating resins
196			IEC 60893-1 (2004-01), Insulating materials — Industrial rigid laminated sheets based on thermosetting resins for electrical purposes — Part 1: Definitions, designations and general requirements
197		测试方法标准	IEC 60893-2 (2003-06), Industrial rigid laminated sheets based on thermosetting resins for electrical purposes — Part 2: Methods of test
198		材料技术标准	IEC 60893-3-3-2012, Insulating materials. Industrial rigid laminated sheets based on thermosettingresins for electrical purposes — Part 3-3: Specifications for individual materials — Requirements for rigidlaminated sheets

续表

序号	材料分类	标准类型	标准名称
199			IEC 60893-3-6-2003, Insulating materials — Industrial rigid laminated sheets based on thermosetting resins for electrical purposes — Part 3-6: Specifications for individual materials; Requirements for rigid laminated
200		测试方法标准	IEC 62329-2 (2006-07), Heat-shrinkable moulded shapes — Part 2: Methods of test
201			IEC 62011-2 (2004-01), Insulating materials — Industrial, rigid, moulded, laminated tubes and rods of rectangular and hexagonal cross-section, based on thermosetting resins for electrical purposes — Part 2: Methods of test
202			IEC 61212-2 (2006-04), Insulating materials — Industrial rigid round laminated tubes and rods based on thermosetting resins for electrical purposes — Part 2: Methods of test
203		应用技术标准	IEC 62011-3-1 (2003-08), Insulating materials — Industrial rigid moulded laminated tubes and rods of rectangular and hexagonal cross-section based on thermosetting resins for electrical purposes — Part 3-1: Specifications for individual materials — Tubes and rods of rectangular and hexagonal cross-section
204			IEC 62011-1 (2002-05), Insulating materials — Industrial, rigid, moulded, laminated tubes and rods of rectangular and hexagonal cross-section based on thermosetting resins for electrical purposes — Part 1: Definitions, designations and general requirements
205			IEC 61212-3-2 (2013-04), Insulating materials — Industrial rigid round laminated tubes and rods based on thermosetting resins for electrical purposes — Part 3: Specifications for individual materials — Sheet 2: Round laminated moulded tubes
206			IEC 61212-3-1 (2013-04), Insulating materials — Industrial rigid round laminated tubes and rods based on thermosetting resins for electrical purposes — Part 3: Specifications for individual materials — Sheet 1: Round laminated rolled tubes
207			IEC/TR 60893-4 (2003-02), Insulating materials — Industrial rigid laminated sheets based on thermosetting resins for electrical purposes — Part 4: Typical values
208			IEC 60893-3-7 ed2.0 (2003-11), Insulating materials — Industrial rigid laminated sheets based on thermosetting resins for electrical purposes — Part 3-7: Specifications for individual materials — Requirements for rigid laminated sheets based on polyimide resins

续表

序号	材料分类	标准类型	标准名称
209	高分子涂覆改性材料	通用基础标准	IEC 61086-1 (2004-01), Coatings for loaded printed wire boards (conformal coatings) — Part 1: Definitions, classification and general requirements
210			IEC 61086-3-1 (2004-02), Coatings for loaded printed wire boards (conformal coatings) — Part 3-1: Specifications for individual materials — Coatings for general purpose (Class 1), high reliability (Class 2) and aerospace (Class 3)
211			IEC 61086-1 (2004-01), Coatings for loaded printed wire boards (conformal coatings) — Part 1: Definitions, classification and general requirements
212		测试方法标准	IEC 61086-2 (2004-02), Coatings for loaded printed wire boards (conformal coatings) — Part 2: Methods of test
213			IEC 61086-2 (2004-02), Coatings for loaded printed wire boards (conformal coatings) — Part 2: Methods of test
214			IEC 61086-3-1 (2004-02), Coatings for loaded printed wire boards (conformal coatings) — Part 3-1: Specifications for individual materials — Coatings for general purpose (Class 1), high reliability (Class 2) and aerospace (Class 3)
215	高分子薄膜材料	应用技术标准	IEC 60674-3-1, Plastic films for electrical purposes — Part 3: Specifications for individual materials — Sheet 1: Biaxially oriented polypropylene (PP) films for capacitors
216			IEC 60674-3-1, Plastic films for electrical purposes — Part 3: Specifications for individual materials — Sheet 1: Biaxially oriented polypropylene (PP) films for capacitors
217			IEC 60674-3-1, Plastic films for electrical purposes — Part 3: Specifications for individual materials — Sheet 1: Biaxially oriented polypropylene (PP) film for capacitors
218			IEC 60674-3-2, Specification for plastic films for electrical purposes — Part 3: Specifications for individual materials — Sheet 2: Requirements for balanced biaxially oriented polyethylene terephthalate (PET) films used for electrical insulation
219			IEC 60674-3-3 (1992-04), Specification for plastic films for electrical purposes — Part 3: Specifications for individual materials — Sheet 3: Requirements for polycarbonate (PC) films used for electrical insulation

续表

序号	材料分类	标准类型	标准名称
220			IEC 60674-3-4 (1993-03), Specification for plastic films for electrical purposes — Part 3: Specifications for individual materials — Sheets 4 to 6: Requirements for polyimide films used for electrical insulation
221			IEC 60674-3-7 (1992-04), Specification for plastic films for electrical purposes — Part 3: Specifications for individual materials — Sheet 7: Requirements for fluoroethylene-propylene (FEP) films used for electrical insulation
222			IEC 61881-1 (2010-08), Railway applications — Rolling stock equipment — Capacitors for power electronics — Part 1: Paper/plastic film capacitors
223		测试方法标准	IEC 60674-2, Specification for plastic films for electrical purposes — Part 2: Methods of test
224			IEC 61234-1 (1994-03), Method of test for the hydrolytic stability of electrical insulating materials — Part 1: Plastic films
225			IEC 60674-2 (2001-10), Amendment 1 — Specification for plastic films for electrical purposes — Part 2: Methods of test
226		应用技术标准	IEC 60384-2 (2011-12), Fixed capacitors for use in electronic equipment — Part 2: Sectional specification — Fixed metallized polyethylene terephthalate film dielectric d. c. capacitors
227			IEC 60384-2-1 (2005-11), Fixed capacitors for use in electronic equipment — Part 2: Sectional specification — Fixed metallized polyethylene terephthalate film dielectric d. c. capacitors
228			IEC 60384-2 (2011-12), Fixed capacitors for use in electronic equipment — Part 2: Sectional specification — Fixed metallized polyethylene terephthalate film dielectric d. c. capacitors
229			IEC 60384-2-1 (2005-11), Fixed capacitors for use in electronic equipment — Part 2-1: Blank detail specification: Fixed metallized polyethylene-terephthalate film dielectric d. c. capacitors — Assessment levels E and EZ
230			IEC 60384-11-1 (2008-02), Fixed capacitors for use in electronic equipment — Part 11-1: Blank detail specification — Fixed polyethylene terephthalate film dielectric metal foil d. c. capacitors — Assessment level EZ

续表

序号	材料分类	标准类型	标准名称
231			IEC 60384-16-1 (2005-11), Fixed capacitors for use in electronic equipment — Part 16-1: Blank detail specification: Fixed metallized polypropylene film dielectric d. c. capacitors — Assessment levels E and EZ
232			IEC 60384-17 (2005-11), Fixed capacitors for use in electronic equipment — Part 17: Sectional specification: Fixed metallized polypropylene film dielectric a. c. and pulse capacitors
233			IEC 60384-19-1 (2006-01), Fixed capacitors for use in electronic equipment — Part 19-1: Blank detail specification — Fixed metallized polyethylene-terephthalate film dielectric surface mount d. c. capacitors — Assessment level EZ
234			IEC 60454-3-11 (2007-05), Pressure-sensitive adhesive tapes for electrical purposes — Part 3: Specifications for individual materials — Sheet 11: Polyester film combinations with glass filament, creped cellulosic paper, polyester non-woven, epoxy and pressure-sensitive adhesive
235			IEC 60454-3-12 ed2.0 (2006-01), Pressure-sensitive adhesive tapes for electrical purposes — Part 3: Specifications for individual materials — Sheet 12: Requirements for polyethylene and polypropylene film tapes with pressure sensitive adhesive
236			IEC 60454-3-14 ed1.0 (2001-07), Pressure-sensitive adhesive tapes for electrical purposes — Part 3: Specifications for individual materials — Sheet 14: Polytetrafluoroethylene film tapes with pressure-sensitive adhesiv
237			IEC 60674-3-1 (2011-12), Plastic films for electrical purposes — Part 3: Specifications for individual materials — Sheet 1: Biaxially oriented polypropylene (PP) films for capacitors
238			IEC 60674-3-1 (1998-03), Plastic films for electrical purposes — Part 3: Specifications for individual materials — Sheet 1: Biaxially oriented polypropylene (PP) film for capacitors
239			IEC 60674-3-1 (2011-09), Amendment 1 — Plastic films for electrical purposes — Part 3: Specifications for individual materials — Sheet 1: Biaxially oriented polypropylene (PP) film for capacitors

续表

序号	材料分类	标准类型	标准名称
240			IEC 60674-3-3 (1992-04), Specification for plastic films for electrical purposes — Part 3: Specifications for individual materials — Sheet 3: Requirements for polycarbonate (PC) films used for electrical insulation
241			IEC 60674-3-4 (1993-03), Specification for plastic films for electrical purposes — Part 3: Specifications for individual materials — Sheets 4 to 6: Requirements for polyimide films used for electrical insulation
242			IEC 60674-3-8 (2011-07), Plastic films for electrical purposes — Part 3: Specifications for individual materials — Sheet 8: Balanced biaxially oriented polyethylene naphthalate (PEN) films used for electrical insulation
243			IEC 62011-1 (2002-05), Insulating materials — Industrial, rigid, moulded, laminated tubes and rods of rectangular and hexagonal cross-section based on thermosetting resins for electrical purposes — Part 1: Definitions, designations and general requirements
244	电力学材料	通用基础标准	IEC 62011-2 (2004-01), Insulating materials — Industrial, rigid, moulded, laminated tubes and rods of rectangular and hexagonal cross-section, based on thermosetting resins for electrical purposes — Part 2: Methods of test
245			IEC 62011-3-1 (2003-08), Insulating materials — Industrial rigid moulded laminated tubes and rods of rectangular and hexagonal cross-section based on thermosetting resins for electrical purposes — Part 3-1: Specifications for individual materials — Tubes and rods of rectangular and hexagonal cross-section
246			IEC 60793-2-40 (2009-04), Optical fibres — Part 2-40: Product specifications — Sectional specification for category A4 multimode fibres
247	高档合成纤维	通用基础标准	IEC 61068-1 (1991-06), Specification for polyester fibre woven tapes — Part 1: Definitions, designation and general requirements
248			IEC 61068-3-1 (1995-02), Polyester fibre woven tapes — Part 3: Specifications for individual materials — Sheet 1: Tapes woven on conventional or shuttleless looms

续表

序号	材料分类	标准类型	标准名称
249			IEC 61754-20（2012-04），Fibre optic interconnecting devices and passive components — Fibre optic connector interfaces — Part 20: Type LC connector family
250			IEC 61754-21（2005-03），Fibre optic connector interfaces — Part 21: Type SMI connector family for plastic optical fibre
251		测试方法标准	IEC 61068-2（1991-06），Specification for polyester fibre woven tapes — Part 2: Methods of test
252			IEC 61068-1（1991-06），Specification for polyester fibre woven tapes — Part 1: Definitions, designation and general requirements
253			IEC 61068-2（1991-06），Specification for polyester fibre woven tapes — Part 2: Methods of test
254			IEC 61068-3-1（1995-02），Polyester fibre woven tapes — Part 3: Specifications for individual materials — Sheet 1: Tapes woven on conventional or shuttleless looms
255		应用技术标准	IEC 62148-4（2003-06），Fibre optic active components and devices — Package and interface standards — Part 4: PN 1x9 plastic optical fibre transceivers
256			IEC 62149-6（2003-09），Fibre optic active components and devices — Performance standards — Part 6: 650nm 250Mbit/s plastic optical fibre transceivers
257			IEC 62300（2004-11），Consumer audio/video equipment digital interface with plastic optical fibre
4. 特种精细化工材料			
258	油墨	材料技术标准	IEC 61249-5-4-1996, Materials for interconnection structures — Part 5: Sectional specification set for conductive foils and films with or without coatings — Section 4: Conductive inks
259			IEC 61249-8-7-1996, Materials for interconnection structures — Part 8: Sectional specification set for non-conductive films and coatings — Section 7: Marking legend inks
260	涂料	通用基础标准	IEC 61086-1-2004, Coatings for loaded printed wire boards (conformal coatings) — Part 1: Definitions, classification and general requirements
261		测试方法标准	IEC 61086-2-2004, Coatings for loaded printed wire boards (conformal coatings) — Part 2: Methods of test

续表

序号	材料分类	标准类型	标准名称
262			IEC 60404-12-1992, Magnetic materials — Part 12: Guide to methods of assessment of temperature capability of interlaminar insulation coatings
263			IEC 60793-1-21-2001, Optical fibres — Part 1-21: Measurement methods and test procedures — Coating geometry
264			IEC 60793-1-32-2010, Optical fibres — Part 1-32: Measurement methods and test procedures — Coating strippability
265			IEC 61086-3-1-2004, Coatings for loaded printed wire boards (conformal coatings) — Part 3-1: Specifications for individual materials — Coatings for general purpose (Class 1), high reliability (Class 2) and aerospace (Class 3)
266		材料技术标准	IEC 60455-3-11-1988, Specification for solventless polymerisable resinous compounds used for electrical insulation — Part 3: Specifications for individual materials — Sheet 11 : Epoxy resin-based coating powders
267			IEC 61249-8-8-1997, Materials for interconnection structures — Part 8: Sectional specification set for non-conductive films and coatings — Section 8: Temporary polymer coatings
268			IEC 60684-3-403 to 405-2002, Flexible insulating sleeving — Part 3: Specifications for individual types of sleeving — Sheets 403 to 405: Glass textile sleeving with acrylic based coating
269			IEC 60684-3-406 to 408-2003, Flexible insulating sleeving — Part 3: Specifications for individual types of sleeving — Sheets 406 to 408: Glass textile sleeving with PVC coating
270		应用技术标准	IEC 60684-3-409-1999, Flexible insulating sleeving — Part 3: Specifications for individual types of sleeving — Sheet 409: Glass textile sleeving with polyurethane (PUR) -based coating
271			IEC 60684-3-420 to 422-2002, Flexible insulating sleeving — Part 3: Specification for individual types of sleeving — Sheets 420 to 422: Polyethylene terephthalate textile sleeving with acrylic based coating
272	添加剂	测试方法标准	IEC 60666-2010, Detection and determination of specified additives in mineral insulating oils

续表

序号	材料分类	标准类型	标准名称
273			IEC 60371-3-4 AMD 1-2006, Specifications for insulating materials based on mica — Part 3: Specifications for individual materials — Sheet 4: Polyester film-backed mica paper with a B-stage epoxy resin binder — Amendment 1
274			IEC 60371-3-6 AMD 1-2006, Specification for insulating materials based on mica — Part 3: Specifications for individual materials — Sheet 6: Glass-backed mica paper with a B-stage epoxy resin binder — Amendment 1
275			IEC 60371-3-7 AMD 1-2006, Insulating materials based on mica — Part 3: Specifications for individual materials — Sheet 7: Polyester film mica paper with an epoxy resin binder for single conductor taping — Amendment 1
276			IEC 60454-3-1 Edition 2.1-2002, Pressure-sensitive adhesive tapes for electrical purposes — Part 3: Specifications for individual materials — Sheet 1: PVC film tapes with pressure-sensitive adhesive
277	粘合剂	应用技术标准	IEC 60454-3-2-2006, Pressure-sensitive adhesive tapes for electrical purposes — Part 3: Specifications for individual materials — Sheet 2: Polyester film tapes with rubber thermosetting or acrylic crosslinked adhesives
278			IEC 60454-3-4-2007, Pressure-sensitive adhesive tapes for electrical purposes — Part 3: Specifications for individual materials — Sheet 4: Cellulose paper, creped and non-creped, with rubber thermosetting adhesive
279			IEC 60454-3-7-1998, Pressure-sensitive adhesive tapes for electrical purposes — Part 3: Specifications for individual materials — Sheet 7: Polyimide film tapes with pressure-sensitive adhesive
280			IEC 60454-3-11-2007, Pressure-sensitive adhesive tapes for electrical purposes — Part 3: Specifications for individual materials — Sheet 11: Polyester film combinations with glass filament, creped cellulosic paper, polyester non-woven, epoxy and pressure-sensitive adhesive
281			IEC 60454-3-12-2006, Pressure-sensitive adhesive tapes for electrical purposes — Part 3: Specifications for individual materials — Sheet 12: Polyethylene film tapes with pressure-sensitive adhesive

续表

序号	材料分类	标准类型	标准名称
282			IEC 60454-3-14-2001, Pressure-sensitive adhesive tapes for electrical purposes — Part 3: Specifications for individual materials — Sheet 14: Polytetrafluoroethylene film tapes with pressure-sensitive adhesive
283			IEC 60454-3-19-2003, Pressure-sensitive adhesive tapes for electrical purposes — Part 3: Specifications for individual materials — Sheet 19: Tapes made from various backing materials with pressure-sensitive adhesive on both sides
284			IEC/PAS 61249-3-1-2007, Materials for printed boards and other interconnecting structures — Part 3-1: Copper-clad laminates for flexible boards (adhesive and non-adhesive types)
285	填料	测试方法标准	IEC 60811-605-2012, Electric and optical fibre cables — Test methods for non-metallic materials — Part 605: Physical tests — Measurement of carbon black and/or mineral filler in polyethylene compounds
286	石油润滑油	通用基础标准	IEC 61221-2004, Petroleum products and lubricants — Triaryl phosphate ester turbine control fluids (category ISO-L-TCD) — Specifications
5. 前沿新型材料			
287		测试方法标准	IEC 62624, Test methods for measurement of electrical properties of carbon nanotubes
288			IEC/PAS 62565-2-1, Nanomanufacturing — Material specifications — Part 2-1: Single-wall carbon nanotubes — Blank detail specification
289	纳米材料		IEC/TS 62607-2-1, Nanomanufacturing — Key control characteristics — Part 2-1: Carbon nanotube materials — Film resistance
290		材料技术标准	IEC/TS 62622, Nanotechnologies — Description, measurement and dimensional quality parameters of artificial gratings
291			IEC/TR 62632, Nanoscale electrical contacts and interconnects
292			IEC/TR 62834, nanoelectronics standardization roadmap
293	超材料	通用基础标准	IEC 60050-815, International Electrotechnical Vocabulary — Part 815: Superconductivity
294		材料技术标准	IEC 61788 系列标准, Superconductivity

续表

序号	材料分类	标准类型	标准名称
295	智能材料	材料技术标准	ISO/IEC/IEEE 21450, Information technology — Smart transducer interface for sensors and actuators — Common functions, communication protocols, and Transducer Electronic Data Sheet (TEDS) formats
296	智能材料	材料技术标准	ISO/IEC/IEEE 21451-1, Information technology — Smart transducer interface for sensors and actuators — Part 1: Network Capable Application Processor (NCAP) information model
297	智能材料	材料技术标准	ISO/IEC/IEEE 21451-2, Information technology — Smart transducer interface for sensors and actuators — Part 2: Transducer to microprocessor communication protocols and Transducer Electronic Data Sheet (TEDS) formats
298	智能材料	材料技术标准	ISO/IEC/IEEE 21451-4, Information technology — Smart transducer interface for sensors and actuators — Part 4: Mixed-mode communication protocols and Transducer Electronic Data Sheet (TEDS) formats
299	智能材料	材料技术标准	ISO/IEC/IEEE 21451-7, Information technology — Smart transducer interface for sensors and actuators — Part 7: Transducer to radio frequency identification (RFID) systems communication protocols and Transducer Electronic Data Sheet (TEDS) formats
300	智能材料	材料技术标准	ISO/IEC 29143, Information technology — Automatic identification and data capture techniques — Air interface specification for Mobile RFID interrogators
301	智能材料	材料技术标准	IEC 60454-3-4, Pressure-sensitive adhesive tapes for electrical purposes — Part 3: Specifications for individual materials — Sheet 4: Cellulose paper, creped and non-creped, with rubber thermosetting adhesive
302	智能材料	材料技术标准	IEC 60454-3-8, Pressure-sensitive adhesive tapes for electrical purposes — Part 3: Specifications for individual materials — Sheet 8 — Woven fabric tapes with pressure-sensitive adhesive based on glass, cellulose acetate alone or combined with viscose fibre
303	智能材料	材料技术标准	IEC 60454-3-11, Pressure-sensitive adhesive tapes for electrical purposes — Part 3: Specifications for individual materials — Sheet 11: Polyester film combinations with glass filament, creped cellulosic paper, polyester non-woven, epoxy and pressure-sensitive adhesive

续表

序号	材料分类	标准类型	标准名称
304			IEC/PAS 60539-1-1, Directly heated negative temperature coefficient thermistors — Part 1-1: Blank detail specification — Sensing application — Assessment level EZ
305			IEC/PAS 60539-1-1, Directly heated negative temperature coefficient thermistors — Part 1-1: Blank detail specification — Sensing application — Assessment level EZ
306			IEC 60539-2, Directly heated negative temperature coefficient thermistors — Part 2: Sectional specification — Surface mount negative temperature coefficient thermistors
307			IEC 60584-2 ed1.0 (1982-01), Thermocouples — Part 2: Tolerances
308			IEC 60730-1, Automatic electrical controls — Part 1: General requirements
309			IEC 60730-2-3, Automatic electrical controls for household and similar use — Part 2-3: Particular requirements for thermal protectors for ballasts for tubular fluorescent lamps
310			IEC 60730-2-4, Automatic electrical controls for household and similar use — Part 2-4: Particular requirements for thermal motor protectors for motor-compressors of hermetic and semi-hermetic type
311			IEC 60730-2-6, Automatic electrical controls for household and similar use — Part 2-6: Particular requirements for automatic electrical pressure sensing controls including mechanical requirements
312			IEC 60730-2-9, Automatic electrical controls for household and similar use — Part 2-9: Particular requirements for temperature sensing controls
313			IEC 60730-2-9, Automatic electrical controls for household and similar use — Part 2-9: Particular requirements for temperature sensing controls
314			IEC 60730-2-9, Amendment 1 — Automatic electrical controls for household and similar use — Part 2-9: Particular requirements for temperature sensing controls
315			IEC 60730-2-10, Automatic electrical controls for household and similar use — Part 2-10: Particular requirements for motor-starting relays

续表

序号	材料分类	标准类型	标准名称
316			IEC 60730-2-13, Automatic electrical controls for household and similar use — Part 2-13: Particular requirements for humidity sensing controls
317			IEC 60730-2-15, Automatic electrical controls for household and similar use — Part 2-15: Particular requirements for automatic electrical air flow, water flow and water level sensing controls
318			IEC 60730-2-19, Automatic electrical controls for household and similar use — Part 2-19: Particular requirements for electrically operated oil valves, including mechanical requirements
319			IEC 60737, Nuclear power plants — Instrumentation important to safety — Temperature sensors (in-core and primary coolant circuit) — Characteristics and test methods
320			IEC 60738-1, Thermistors — Directly heated positive temperature coefficient — Part 1: Generic specification
321			IEC 60738-1-1, Thermistors — Directly heated positive step-function temperature coefficient — Part 1-1: Blank detail specification — Current limiting application — Assessment leve EZ
322			IEC 60738-1-2, Thermistors — Directly heated positive step-function temperature coefficient — Part 1-2: Blank detail specification — Heating element application — Assessment level EZ
323			IEC 60738-1-3, Thermistors — Directly heated positive step-function temperature coefficient — Part 1-3: Blank detail specification — Inrush current application — Assessment level EZ
324			IEC 60738-1-4, Thermistors — Directly heated positive step-function temperature coefficient — Part 1-4: Blank detail specification — Sensing application — Assessment level EZ
325			IEC 60746-4, Expression of performance of electrochemical analyzers — Part 4: Dissolved oxygen in water measured by membrane covered amperometric sensors
326			IEC 60747-14-1, Semiconductor devices — Part 14-1: Semiconductor sensors — Generic specification for sensors
327			IEC 60747-14-2, Semiconductor devices — Part 14-2: Semiconductor sensors — Hall elements

续表

序号	材料分类	标准类型	标准名称
328			IEC 60747-14-3, Semiconductor devices — Part 14-3: Semiconductor sensors — Pressure sensors
329			IEC 60747-14-5, Semiconductor devices — Part 14-5: Semiconductor sensors - PN-junction semiconductor temperature sensor
330			IEC 60751, Industrial platinum resistance thermometers and platinum temperature sensors
331			IEC 60947-5-1, Low-voltage switchgear and controlgear — Part 5-1: Control circuit devices and switching elements — Electromechanical control circuit devices
332			IEC 61043, Electroacoustics — Instruments for the measurement of sound intensity Measurements with pairs of pressure sensing microphones
333			IEC 61051-1, Varistors for use in electronic equipment — Part 1: Generic specification
334			IEC 61051-2, Varistors for use in electronic equipment — Part 2: Sectional specification for surge suppression varistors
335			IEC 61051-2, Varistors for use in electronic equipment — Part 2: Sectional specification for surge suppression varistors
336			IEC 61051-2-2, Varistors for use in electronic equipment — Part 2: Blank detail specification for zinc oxide surge suppression varistors — Assessment level E
337			IEC 61643-331, Components for low-voltage surge protective devices — Part 331: Specification for metal oxide varistors (MOV)
338			IEC 61207-2, Expression of performance of gas analyzers — Part 2: Oxygen in gas (utilizing high-temperature electrochemical sensors)
339			IEC 61496-2, Safety of machinery — Electro-sensitive protective equipment — Part 2: Particular requirements for equipment using active opto-electronic protective devices (AOPDs)
340			IEC 61496-3, Safety of machinery — Electro-sensitive protective equipment — Part 3: Particular requirements for Active Opto-electronic Protective Devices responsive to Diffuse Reflection (AOPDDR)
341			IEC/TR 61496-4, Safety of machinery — Electro-sensitive protective equipment — Part 4: Particular requirements for equipment using vision based protective devices (VBPD)

续表

序号	材料分类	标准类型	标准名称
342			IEC 61520, Metal thermowells for thermometer sensors — Functional dimensions
343			IEC 61757-1, Fibre optic sensors — Part 1: Generic specification
344			IEC/TS 61994 系列标准, Piezoelectric and dielectric devices for frequency control and selection — Glossary
345			IEC 62026 系列标准, Low-voltage switchgear and controlgear — Controller-device interfaces (CDIs)
346			IEC 62243, Artificial Intelligence Exchange and Service Tie to All Test Environments (AI-ESTATE)
347			IEC 62319-1-1, Polymeric thermistors — Directly heated positive step function temperature coefficient — Part 1-1: Blank detail specification — Current limiting application
348			IEC/TR 62331, Pulsed field magnetometry
349			IEC/TS 62370, Electroacoustics — Instruments for the measurement of sound intensity — Electromagnetic and electrostatic compatibility requirements and test procedures
350			IEC 62464 系列标准, Magnetic resonance equipment for medical imaging
351			IEC/TR 62797, International comparison of measurements of the magnetic moment using vibrating sample magnetometers (VSM) and superconducting quantum interference device (SQUID) magnetometers
352			IEC 60825-1, Safety of laser products — Part 1: Equipment classification and requirements
353			IEC 60825-2, Safety of laser products — Part 2: Safety of optical fibre communication systems (OFCS)
354	光电材料	安全技术标准	IEC/TR 60825-3, Safety of laser products — Part 3: Guidance for laser displays and shows
355			IEC 60825-4, Safety of laser products — Part 4: Laser guards
356			IEC/TR 60825-5, Safety of laser products — Part 5: Manufacturer's checklist for IEC 60825-1
357			IEC/TR 60825-8, Safety of laser products — Part 8: Guidelines for the safe use of laser beams on humans

续表

序号	材料分类	标准类型	标准名称
358			IEC/TR 60825-9, Safety of laser products — Part 9: Compilation of maximum permissible exposure to incoherent optical radiation
359			IEC 60825-12, Safety of laser products — Part 12: Safety of free space optical communication systems used for transmission of information
360			IEC/TR 60825-13, Safety of laser products — Part 13: Measurements for classification of laser products
361			IEC/TR 60825-14, Safety of laser products — Part 14: A user's guide
362			IEC/TR 60825-17, Safety of laser products — Part 17: Safety aspects for use of passive optical components and optical cables in high power optical fibre communication systems
363			IEC 61231, International lamp coding system (ILCOS)
364			IEC 61231 (2010-01), International lamp coding system (ILCOS)
365			IEC 61280-2-8 (2003-02), Fibre optic communication subsystem test procedures — Digital systems — Part 2-8: Determination of low BER using Q-factor measurements
366			IEC 61300-3-2, Fibre optic interconnecting devices and passive components — Basic test and measurement procedures — Part 3-2: Examination and measurements — Polarization dependent loss in a single-mode fibre optic device
367		测试方法标准	IEC 60332 系列标准, Tests on electric and optical fibre cables under fire conditions
368			IEC 61211, Insulators of ceramic material or glass for overhead lines with a nominal voltage greater than 1000 V — Impulse puncture testing in air
369			IEC 60306-1, Measurement of photosensitive devices — Part 1: Basic recommendations
370		材料技术标准	IEC 60306-2, Measurement of photosensitive devices — Part 2: Methods of measurement of phototubes
371			IEC 60306-3, Measurement of photosensitive devices — Part 3: Methods of measurement of photoconductive cells for use in the visible spectrum

续表

序号	材料分类	标准类型	标准名称
372			IEC 60306-4, Measurement of photosensitive devices — Part 4: Methods of measurement for photo-multipliers
373			IEC 60317-50, Specifications for particular types of winding wires — Part 50: Glass-fibre wound silicone resin or varnish impregnated, bare or enamelled round copper wire, temperature index
374			IEC 60357, Tungsten halogen lamps (non vehicle) — Performance specifications
375			IEC 60404-6, Magnetic materials — Part 6: Methods of measurement of the magnetic properties of magnetically soft metallic and powder materials at frequencies in the range 20 Hz to 200 kHz by the use of ring specimens
376			IEC 60432-1, Incandescent lamps — Safety specifications — Part 1: Tungsten filament lamps for domestic and similar general lighting purposes
377			IEC 60432-3, Incandescent lamps — Safety specifications — Part 3: Tungsten halogen lamps (non-vehicle)
378			IEC 60598-2-2, Luminaires — Part 2-2: Particular requirements — Recessed luminaires
379			IEC 60747-5-4, Semiconductor devices — Discrete devices — Part 5-4: Optoelectronic devices — Semiconductor lasers
380			IEC 60747-5-5, Semiconductor devices — Discrete devices — Part 5-5: Optoelectronic devices — Photocouplers
381			IEC 60747-5-5, Semiconductor devices — Discrete devices — Part 5-5: Optoelectronic devices — Photocouplers
382			IEC 60794-3-11, Optical fibre cables — Part 3-11: Outdoor cables — Product specification for duct, directly buried, and lashed aerial single-mode optical fibre telecommunication cables
383			IEC 60811-607, Electric and optical fibre cables — Test methods for non-metallic materials — Part 607: Physical tests — Test for the assessment of carbon black dispersion in polyethylene and polypropylene
384			IEC 60903 ed2.0, Live working — Gloves of insulating material

续表

序号	材料分类	标准类型	标准名称
385			IEC 60904-2, Photovoltaic devices — Part 2: Requirements for reference solar devices
386			IEC 60904-5, Photovoltaic devices — Part 5: Determination of the equivalent cell temperature (ECT) of photovoltaic (PV) devices by the open-circuit voltage method
387			IEC 60904-7, Photovoltaic devices — Part 7: Computation of the spectral mismatch correction for measurements of photovoltaic devices
388			IEC 61109, Composite suspension and tension insulators for a. c. systems with a nominal voltage greater than 1000 V — Definitions, test methods and acceptance criteria
389			IEC 61249-5-4-1996, Materials for interconnection structures — Part 5: Sectional specification set for conductive foils and films with or without coatings — Section 4: Conductive inks
390			IEC/TR 61282-9, Fibre optic communication system design guides — Part 9: Guidance on polarization mode dispersion measurements and theory
391			IEC 61747-3, Liquid crystal display devices — Part 3: Liquid crystal display (LCD) cells — Sectional specification
392			IEC 61747-4, Liquid crystal display devices — Part 4: Liquid crystal display modules and cells — Essential ratings and characteristics
393			IEC 61755 系列标准, Fibre optic connector optical interfaces
394			IEC 61757-1 Fibre optic sensors
395			IEC 61834-3, Recording — Helical-scan digital video cassette recording system using 6. 35 mm magnetic tape for consumer use (525-60, 625-50, 1125-60 and 1250-50 systems) — Part 3: HD format for 1125-60 and 1250-50 systems
396			IEC 61952-2008, Insulators for overhead lines — Composite line post insulators for a. c. systems with a nominal voltage greater than 1000 V — Definitions, test methods and acceptance criteria
397			IEC 61978-1, Fibre optic interconnecting devices and passive components — Fibre optic passive chromatic dispersion compensators
398			IEC 61988-1, Plasma display panels — Part 1: Terminology and letter symbols

续表

序号	材料分类	标准类型	标准名称
399			IEC 61988-2-1, Plasma display panels — Part 2-1: Measuring methods — Optical and optoelectrical
400			IEC 61988-2-2, Plasma display panels — Part 2-2: Measuring methods — Optoelectrical
401			IEC 61988-2-3, Plasma display panels — Part 2-3: Measuring methods — Image quality: defects and degradation
402			IEC 61988-2-4, Plasma display panels — Part 2-4: Measuring methods — Visual quality: Image artifacts
403			IEC 61988-2-5, Plasma display panels — Part 2-5: Measuring methods — Acoustic noise
404			IEC 61988-3-1, Plasma display panels — Part 3-1: Mechanical interface
405			IEC 61988-3-2, Plasma display panels — Part 3-2: Interface — Electrical interface
406			IEC 61988-4, Plasma display panels — Part 4: Climatic and mechanical testing methods
407			IEC 61988-4-2, Plasma display panels — Part 4-2: Environmental testing methods — Panel strength
408			IEC 61988-5, Plasma display panels — Part 5: Generic specification
409			IEC 62002-1, Mobile and portable DVB-T/H radio access — Part 1: Interface specification
410			IEC 62007-1, Semiconductor optoelectronic devices for fibre optic system applications — Part 1: Specification template for essential ratings and characteristics
411			IEC 62007-2, Semiconductor optoelectronic devices for fibre optic system applications — Part 2: Measuring methods
412			IEC 62231-2006, Composite station post insulators for substations with a. c. voltages greater than 1000 V up to 245 kV — Definitions, test methods and acceptance criteria
413			IEC 62275-2006, Cable management systems — Cable ties for electrical installations

续表

序号	材料分类	标准类型	标准名称
414			IEC 62341-1-1, Organic light emitting diode (OLED) displays — Part 1-1: Generic specifications
415			IEC 62341-1-2, Organic light emitting diode displays — Part 1-2: Terminology and letter symbols
416			IEC 62341-5, Organic light emitting diode (OLED) displays — Part 5: Environmental testing methods
417			IEC 62341-5-2, Organic light emitting diode (OLED) displays — Part 5-2: Mechanical endurance testing methods
418			IEC 62341-5-3, Organic light emitting diode (OLED) displays — Part 5-3: Measuring methods of image sticking and lifetime
419			IEC 62341-6-1, Organic light emitting diode (OLED) displays — Part 6-1: Measuring methods of optical and electro-optical parameters
420			IEC 62341-6-2, Organic light emitting diode (OLED) displays — Part 6-2: Measuring methods of visual quality and ambient performance
421			IEC 62341-6-3, Organic light emitting diode (OLED) displays — Part 6-3: Measuring methods of image quality
422			IEC 62496-2-4, Optical circuit boards — Basic test and measurement procedures — Part 2-4: Optical transmission test for optical circuit boards without input/output fibres
423			IEC/TR 62572-2, Fibre optic active components and devices — Reliability standards — Part 2: Laser module degradation
424			IEC 62572-3, Fibre optic active components and devices — Reliability standards — Part 3: Laser modules used for telecommunication
425			IEC 62595-1-1, LCD backlight unit — Part 1-1: Generic specification
426			IEC 62595-1-2, LCD backlight unit — Part 1-2: Terminology and letter symbols
427			IEC 62595-2, LCD backlight unit — Part 2: Electro-optical measurement methods of LED backlight unit
428			IEC 62621-2011, Railway applications — Fixed installations — Electric traction — Specific requirements for composite insulators used for overhead contact line systems

续表

序号	材料分类	标准类型	标准名称
429			EC 62629-1-2, 3D display devices — Part 1-2: Generic — Terminology and letter symbols
430			IEC 62629-12-1, 3D Display devices — Part 12-1: Measuring methods for stereoscopic displays using glasses — Optical
431			IEC 62629-22-1, 3D display devices — Part 22-1: Measuring methods for autostereoscopic displays — Optical
432			IEC 62679-3-2, Electronic paper display — Part 3-2: Measuring method — Electro-optical
433			IEC/TR 62728, Display technologies — LCD, PDP and OLED — Overview and explanation of differences in terminology
434		应用技术标准	IEC/TR 61496 系列标准, Safety of machinery — Electro-sensitive protective equipment
435			IEC 61947 系列标准, Electronic projection — Measurement and documentation of key performance criteria — Part 1: Fixed resolution projectors
436			IEC 61966 系列标准, Multimedia systems and equipment — Colour measurement and management
437			IEC 60050-482, International Electrotechnical Vocabulary — Part 482: Primary and secondary cells and batteries
438			IEC 60647, Dimensions for magnetic oxide cores intended for use in power supplies (EC-cores)
439			IEC 61427-1, Secondary cells and batteries for renewable energy storage — General requirements and methods of test — Part 1: Photovoltaic off-grid application
440	新能源材料	通用基础标准	IEC 61429, Marking of secondary cells and batteries with the international recycling symbol ISO 7000-1135
441			IEC/TR 61431, Guide for the use of monitor systems for lead-acid traction batteries
442			IEC 61434, Secondary cells and batteries containing alkaline or other non-acid electrolytes — Guide to designation of current in alkaline secondary cell and battery standards
443			IEC/TS 62282-1, Fuel cell technologies — Part 1: Terminology

续表

序号	材料分类	标准类型	标准名称
444		安全技术标准	IEC/TR 61438, Possible safety and health hazards in the use of alkaline secondary cells and batteries — Guide to equipment manufacturers and users
445			IEC 62281, Safety of primary and secondary lithium cells and batteries during transport
446			IEC 62485-2, Safety requirements for secondary batteries and battery installations — Part 2: Stationary batteries
447			IEC 62485-3, Safety requirements for secondary batteries and battery installations — Part 3: Traction batteries
448		测试方法标准	IEC/TS 61430, Secondary cells and batteries — Test methods for checking the performance of devices designed for reducing explosion hazards — Lead-acid starter batteries
449		材料技术标准	IEC 60428, Standard cells
450			IEC 60622, Secondary cells and batteries containing alkaline or other non-acid electrolytes — Sealed nickel-cadmium prismatic rechargeable single cells
451			IEC 60623, Secondary cells and batteries containing alkaline or other non-acid electrolytes — Vented nickel-cadmium prismatic rechargeable single cells
452			IEC 60951-1, Nuclear power plants — Instrumentation important to safety — Radiation monitoring for accident and post-accident conditions — Part 1: General requirements
453			IEC 60952-1, Aircraft batteries — Part 1: General test requirements and performance levels
454			IEC 60952-2, Aircraft batteries — Part 2: Design and construction requirements
455			IEC 60952-3, Aircraft batteries — Part 3: Product specification and declaration of design and performance (DDP)
456			IEC 60965, Nuclear power plants — Control rooms — Supplementary control points for reactor shutdown without access to the main control room
457			IEC 61951-1, Secondary cells and batteries containing alkaline or other non-acid electrolytes — Portable sealed rechargeable single cells — Part 1: Nickel-cadmium

续表

序号	材料分类	标准类型	标准名称
458			IEC 61951-2, Secondary cells and batteries containing alkaline or other non-acid electrolytes — Portable sealed rechargeable single cells — Part 2: Nickel-metal hydride
459			IEC 61959, Secondary cells and batteries containing alkaline or other non-acid electrolytes — Mechanical tests for sealed portable secondary cells and batteries
460			IEC 61960, Secondary cells and batteries containing alkaline or other non-acid electrolytes — Secondary lithium cells and batteries for portable applications
461			IEC 61982, Secondary batteries (except lithium) for the propulsion of electric road vehicles — Performance and endurance tests
462			IEC/TR 62060, Secondary cells and batteries — Monitoring of lead acid stationary batteries — User guide
463			IEC 62259, Secondary cells and batteries containing alkaline or other non-acid electrolytes — Nickel-cadmium prismatic secondary single cells with partial gas recombination
464			IEC 62282-2, Fuel cell technologies — Part 2: Fuel cell modules
465			IEC 62282-3-100, Fuel cell technologies — Part 3-100: Stationary fuel cell power systems — Safety
466			IEC 62282-3-200, Fuel cell technologies — Part 3-200: Stationary fuel cell power systems — Performance test methods
467			IEC 62282-3-201, Fuel cell technologies — Part 3-201: Stationary fuel cell power systems — Performance test methods for small fuel cell power systems
468			IEC 62282-3-300, Fuel cell technologies — Part 3-300: Stationary fuel cell power systems — Installation
469			IEC 62282-5-1, Fuel cell technologies — Part 5-1: Portable fuel cell power systems — Safety
470			IEC 62282-6-100, Fuel cell technologies — Part 6-100: Micro fuel cell power systems — Safety
471			IEC 62282-6-200, Fuel cell technologies — Part 6-200: Micro fuel cell power systems — Performance test methods

续表

序号	材料分类	标准类型	标准名称
472			IEC 62282-6-300, Fuel cell technologies — Part 6-300: Micro fuel cell power systems — Fuel cartridge interchangeability
473			IEC/TS 62282-7-1, Fuel cell technologies — Part 7-1: Single cell test methods for polymer electrolyte fuel cell (PEFC)
474			IEC 62646, Nuclear power plants — Control rooms — Computer based procedures
475			IEC 62660-1, Secondary lithium-ion cells for the propulsion of electric road vehicles — Part 1: Performance testing
476			IEC 62660-2, Secondary lithium-ion cells for the propulsion of electric road vehicles — Part 2: Reliability and abuse testing
477			IEC/PAS 62282-6-150, Fuel cell technologies — Part 6-150: Micro fuel cell power systems — Safety — Water reactive (UN Devision 4.3) compounds in indirect PEM fuel cells